GETTING FREE

GETTING FREE

GETTING FREE

A Handbook
for Women in Abusive Relationships

Expanded Second Edition

by Ginny NiCarthy
With a New Introduction by the Author

The Seal Press

Published by The Seal Press, P.O. Box 13, Seattle, Washington 98111.

Cover and book design by Rachel da Silva and Barbara Wilson.

Library of Congress Cataloging-in-Publication Data

NiCarthy, Ginny.
    Getting free.

    Bibliography: p.
    1. Abused women—United States—Handbooks, manuals, etc.
I. Title.
HV6626.N5 1986   362.8'3   86-3774
ISBN 0-931188-37-7 (pbk.)

10 9 8 7 6 5

Second edition.

Acknowledgements

I couldn't have learned what I did about the problems of abused women if my colleagues Naomi Gottlieb, Holly Moss and Cheryl Richey hadn't supported my establishment of the Abused Women's Network as a project of the Women's Institute. Their dedication never flagged, even when the Network seemed at times to be engulfing the Institute. In the early phases of the book, women at New Beginnings Shelter For Battered Women, the Abused Women's Network and the downtown YWCA groups read each chapter as it was written and gave me invaluable comments. If I became discouraged there was always one of them urging me on so they could read the next chapter. For reasons of confidentiality, I can't name those women, but I want them to know it might never have been finished at all, had it not been for their enthusiasm.

Rachel da Silva and Barbara Wilson took a risk when they decided to depart from their usual publications of literature. Knowing that others had turned down *Getting Free* because they thought there wasn't enough of a market, they wanted to take the chance because they knew there was a need. The book exists because of their decision and their courage to see it through.

A core of fundraisers planned and produced events, fliers, tee shirts and even the traditional baked goods: Linda Golaszewski, Mary Hambly, Marsha Kelley, Jane Cahill. I'm especially grateful to Rachel da Silva for the numerous hours and imaginative work that went into fundraising events and products, as well as editing and every phase of the book's production. Faith Conlon dedicated countless hours to editing and helping in organizational problems. Carol Richard's comments and suggestions, enriched by provocative conversations about the lives of abused women and their children restimulated my excitement in the later stages of the book.

I thank the following people for reading either substantial portions of the book or a chapter or two in their areas of expertise: Gay Abarbanell, Sally Buckley, Cathy Cado, Jane Cahill, Susan Crane, Deborah De Wolfe, Ann Fetter, Kay Frank, Wanda Fullner,

Karen Kaur, Ruth McCormick, Karen Merriam, Carol Richards, Julee Rosanoff, Cathy Schmitz. Ann Halloran was especially useful in making suggestions about substantive matters as well as my stylistic habits.

I thank my friends for their patience when I disappeared for weeks or months at a time and for their encouragement to keep writing: Ruth Crow, Sue Davidson, Kathy Draper, Ruth Goodman, Naomi Gottlieb, Lisa Hicks, Jane Klassen, my daughter Iskra Johnson and Ruth McCormick. My son Nathan Crow was an enthusiastic supporter from the beginning and Matthew Crow's patience with my demands for a silent household made the last stages of the manuscript revisions bearable.

Sandy Brown typed the early versions with wonderful swiftness and accuracy. Lisa Thomas waded through at least two pasted-together, re-written versions, unerringly deciphering the meaning and turning apparent chaos into order.

And Barbara Wilson. What can I say? I imagine she would never have agreed to this project had she foreseen what it would do to her life for a year or more. Her ability to organize material and cut through to the essentials is invaluable. Her patience with my periodic urges to add new material and her humorous perspective on the task at hand made the burdensome tolerable and the tedious fun.

Additional Acknowledgments for the Expanded Second Edition:

I want to thank Sandra Coffman and Ruth Crow for insightful comments on the emotional abuse and teen abuse chapters, respectively.

Conversations with many people about lesbian abuse have helped me begin to understand it. Among those who contributed to my thinking are Jay Craver, Sandra Coffman, Ruth Crow, Tina Ephron, Pam Hansen, Debbie Hamolsky, Barbara Hart, Dan Kelleher, Julee Rosanoff, Sunny Schwartz and especially Anne Harvey, my co-leader in a group for lesbians with abusive anger problems. I'm especially grateful to the participants in that group, in particular the two who have met with Anne and me for a year to analyze and evaluate our work. For reasons of confidentiality they will not be named.

I'm grateful to the high school students in my workshops on "Addictive Love and Abuse" for being open about their feelings and ideas, and I learned a great deal from Anne Meunchow as we co-led two of those groups.

My understanding of emotional abuse has grown over the years with each client I see, each group I lead and each friend I speak to. Karen Merriam helped me see certain patterns clearly and I particularly appreciate Diana E. H. Russell's work in bringing to light the "Chart of Coercion."

To

Jane Klassen

who gave me both moral and material support at the conception of the book, when I most needed it.

and to

all the abused women I met through the Abused Women's Network, New Beginnings Shelter For Battered Women and the Women's Counseling Group, and to the formerly abused women who gave generously of their time for long interviews. Whatever I know, I've learned from them.

CONTENTS

INTRODUCTION

If you were battered before the mid-1970s you probably didn't know of any shelters that would provide you refuge, because they were still almost unheard of. If you had a vague feeling the police wouldn't help or prosecutors wouldn't take the law seriously, you were most likely right. State laws against woman battering had been on the books for many years, but provided little or no protection because they were usually ignored by police and prosecutors. If you went to a hospital after being battered you probably were asked few questions about your injuries, and if you uneasily lied about how you got them, perhaps medical personnel were relieved to let you off the hook by pretending to believe you. There was good reason to fear that if you told anyone you were beaten, they either wouldn't believe you or would blame you for it. If you saw a therapist or confided in your minister, chances are you were told to stop provoking your man, and advised to tough it out. Books, movies and television seldom portrayed women who were battered, and then only as unsympathetic characters who deserved what they got.

The Beginning of Change

By 1975 women who had survived violent relationships, along with feminists and other concerned women, had begun the movement against battering, which soon became a groundswell of activity. Volunteers and meagerly paid workers in shelters and safe homes worked around the clock to create safe places for women who were in danger, and as those of us working in the movement learned more about the problem, we raised the awareness of professionals and media workers throughout the country. By 1978 things had begun to change, although many women who needed refuge and other help didn't yet realize it was becoming available. Nearly all states provided shelter, though it was not always easy to find and in some areas you might have had to travel several hundred miles to take advantage of it.

If you're in a dangerous relationship now, it might be impossible to imagine helping other women or doing much of anything that requires initiative or imagination or energy. But many of the women who did the important work of organizing shelters, safe homes, state coalitions and the national movement against battering were women like you. Having just begun to create safe and autonomous lives for themselves, they then extended themselves to help others save themselves. In many cases their work was an important way of reinforcing their own capacity to survive. They acquired skills as they were needed, often by trial and error, and lobbied for legal changes, made films and slide shows, gave speeches and changed medical protocols. Slowly, and then dramatically, they began to change the position of battered women in the U.S., while similar organizations moved in the same direction in the British Isles and Western Europe.

In the late 1970s some books began to discuss battering as a serious and pervasive social problem, but by 1982 Del Martin's book, *Battered Wives,* was still the only publication accessible to the general reader, and if you were looking for something specifically addressed to how you could change your situation, there was nothing for you. The word was just beginning to get out that if you were battered, you were not the one at fault. But there were mixed messages. Marital rape, for instance, was still considered a husband's legal right, though women in the anti-rape movement had tried to change the laws.

Although those of us involved in the movement tried to spread the knowledge we'd acquired that battering affected all women, there were some we weren't helping much. If you were an abused teenager or a woman battered by a boyfriend, you might have assumed from the general silence on the subject that your problem was unique. Most movement activity was carried out by white women; if you were a woman of color seeking help, you might have thought "battered women" didn't mean you. If you were a lesbian being battered, you were probably well aware that almost no one was willing to speak about lesbian abuse. There were a few groups for men who battered, but most women couldn't hope for any help, even for a man who wanted to change.

I worked on the first edition of *Getting Free* during the period of rapid movement growth from 1977 to 1981. Most of it was written while I was directing the Abused Women's Network in Seattle and leading groups at New Beginnings Shelter for Battered Women and the Seattle YWCA. Each chapter developed from what women who struggled to get free of violent partners taught me about how they changed their lives. Those were the days of CETA workers, large numbers of volunteers and unstable shoestring budgets. We were flying by the seat of our pants, but providing shelter and support for hundreds of thousands of women and children.

Between 1982 and 1986 shelters and safe homes proliferated. State after state passed laws recognizing that it's a crime for a husband to rape his wife; more recently, new laws in some states make arrest mandatory where there is reasonable cause to suspect battering. Hospitals have special protocols for treating patients when battering is suspected. More than one nurse has shepherded a wounded, frightened woman out the back door of a hospital to a shelter to avoid the husband in the waiting room. Ministers and therapists have been educated to understand that a woman who has been battered does not like it and has many reasons to fear leaving her partner.

Although few methods have been found to discover and stop it, information about the pervasiveness of elder abuse has begun to appear. Teenage and date battering have also recently come to public attention, and many shelter workers are developing high school curriculae to prevent it. Lesbians have begun to speak out about battering, and here and there a few programs are being established to provide shelter and other services. In some parts of the country special programs for women of color are available. The National Coalition Against Domestic Violence has made a commitment to promote help for all women, including lesbians and women of color. The first stages of that commitment are education and consciousness raising within the movement about racism and homophobia (fear of lesbians and homosexuals).

It is hard to believe that many publishers turned down *Getting Free* because it was "directed to a rather limited market," or because they doubted that the women who need it would buy it. Seal Press' faith in the book and confidence that the women who need it will find it has been validated by its sales. Since 1980 public awareness of battering as a widespread social problem has grown, until nearly everyone has at least seen a television program about it. The TV movie production of *The Burning Bed,* for example, was a widely viewed and well-publicized program, and shelter telephones rang continually for weeks after it was aired. Although women still give many reasons for staying with men who batter, fewer and fewer of them automatically assume they deserve to be abused or that they could have prevented it. Even though individual men still try to promote the idea that the women are to blame for the violence done to them, society's message has changed to a large extent.

This is not to say that the problem is essentially solved. Far from it. Men continue to batter and women continue to fall in love with them in spite of the danger. Even with the sweeping reforms that have occurred, you may still have encountered a police officer, judge, therapist or minister whose attitudes about battering have not caught up to the 1980s. The important thing is that if you have that kind of bad luck you are more likely to recognize that this is someone who is not going to help you and who might even do you harm. Unless you are in a very small community you can find someone else who will give you the kind of positive aid you need.

What About the Future?

Lest we become too complacent, we need to be alert to political threats from those who believe that it is better to risk death from a violent man than to change the family living arrangement. Those who are vocal about that view are growing even as the battered women's movement is expanding. The success of the movement in gaining government financial support on local, state and federal levels also presents certain dangers. Federal government budget cuts may mean that shelters and other services are threatened with closure. If the worst happens, we will have to return to our grass roots and work with volunteers and minimum budgets. But the movement is too entrenched, now, to die, and too important to individual women to allow silence about battering to prevail.

The word is out, not just in the United States, but all over the world. In Nairobi, at the United Nations Forum '85 conference to mark the end of the Decade of Women, I had the privilege of participating in the establishment of the International Network Against Violence Against Women. Many of the ideas in our resolutions were incorporated in a resolution passed by the United Nations at the official governmental conference. The U.N. resolution will not end battering, but it says to every nation in the world "This is a serious problem. This is wrong. This must be stopped everywhere in the world." Women everywhere are working to stop all forms of violence against women, and the campaign against battering by intimate partners is seen by many as the cornerstone of it all.

Women of all sorts have told me *Getting Free* has helped them, but much has been learned since I completed the book in 1981. Although all of the new information can't be included in this edition, some of it is incorporated into three new chapters at the end of the book, designed for abused women in particular situations.† If you're a teenager or her parent, you'll find Chapter 22 useful. Chapter 23 is written for you if you're a lesbian, and the last chapter is for any woman who has been emotionally abused. You may want to read them first, since they include suggestions on how to find and use the sections of the book that are most pertinent to you. Whatever your situation, it is my hope that *Getting Free* will help you tap into your own resources, so you can develop a life of peace and freedom.

Ginny NiCarthy
Seattle, 1986

† See also the following recent publications:
Evelyn C. White, *Chain Chain Change: For Black Women Dealing with Physical and Emotional Abuse,* The Seal Press, 1985.
Myrna M. Zambrano, *Mejor Sola Que Mal Acompañada: For the Latina in an Abusive Relationship/Para la Mujer Golpeada,* The Seal Press, 1985.
Ginny NiCarthy, Karen Merriam and Sandra Coffman, *Talking It Out: A Guide To Groups For Abused Women,* The Seal Press, 1984.
Kerry Lobel, ed. *Naming the Violence: Speaking Out About Lesbian Battering,* The Seal Press, forthcoming 1986.

WHO THE BOOK IS FOR

If you're a woman who has been physically or emotionally abused by a man you were intimately involved with, this book is for you. If you're still involved with the man, it may help you leave him. If you've already left him, or if you're abused by a child or a lover of the same sex or a parent, you'll also find parts of it useful. It may also help you if you're a professional counselor, a friend to a woman who's abused, or if you want to guard against becoming involved in such a relationship yourself.

Many of the ideas and activities in the book are directed to women who have been subjected to frequent and dangerous beatings over a long period of time and who are married or have children. Many are directed to women who have numerous fears, low self-esteem, little money and few contacts with anyone other than the violent man. All of those women are likely to need a lot of help to change their lives. But most of the book applies to any woman who's been physically, sexually or emotionally abused by anyone she's in an intimate relationship with. If you've "only" been abused once, the book will give you an idea of how hard it is to separate from the man when the abuse grows worse and the relationship lasts longer. Some questions may help you understand whether you've been abused or not.

PHYSICAL ABUSE

Since the problem has come to public attention, many women have asked themselves, "Am I abused?" "Am I a battered woman?" In this book I use "battered" to refer to physical assault. "Abuse" includes physical, sexual or emotional attacks, ranging from mild to lethal. The word you use to describe your situation is not important. It is important to recognize what's being done to you and to know you don't have to take it. Has your intimate partner done any of these things to you?
- pushed or shoved you
- held you to keep you from leaving
- slapped or bit you
- kicked or choked you

- hit or punched you
- thrown objects at you
- locked you out of the house
- abandoned you in dangerous places
- refused you help when you were sick, injured or pregnant
- subjected you to reckless driving
- forced you off the road or kept you from driving
- raped you
- threatened or hurt you with a weapon

Which of those acts happened repetitively? Which of them resulted in bruises, cuts or broken bones? Which of them were aimed at specific parts of your body, indicating the man was in control of his actions? Which required medical treatment, hospitalization or resulted in permanent injury or disfigurement?

How many times or how often have you been assaulted one way or another? How many of them could have resulted in serious injury if the man had miscalculated? Have the assaults stayed about the same in frequency, or are they changing? If changing, how?

Perhaps by the time you answered the last question you became convinced you're battered. Or maybe the more dangerous assaults at the end of the questions caused you to think you're not so bad off, since you haven't had any broken bones or had a gun held to your head, yet.

Although some items are clearly more dangerous than others, almost all of them are potentially dangerous and all show a lack of respect and an effort to intimidate and control you. Many men and women occasionally push, hold or slap each other, but that doesn't necessarily make it right. If everyone in your neighborhood or family has always done those things, that doesn't mean you have to continue the pattern. One problem with accepting a certain level of abuse is that there's a tendency for the abusive man to interpret it as permission to escalate the assaults into more dangerous and more frequent acts. You're the only one who can decide how much is too much and what you're ready to do about it.

SEXUAL ABUSE

Sexual abuse is so common that it too is beginning to seem almost normal to some people. Women have historically had so little to say about their sexuality that it's a very confusing area for many of us. Ask yourself whether your partner has done any of these things to you:

- told anti-woman jokes or made demeaning remarks about women

- treated women as sex objects
- been jealously angry, assuming you would have sex with any available man
- insisted you dress in a more sexual way than you wanted
- minimized the importance of your feelings about sex
- criticized you sexually
- insisted on unwanted and uncomfortable touching
- withheld sex and affection
- called you sexual names like "whore," "frigid"
- forced you to strip when you didn't want to
- publicly showed sexual interest in other women
- had affairs with other women after agreeing to a monogamous relationship
- forced sex with him or others or forced you to watch others
- forced particular unwanted sexual acts
- forced sex after beating
- forced sex when you were sick or it was a danger to your health
- forced sex for the purpose of hurting you with objects or weapons
- committed sadistic sexual acts

Have you been less interested in sex since you became involved with your partner or since he made particular demands? Do you feel less physically attractive than you did before? Do you feel sexually humiliated or ashamed, or do you believe no one else would want you sexually? Are you afraid to initiate what you want sexually?

You might give in to your partner's wish because you truly want to, and you know he'll do the same for you. But if you give in because you're afraid not to, or because you know he'll keep at you until he wears you down, it will be an important step to admit that he's really forcing you.

EMOTIONAL ABUSE

Emotional abuse is sometimes even harder than sexual abuse to define and recognize. Almost everyone does it at some time or other and many couples develop a habit of hurling insults at each other. It's often hard to determine who did what to whom first, especially if the injury is delivered in a subtle way. How many of these things has your partner done to you?
- ignored your feelings
- ridiculed or insulted women as a group
- ridiculed or insulted your most valued beliefs, your religion, race, heritage or class
- withheld approval, appreciation or affection as punishment

- continually criticized you, called you names, shouted at you
- insulted or drove away your friends or family
- humiliated you in private or public
- refused to socialize with you
- kept you from working, controlled your money, made all decisions
- refused to work or share money
- took car keys or money away
- regularly threatened to leave or told you to leave
- threatened to hurt you or your family
- punished or deprived the children when he was angry at you
- threatened to kidnap the children if you left him
- abused pets to hurt you
- told you about his affairs
- harassed you about affairs he imagined you were having
- manipulated you with lies and contradictions

The list could extend to countless pages and is more difficult to put in order of less damaging to more damaging behavior because the subtleties and frequency can make them mere slights or devastating humiliations. If there are things you were subjected to that don't fit into any of the items above, write them down.

If you did some of those things to your partner, the picture might be confusing. If you want to assign blame, it could make a difference who started it, who did what, most and worst. But the first thing to recognize is whether you were abused. Once you see that, you can evaluate the consequences. If you're still in the relationship or have only recently left it, you might not be able to tell yet what the long-range damage is, but answering the following questions may give you some ideas about it.

Did you often doubt your judgment or wonder if you were "crazy"? Were you often afraid of your partner and did you express your opinion less and less freely? Did you develop fears of other people and tend to see others less often? Did you spend a lot of time watching for his bad, and not so bad, moods before bringing up a subject? Did you ask permission to spend money, take classes or socialize with friends, and have fears of doing the wrong thing or getting in trouble? Did you lose confidence in your abilities, become increasingly depressed and feel trapped and powerless?

If you answered "Yes" to many of those questions it's probable you changed as a result of being abused. If you feel you deserved to be abused because you also abused your partner, consider that your actions don't negate the problem. Rather, they indicate you have two problems: your abuse and his. If you make a commitment to respect and protect yourself, you may find yourself being less abusive, as well.

HOW TO READ THE BOOK

You might want to read the book straight through, particularly if you're currently in the "honeymoon" phase of an abusive relationship, when your man is sorry he abused you and trying to make up for it. You'll read first about some of the political and social aspects of abuse and historical changes in marriage and the family. With those ideas as background, you'll be encouraged to weigh your obligations to yourself and the relationship, so that by the last chapter of Section I you'll be better prepared to decide whether to leave the man or stay with him. The next sections give advice on how to choose and evaluate professional helpers and how to be your own counselor. Section IV discusses various practical and emotional problems you'll encounter if you decide to leave the man. The final section relates experiences of women who were battered and who left their partners, and includes some advice from them.

If you're in crisis, you may decide to start with Chapter 6, "Making the Decision," or Chapter 14, "The First Week," which discusses the pros and cons of moving into a shelter or staying with relatives.

If you believe you can never change your life or that you'll be in a worse situation if you leave the man, you might want to begin with the last chapter. When you see that others, not so different from you, have gotten free and radically changed their lives, you might turn to Chapter I and read the rest of the book straight through. If you are so depressed or filled with self-hatred that you're nearly immobilized, you can start with Chapter 10, "How To Be Your Own Counselor."

Begin with the part of the book that looks most useful to you. You may re-read some chapters and they'll have different meanings to you at different times, depending on your situation and what changes you've made in how you think about yourself, your man and your life.

If there's an area of concern that isn't covered in one separate chapter, look in the table of contents for the parts of chapters that will tell you what you want to know. If you have a rule that says you must read a book from beginning to end, without "skipping," please consider breaking it now. This could be an opportunity to take the first step toward doing what's good for you, rather than following other people's outmoded rules. Feel free also to break that old rule about never writing in a book. This one is meant to be written in. Just be sure you keep it in a safe place.

Getting Free began as a slender volume to be easily slipped into purse or pocket, but has continually threatened to grow impossibly fat. My editors and I had to restrain ourselves often, limiting the content to the most immediately necessary subjects and to mere overviews of some of them. The bibliographies for each chapter at the end of the book compensate for necessary omissions, and we hope you'll read many of the books suggested. Libraries are still almost free, so try a number of books and when you find one that bears more than one reading, consider buying it. Most of the recommended books are reasonably priced paperbacks.

Most bookstores have "Self-help" and "Women's" sections, and you'll find most of the books I've listed in one or the other. A few have a general religious orientation, a few lean toward interpersonal and sexual freedom, and most are in between. All the books have been useful to me or to someone I know. But don't take my word. Read a few pages of several books and decide for yourself whether it's boring or stimulating and whether the author shares at least some of your values.

If you're a professional counselor or a friend of an abused woman, read *Getting Free* yourself and then pass it on to your client or friend, suggesting she read whatever parts seem most appropriate for her situation. She may be able to focus on only one small part at a time, depending on how great a crisis she's in. Encourage her to write in the book and to do the activities. Offer to keep the book in a safe place for her, if it's likely to be found by her partner. If some of the activities aren't appropriate for her special situation, the two of you can make whatever modifications are useful.

There remains a great deal to be learned about abuse, and it's my hope that whoever reads this book will view it not so much as the answer but as one of the first steps in understanding a problem that affects us all. Professionals, victims, women and men need to teach each other so that we can put an end to violence.

GETTING FREE

SECTION I

Making the Decision to Leave or Stay

Chapter 1

SOCIAL AND POLITICAL ASPECTS OF ABUSE

One of the most painful aspects of being abused by a man you love is a feeling of being alone with the problem. That emotional isolation often leads to a feeling of "I must be crazy." Fortunately, this situation is changing as more people are learning that abuse of women by their male partners is widespread. Somewhere between twenty-five and fifty percent of women who have intimate relationships with men will be physically abused by them at least once. Emotional abuse is even more prevalent.

Although individual women can be helped to foresee, prevent and leave violent relationships, the problem won't disappear until there are basic changes in the society as a whole. All of us, including those in positions of authority, will have to revise the widely held idea that violence is an acceptable way to solve problems. In addition, we'll have to reexamine and restructure the quality of women's and men's lives and the ways they relate to each other. In this chapter I'll give an overview of woman abuse in society, present theories about why it happens and suggest possibilities for change.

THE HISTORY OF BATTERING

Increased awareness of violence against women causes some of us to wonder if it's getting worse. Documentation of the problem is uncertain, incomplete and recent. It's impossible to tell for sure whether battering was more common in the past, but there are some indications it was. The British philosopher, John Stuart Mill, commented on the subject in 1869:

> From the earliest twilight of human society, every woman...was found in a state of bondage to some man... How vast is the number of men in any great country, who are little higher than brutes, and...this never prevents them from being able, through the laws of marriage, to obtain a victim... The vilest malefactor has some wretched woman tied to him, against whom he can commit any atrocity except killing her... and even that he can do without too much danger of legal penalty.

3

Until very recently women were considered the property of men. They belonged to their fathers until marriage and then became the property of their husbands. And men had the right to treat their property as they wished. In British common law, husbands were authorized to "chastise" their wives with "any reasonable instrument." Later the law was modified so that men could beat their wives so long as the weapon was no thicker than a man's thumb — which is how the phrase "rule of thumb" came into use.

United States laws were greatly influenced by British common law and the right and obligation of a husband to discipline his wife was retained in this country. In the last quarter of the nineteenth century a few states took that right away, yet those who continued to exercise it were still protected from prosecution. A North Carolina judge stated, "If no permanent injury has been inflicted nor malice nor dangerous violence shown by the husband, it is better to draw the curtain, shut out the public gaze, and leave the parties to forget and forgive." We may imagine that many wives did forgive over and over again, just as they do today.

As recently as 1962, a woman who wanted to sue her husband for assault damages was turned down by a California Supreme Court judge because to hear the case "would destroy the peace and harmony of the home, and thus would be contrary to the policy of the law."

Proverbs and poetry illustrate the historical acceptance of the idea that it's natural for men to control women and for male violence to support the concept of male superiority. Old English Proverb: "A spaniel, a woman and a hickory tree, the more ye beat them, the better they be"; Alfred Lord Tennyson: "Man is the hunter, woman his game"; Russian proverb: "A wife may love a husband who never beats her, but she doesn't respect him." Paradoxically, while most societies have assumed that men must use violence to control women, the prevalence of these violent actions has been systematically denied and hidden.

Minimizing the Problem

The nineteenth century judge's instruction to "draw the curtain" is still followed by many members of the medical and counseling professions as well as by the judiciary. Doctors and nurses typically avoid asking battered women for details about injuries or pretend to believe patients' fabricated stories of falling down stairs or running into doors. Therapists often fail to recognize abuse and accept a couple's denial or minimization of the violence. Police are trained to defuse the situation and to dissuade women from filing charges; prosecutors typically are reluctant to prosecute and judges to convict or sentence.

Small wonder that the abused women feels isolated and "crazy" when it appears that doctors, lawyers and police are conspiring to deny the existence or seriousness of her condition or to assign the blame to her. Relatives and friends may also play into the woman's self-doubt by refusing to believe her. Many violent men insist that their women end relationships with everyone else. When an abused woman is the only person who knows of or admits to what's going on and the violent man defines the situation as not dangerous, not his fault and not important, she begins to think there's something wrong with her.

Changing Attitudes

Alongside these persistent attitudes, new ones have begun to develop. Major changes began in the 1970s. We began to recognize the problem and to talk about it out loud; to understand that the victim neither asks for it, nor wants it, nor deserves it; to assign responsibility to the person who is violent; to support a woman who wants to prosecute and who chooses to leave a violent man.

Now that the curtain has been opened to expose the danger and the pain of violent relationships, it's possible to work on changing laws, retraining police and educating prosecutors, judges, therapists and medical personnel as well as the general public. All of this is being done. And we can seriously address the questions, "Why does he batter?" "Why does she stay?" and "Why does he stay?"

THE MASCULINE ROLE

What does it mean to be a man? Therapists questioned in a 1968 survey said that the healthy mature man is very aggressive, dominant, self-confident, independent, active, competitive, decisive, knows the ways of the world, is not easily influenced nor excitable in minor crises, and when he is emotional he almost always hides it.† Some therapists have changed their attitudes since the survey was made, but many have not.

Imagine for a moment what it's like for a man to try to live up to that image. The definition of masculinity is fostered directly and indirectly by all of our institutions: the church and the government assume the man to be the authoritative and financial head of the household; schools picture males as adventurous, strong and brave in primary readers and high school history

†Inge K. Broverman, et al. "Sex-Role Stereotypes and Clinical Judgments of Mental Health," *Journal of Consulting and Clinical Psychology*, 34:i (1970), pp. 1-7.

textbooks; television shows depict men as violent and powerful.

Family members support the notion that even newborn male infants are better coordinated, more alert, hardier and stronger than female infants. It's ironic that even though most people believe males are born with certain traits, all institutions put pressure on males to develop those same traits and punish those who don't conform. No one explains why the social pressure is necessary if that's the way males naturally are. It's considered appropriate and necessary for even very young boys to be active, brave competitive and strong, and to hide their emotions. Parents are proud when their male toddler holds back his tears and picks himself up from a fall, and they're pleased when their son persists in sticking out a game without tears or complaint, even though he's hurt by a ball or another player. He's rewarded for his bravery and physical toughness and punished if he acts "like a sissy" or "like a girl" or a coward.

Boys may be given a general message not to fight, but they're also taught, as a matter of pride, never to let another boy get away with hitting them. "Don't fight, but if you're hit first, fight back."

Boys dream of being famous race car drivers, boxers or football heroes but as they grow older it becomes more and more difficult to live up to the image of the dominant, worldly, self-confident, aggressive, decisive male. How does a person pull that off if he's sixteen years old — or twenty-three or forty-five — and he's rarely left the town where he grew up, he's never had a permanent job, or if he knows he's stuck in the tedious job he's held for twenty years? What does he do when he feels weak, vulnerable or dependent? Or when he doesn't know how to do what needs to be done — whether it's fixing the stopped-up kitchen sink, finding his way in a strange city or handling a financial problem?

Many men, faced with a threat to their masculine image, try to hide their fears in bluff and bluster. They act as if they're confident and strong, independent and competent, regardless of how they feel. Sometimes this bravado helps them learn to perform tasks well. But, when they can't perform up to their standards of masculinity, they may lash out verbally or physically, blaming whoever is handy, in order to save face. In either case the unacceptable feelings of helplessness, weakness, dependency or incompetency are buried in a seemingly safe place, beneath conscious awareness. A great deal of pain is buried with them.

These feelings of failure or inadequacy are experienced by many men who have both low and high status jobs and include some who give the impression of self-confidence. Often it is only his wife who knows how vulnerable such a man feels and how fearful he is of being found out to be less than the ideal of masculinity.

A few men are fortunate enough to have been allowed and even encouraged as youngsters to express the "nonmasculine" traits of dependency, vulnerability, and emotionality. Others learn to do that as adults, through hard work and the courage to risk feeling vulnerable. In either case they'll be able to face problems with a realistic assessment of the challenge and to accept their fears and hopes about their capacity to meet it.

WHY DO MEN BATTER?

Why would a man use the person he loves as a punching bag? It's a cliche that there's a fine line between love and hate and that "You always hurt the one you love." Intimate relationships cause some people to feel vulnerable and dependent. If one person loves or seems to love more than the other, those feelings will be exaggerated in the one who loves most and will contribute to his or her giving the partner power. Many of us feel hostility toward those who have power over us. For men, who aren't supposed to be either dependent or powerless, love sometimes produces feelings of resentment, even rage, especially when the loved one who holds that power is "merely" a female, a person who's supposed to be inferior. It can be experienced as intolerable humiliation, though it may seldom be expressed or even recognized as such. The more vulnerable the man feels, and the more important invulnerability is to his idea of masculinity, the more he may hate the one he also loves.

Permission To Batter

Another important contributing factor is that men have society's implied permission to hit their wives or girlfriends. It's probably true that most people would say men shouldn't hit the women they love (or anyone else that they care for or who is smaller and weaker than themselves). But we've seen that historically this idea exists side by side with the traditional assumption that men should be able to control their wives by whatever means necessary. Traditional ideas die hard.

In one study, over half of a sample of husbands indicated they would be jealous if their wives were unfaithful and that they would probably respond with some form of violence.† The response of strangers to male violence against women supports the idea that such a reaction is acceptable. Both experimental and real life situations indicate that a woman assaulted by a man in public

†Suzanne Steinmetz and Murray Straus, eds., *Violence in the Family* (New York: Harper and Row, 1974), p. 80.

will not be helped by passersby.

Friends may blame the victim for being in the situation at all, family members may not believe that it's happening and therapists are likely to ask what the woman did to provoke it. Although none of these people state in so many words that they approve of the violence, denial of the battering or the implication that the victim is at fault has the effect of giving the man a "hitting license," especially if the batterer is the victim's husband. He can be quite confident that his friends and family — and perhaps even hers — will stick by him; he probably won't go to jail or even be questioned by police. The social sanctions that keep most of us from acting on violent impulses don't operate in the arena of marriage.

Interpersonal Conflicts and Stresses

The question of why men batter is often confused with why men become angry at the women they love. A relationship between lovers or family members involves a continual chain of action and reaction, so that it's easy for a man who hits to say it's the woman's sarcasm (or coldness, drinking, poor housekeeping, extravagance) that caused it. Therapists have often taken this view and focused on what the women can do differently to cause change in the men.

Certainly couples trigger feelings in each other, and often they are related simply to expectations, needs and wants at the moment the exchange takes place. They're just as likely to be the result of a history of exchanges between the couple. A man who's had several extramarital affairs will get a different response from his wife when he says he has to work late at the office than will a hard worker whose wife feels confident he's faithful to her.

An angry response can also be displaced from a relationship with another person. "You're reacting just like my mother/father/third grade teacher." Or it can be a result of stress. Real world problems like job loss or a sick child can cause tension that easily explodes in anger, given the slightest opportunity. Yet one person's stress is another's challenge; one becomes angry, another depressed and still another works it out in therapy.

Any of these situations can help explain why one person becomes explosively angry and another merely irritated or hurt or worried. None of them explain why one angry person hits his wife, another his child, why one goes out and gets drunk, another verbally lashes out and still another cries or becomes silent and cold or covers up his feelings with jokes. None gives us the answer to why men batter.

Research indicates somewhere around sixty percent of men

who batter grew up in homes where they were beaten or they witnessed one parent battering another. However, this is not an explanation either. What about the other forty percent? And what about those who grew up in abusive homes who didn't batter anyone? R. Emerson and Russell Dobash found in a study in Scotland that only twelve percent of the siblings of batterers were violent to anyone.† Children model parents' behavior, but they also interpret what they see and connect it with other events, ideas and feelings. It's unpredictable how they'll use what they see and which parts of it they'll mimic. (This means that if your children have seen their father batter, there is a possibility of helping them interpret the battering in such a way that they won't want to imitate it.)

What makes a man hit the woman he loves is a varied and complicated mix: internal stress; society's permission to hit interpreted as an individual right; mimicking of violent parents or other role models; interpersonal struggles with the woman and others; feelings of anger, vulnerability, powerlessness and inadequacy; and very few clear actions by the woman, the justice system or others that unequivocally state violence is not allowed.

THE FEMALE ROLE

Women have their image to live up to just as men do. According to the same group of therapists mentioned above, the healthy, mature woman's characteristics are the opposite of the man's: she's very emotional, easily influenced, submissive, excitable, passive, home oriented, unworldly, indecisive and dependent and not at all competitive, adventurous, aggressive, independent or self-confident.

For some women, these characteristics are easier to live up to than those roles men must master. Yet most of us are not easily turned into the marshmallows these traits imply. To the extent we're able to be that kind of woman, we can thank the same institutions that mold the male character: the churches that have traditionally tried to suppress women's sexual power and their independence; the school readers that picture girls as hopelessly frightened of spiders and lizards and the dark; the television and magazine ads that show ninety-pound females who do little other than wash and curl their hair, paint their faces and nails and douse themselves with good smells.

The messages, both subtle and direct, inundate us from infancy on ("Isn't she sweet, pretty, tiny, adorable?"). Gradually, we

---

†R. Emerson Dobash and Russell Dobash, *Violence Against Wives: A Case Against Patriarchy* (New York: The Free Press, 1979), p. 154.

succumb to the idea that we're incapable of making decisions or of acting independently, and that we need protection from major responsibilities as well as from dangerous men. The protector, of course, is that special man in our lives. Many of us are fearful of venturing out at night without male protection and are afraid to live alone. Those of us who work for three or four dollars an hour find it burdensome and depressing to take the entire financial responsibility for ourselves and our children, though many of us must.

As young women we learn that when we are sexually open, we're subject to severe criticism from parents, men, churches and schools. When we assert our independence, show our competence and take responsibility in social interactions men often become angry or hurt and may assume that we're expressing doubts about their ability to handle situations adequately. So when we're at our best — that is, acting openly, independently, competently and responsibly — we face judgments from ourselves and others that are disturbing: "Maybe I'm not a 'real' woman, and maybe my man isn't a 'real' man unless he objects to my independence." Each time we subject ourselves to such a judgment we become less confident and open the door a little bit more to dependency, submissiveness and eventual helplessness.

WHY DO WOMEN STAY?

Those of us who manage to rise above the most damaging aspects of sex role socialization to become strong, adventurous, competent people would like to think we're free of male control and violence. But it isn't necessarily so. Although women who have been abused sometimes fit the stereotype of the submissive, dependent, helpless woman, many are the opposite — strong, independent people. They sometimes hold important, demanding, professional positions as doctors, media performers, teachers, or they may work in traditionally male trades. These women have broken out of the restrictive traditional roles, yet are still capable of falling in love, feeling responsible for what happens in an intimate relationship, and committed to going beyond the last mile to make it work.

Every woman learns as she grows up that to be a "whole person" she must have a male partner. Although divorced, single and widowed women constitute more than forty-two percent of the workforce, and though more than sixteen percent of the whole female population never marries at all, the myth persists that every woman must have a man. A single woman may still feel like a freak who accidentally landed on Noah's Ark. Even though men who are widowed or divorced tend to be more de-

pressed and remarry more quickly than women in similar circumstances, most women believe men get along very well without
them. This contributes to their placing a low value on themselves
and to the fear of never attracting and keeping another man.

Fear of Poverty

The belief that she will be provided for by a man may discourage a woman from taking seriously the need to earn an
adequate income. If she does plan a career, discrimination in the
job market is likely to make it hard to make a good living. If she
leaves paid work for a few years to have children, she's likely to
lose both income and self-confidence.

Even a woman who has a good job will suffer a big loss in
income when she leaves a man, especially if she has custody of
children. The man she's left probably earns much more than she;
child support is almost never enough to cover expenses and it's
often not paid at all. The fear of poverty or a greatly lowered
standard of living is a major reason women stay in abusive situations, hoping year after year it will change and that they won't
have to risk making it on their own.

In addition, women still usually take major responsibility for
the children, are closer to them and want custody of them, which
adds to the financial burden. It may seem impossible to cope with
all the children's emotional needs, including the loss of a father
figure as well as working full time or more. Although many
women do manage to do all that, the reality is, it's a very hard life.
Until a woman has done it, and learned firsthand that it's still
much less painful than depending on a man who can't be depended on, she'll be too afraid to risk leaving.

Love and Guilt

When an abused woman overcomes her fear of poverty and
the pervasive ideas about woman's role and prepares to leave, she
may be faced with the abusive man at his most irresistible: "I
know I'm a brute, but I'm on my knees asking forgiveness... How
could you turn away from me when I most need you... If you
really loved me, you'd forgive and trust me... Look how I'm hurting and how hard I'm trying... I'm afraid I'll fall apart without
you... You're all I have, all I care about..."

In a few sentences he can trigger the woman's addictive love,
(see Chapter 5), her guilt, her concern for him, her feeling that
she's responsible for his life and feelings, her hopefulness, her
idea that she should be a trusting, nurturing, forgiving woman,
and that it would be wrong not to give him another chance,
wrong to turn her back on him just as he's finally really ready to

change.

She unpacks her bags. The cycle begins again.

WHY DO MEN STAY?

If a man feels so hostile to his chosen woman that he regularly hits her, why doesn't he leave? If pressed for an explanation, he too might say that it's love that has him locked helplessly in its grip, though he's more likely to mask his feelings with indignant complaints about the woman. He's unlikely to confess that he feels the need of a woman, and that life without an intimate partner would be intolerable. He may not even be willing to admit to himself the importance of the relationship, because emotional dependency runs counter to the accepted image of masculinity.

Often the man is as dependent on his woman as she is on him, though he may rarely admit it. In their mutual addiction they tend to shut out the rest of the world, she because she's ashamed of her bruises and because he demands that she cut off other relationships; he because he doesn't know how to form relationships and is jealous and fearful of her involvement with others. The more isolated they become, the more dependent they grow, and the more addicted to a relationship they expect to fulfill all their needs. Since no one can fulfill all of another's needs, the continued disappointment leads to increased stress, depression and hostility.

Many men who batter are immature and emotionally dependent, though some successfully hide it in their work and social lives outside the home. They're often addicted to the women they abuse, and they batter in hopes of frightening the women so much that they won't dare "abandon" them. The fear of abandonment often leads to extreme jealousy and to suspicion that a woman will betray her husband with other men, a jealousy often interpreted by both partners as "love."

The batterer believes he can force change by frightening the woman into submission and fidelity, and he, like the woman he victimizes, perpetually renews his hope for change.

WHAT CAN BE DONE?

Since woman abuse is a problem that seems to have been with us since the dawn of history and it's tolerated by all of our institutions, it may seem impossible for you to break out of it.

But that isn't so. For the first time in history, women as a group are saying "No!" to battering, are helping each other get free of dangerous men and are working together to create better lives with and without men. So far, they have changed laws and police procedures and attitudes of medical and counseling professionals, as well as maintaining shelters. There is a lot more to be done, but it's easier for a woman who wants to get out of an abusive situation to get help than at any time in history.

Individual women, with the help of each other, are finding their own ways to protect themselves from violence, usually by separating from dangerous men. The decision — whether to leave or to stay but to make a plan to be relatively safe — is the first hard step in the process of change.

Chapter 2

MARRIAGE AND THE FAMILY: NEW AND TRADITIONAL VALUES

The concepts of family, marriage and loyalty to the man you love each have different meanings to individuals and to religious, cultural and ethnic groups. These ideas don't always keep up with changing customs, so it will be helpful to take a fresh look at what you believe makes sense, whether others agree or not. In this chapter you'll have an opportunity to clarify what you value about marriage and the family.

WHAT IS A FAMILY?

In an age of rapid social change it's hard to know what our obligations are. You said the words "till death do us part," or if you're not married you may have just assumed you'd grow old with your partner, staying by his side through bad times as well as good. You may have grown up believing that unquestioning devotion and loyalty are necessary in marriage and that marriage is the central relationship of everyone's family. Leaving the man, even talking to someone about your relationship problems, may seem unacceptable. When you look back at the family you grew up in, you may remember that there were all kinds of flaws, even dangers, and damaging relationships. But perhaps it's comforting to you that at least the family was together.

When you think of leaving your man and try to imagine yourself as a single person, it seems everywhere you look there are either couples or "complete" family units — a mother and a father and two or more children. You see the couples at movies and restaurants. You see the families at the zoo. You see them — mother, father, athletic-looking boy, slightly younger, pretty little girl — on ads for washing machines, breakfast cereals and living-room rugs. So, of course, that must be what a family is. Oddly, this picture of the two-parent, nuclear, "normal" family persists even among people who have seen or experienced many different kinds of families.

The picture is in stark contrast to the current reality that four and a half million families in the U.S. are headed by women, and, of these, almost half are single mothers with children under eighteen. The nuclear family has been shrinking in both size and number for a generation, and some marriage ceremonies no longer even include the words "till death do us part." In order to gain a new perspective on being a single person, you need to begin thinking of it as a different lifestyle, rather than focusing on negative phrases like "fifth wheel," "broken home," and "father-less family." Being single doesn't mean you'll have a family organism with a permanent gaping hole where the father/husband has been amputated. Like almost twenty-five percent of the families in the nation, yours may be a woman-headed full household or a complete family that has one resident and one nonresident parent.

THE FAMILY IN PERSPECTIVE

Historically the husband was the protector of the wife and children. A woman constantly giving birth couldn't manage economically without a man's support. Nor could he manage without her. A man not only needed a woman to take major responsibility for the children and household tasks, he needed her help economically to supply the food, clothing and other items which are now usually manufactured outside the home. They both needed the children to help out on the farm, in the store or in the home.

Families traditionally have been urged to stay together on moral and religious grounds, and more recently for psychological reasons. However, the stability of the family — still sometimes defined as a gainfully employed father, a mother at home, and 2.5 children — has also served the interests of political and economic institutions. As long as women take primary responsibility for the care and training of the next generation and of most household tasks, men are free to work long hours in factories, business and government. Thus, in a sluggish economy, when there is a surplus of workers, women may be encouraged to stay in the home and have more children through government bonuses and highly restrictive abortion laws.

In the United States it was considered wrong for mothers to leave their children in the hands of other caretakers. During World Wars I and II, however, this practice became acceptable as national priorities made it necessary to employ women in great numbers to promote "the war effort." Thousands of mothers were recruited into factories, their children presumed to be cared for adequately. In many cases childcare was provided at the workplace. But in the postwar years, as soon as the men came home to reclaim those jobs, it was generally agreed upon by heads of industry and government that a woman's place was in the home after all and that the children needed her constant presence. Today, when we have a scarcity of jobs, neither government nor industry see it as important or valuable to provide childcare for working mothers. And once again a movement is afoot to persuade women that their full-time services are needed in the home.

Government decisions and industrial needs are passed on to us in various ways in addition to the obvious ones of laws and company announcements. In a period of just a few years, new messages about social values are transmitted through television news and drama, movies and popular magazines. Depending upon the historical period, it may seem that suddenly "everyone" is talking about having babies, or that all the previously contented homemakers on the block are planning to get paid jobs. Since most of us are uncomfortable with ideas that are different, we begin to change our thinking too, without analyzing exactly who is promoting these new ideas and what their reasons are. We can easily lose sight of what we really want for ourselves.

WHO ARE YOU LISTENING TO?

It's a good idea to ask whose voice it is — besides your own — that gives you messages about your obligations:

"A woman's place is by her husband's side."

"No real woman leaves just because of a few family fights."

"It is the woman's responsibility to see that the family functions harmoniously."

"It must be her fault if he is being violent."

"She should learn to be a better wife."

"You can't run away from your problems."

"The family should stay together through thick and thin and work things out together."

Is it your mother's voice? Your husband's? Your minister's? Counselor's? Your father's? Shut your eyes for a minute and listen to the words that are most familiar to you, whichever words ring true about staying with your man. Who is it that says them?

Once you know where they come from, you can begin to analyze them. Are they what you really believe, or are they just words you've been repeating without thinking about what they mean or why they might be true? What are the reasons that a wife should stick by her husband regardless of how he treats her?

WHAT IS IMPORTANT TO YOU?

Now it's time for you to give some thought to what "family" means to you. What are your values and which of them are most important? What kind of family would best promote those values? Even if you're not married and not a parent now, it's a good idea to examine your values, since your involvement with an abusive partner is likely to include a dream of, or a plan to create, a family unit.

Many people believe that marriage, and even more certainly the family, provide and nourish the development of valued traits and situations: warmth, security (both emotional and financial), peace of mind, stability, companionship, loving and satisfying sex, someone to grow old with, children to carry on the family name and traditions, interdependence, affection, loyalty, and the sharing of responsibilities, worries, work, rewards, and pride in children and accomplishments.

Other people claim that not only do marriage and the family fail to promote these values, but they inhibit the development of freedom, adventure, social and intellectual stimulation, growth, flexibility, independence and individuality. They assert that spouse battering, child abuse and incest are indications that families are too often centers of stress that result in serious physical and emotional damage to family members.

Whether you view your own situation as relatively satisfying or not depends upon your relationship with your partner and your interpretation of that relationship — what values it provides you with, and how important they are. Being married to a gambler will not be so bad if financial security is not of great value to you. You won't be troubled by a "swinging" husband if fidelity isn't important to you. One person's emotional security may be another's boredom.

It's easy to lose sight of what's important when it seems impossible to ever have it. This first exercise will help you focus on the things that were once important to you and that still might be if you let them be. *Fill in the blanks* as honestly as you can.

Activity 1

Activity 1   What's Important To You?

1. If I had twenty-four hours to live, I would try to be with _____

_____and to do

_____

I would not want to be with _____

_____and I would try not to

_____

2. If I were to die, I would like people to say these things about me: _____

_____

_____

3. I hope my children and/or grandchildren won't ever have to__

_____

_____

4. If I had plenty of money, I would _____

_____

_____

5. When the children grow up, I will_____

_____

_____

6. If I were younger, I would_____

_____

_____

7. If it didn't take so long, I would_____

_____

_____

8. Some of the things I wish I had done are _____

_____

_____

9. If I felt better or had more courage, I would _____

_____

_____

Perhaps you filled in the blanks with things that are only the most vaguely felt dreams or wishes, things you'd like to have or do, but don't really expect, and certainly haven't a plan to make happen. Many of us drift along, making the best of a hard life and losing sight of goals and values that were once important to us. If that's what you've done, this is a good time to get them back in your sight again. The next exercise will take you a step farther in recognizing your goals. Without considering how likely you are to achieve them, *circle* each of the following values that's important to you.

Activity 2   **What Are Your Values?**

predictable relationship

security

enough money for comfort

wealth

peace of mind

flexibility

freedom

friends

fun

work

creativity

love

sex

close family

time for family

travel

education

independence

power

fame

glory

respect

achievement

service

leadership

control

being nurtured

nurturing

feeling useful

being well-liked

self-expression

participation in the arts

participation in sports

adventure

excitement

variety

being entertained

leisure time

close relationship

honesty

humor

order

rituals and tradition

shared childcare

integrity

time to read

country living

learning

privacy

meeting new people

To get a clearer view of how you're most likely to achieve your values, *make a list* of all the potential advantages and disadvantages of both married and single life. Use the items you put in the blanks and the circled values from the last two exercises to help you fill in the "Advantages" columns below the examples I've given in the next exercise.

Activity 3   *Advantages and Disadvantages of Marriage and Single Life:*

Marriage		Single Life	
Advantages	Disadvantages	Advantages	Disadvantages
1. Financial security	Financial dependence	1. Financial security	Poverty
2. Companion-ship	Lack of companionship	2. Choice of being alone	Loneliness
3. Reliable sex	Boring sex	3. Better sex	Sexual hassles
4. Share childcare	Total care of kids	4. Total responsibility for kids	No help with kids
5. _____		5. _____	
6. _____		6. _____	
7 _____		7 _____	
8 _____		8 _____	
9 _____		9 _____	
10 _____		10 _____	

WEIGHING THE PROS AND CONS

Notice the seeming contradictions. Whether a particular condition occurs in marriage or as a single person depends upon individual experiences with certain people. If your man has a steady job in an expanding field, good health and is willing to share the money equally, then you have some financial security. But if he's an alcoholic, gets laid off, leaves you for a younger woman, has a heart attack or provides you with only the bare essentials, you have no security. In the latter case you might feel more secure as a single person, providing for yourself.

See how many disadvantages of the single life can also be viewed as advantages. The purpose of doing that is not to make you decide to leave the man, but to help you realize that you have a real choice. "Having to make decisions by myself" can be viewed positively as an opportunity to become more independent.

This is a good time to stop saying: "I can't," "Maybe when the children are older," "I couldn't support the children," "I couldn't take the children from him," "I couldn't leave the children." Try substituting, "If I decided to leave...to support the children...to leave the children...how could I make the best of it?" The problems of single parenting are many, but the solutions are beginning to develop, and being a single parent — even under stress and in poverty — might be a relief and easier in some ways than trying to protect the children from an abusive man.

In order to clarify what values might be achieved in various kinds of relationships, consider what values were prevalent in your original family, as well as in each of the intimate relationships you've had. Compare those values with the ones that typified your life when you weren't in an intimate relationship. Include living alone, in a dormitory or with friends. Note which situations enabled you to achieve your most important values.

How do your particular experiences square with your ideas about advantages and disadvantages of marriage and the single life? If you said an advantage of marriage is companionship, a father for your children or sexual satisfaction, but during two marriages you haven't experienced any of those benefits, you'll need to decide whether your expectations of a husband are unrealistically high or whether you should make some changes in your choice of men.

If you're used to thinking of yourself only as a daughter, wife or mother, you may find these questions bewildering at first. You can expect to take some time evaluating your life as an individual as well as a family member. Whenever you feel you're getting a slightly different slant on your life, return to these questions and change or expand your answers. Some of them will become clearer as you read the rest of the book and gain more understanding of your obligations and your options.

Chapter 3

IS IT EVER RIGHT TO BREAK UP
THE FAMILY?

The family, meaning that nuclear family discussed in the previous chapter, represents to many people all that is good and the best hope for a better world. You may have gotten a message like that from many sources as you were growing up — and with it, the message that it's the woman's role to hold marriage and family together, certainly not to destroy the marriage or break up the family.

If you've decided that what you really want is to end your relationship with the man who abuses you, you may still feel guilty for taking a stand or feel responsible for other people's reactions. This chapter will focus on the question of your obligations to the man, and children or other family members who may be involved.

WHERE DO YOUR GUILT FEELINGS COME FROM?

"He needs me."

"He'll fall apart."

"He'll kill himself."

"He has nothing else."

"I can't deprive him of the kids."

If you're worrying yourself with those kinds of warnings, it's especially important to determine whether they stem from your own reasonable fear based on past experience, or from an attempt by the man, his friends or relatives to induce guilt and to "make" you stay with him. The situation becomes difficult to sort out when a man not only is manipulating your guilt feelings but additionally may be in real danger of "cracking up" or killing himself. Friends, relatives and professionals may tell you it will be on your conscience if your man becomes self-destructive after you leave. Before assessing the value of those judgments, you need to consider several questions. The first is, "Who said it?"

If you're the only person explicitly stating these fears, you should ask yourself whether you've gotten the idea from other people's hints or from their indirectly stated fears. Perhaps those ideas are disguised as innocent questions: "Do you think he'll be able to manage without you?" Or offhand comments: "He really doesn't have much to live for, aside from you and the kids."

If these remarks come from people closer to him than to you, ask yourself further questions before deciding their judgments are right. "Does this person care about me at all? Has she only been hearing the man's interpretation of the relationship? Does she understand what kind of fear I live with every day? Have I ever told her, rather than hinting, or talking in vague generalities, exactly what he does to me?" Unless the person cares for you at least as much as for the man, and unless she thoroughly understands what it is you want to escape, her advice should be taken with a grain of salt. If the advising person is a professional who doesn't really know either of you, there are other questions to ask. (See Section II on GETTING PROFESSIONAL HELP.)

The people who are generous about advising you have experienced the same social conditioning you have, including the idea that you're responsible for the welfare and happiness of your man. Though they may have good intentions, the advice may not be the best thing for you. After listening to the ideas of the caring people in your life, you'll be the one to make the decision and to live with its consequences. It's a big responsibility, and there are no easy answers. You won't be able to hold anyone else responsible for the results of your decisions, no matter how free they were in handing out advice.

SUICIDE AND "CRACKING UP"

The two most frightening possibilities are that the man will kill himself or "go crazy." You shouldn't expect to predict with very much certainty (nor could a professional therapist), whether that will happen. There are some questions, though, that will help you weigh the possibilities.

Has he done it before? If he's tried suicide or had a mental breakdown in the past, that's an indication that he has a poorly developed capacity to handle stress; if you leave him he may repeat his old patterns. But that doesn't mean he'll crack up completely just because you're not there. There may be other factors that will help him handle this situation more constructively than he's handled problems in the past. If he's had emotional problems before he met you, you're not the cause of them.

Has he talked about it? If he threatens self-destructive behavior, it doesn't mean he'll necessarily follow through, nor is silence a certain indication that he won't. Nevertheless, threats of suicide should be taken seriously. There's a commonly held belief that those who talk about suicide don't do it, which is definitely not true.

What Can He Do For Himself?

Even if your man has few friends and isn't close to his family, in an emergency friends may come through and family may become close. Try to find out from them whether they will be supportive if you leave, and if they seem to care, find a way to let them know you're leaving when you make the decision.

The more isolated the man is, the more likely he'll feel he can't handle being "deserted" or "abandoned" by you, and the more self-destructive he's likely to be. Many men who batter have no friends or close relatives and are entirely dependent on one special woman for emotional sustenance. It's as if their emotional survival depends upon a mutually suffocating relationship which fosters mutual helplessness. If you tell the man you're leaving, and especially if there are children who will go with you, he may feel he has nothing to live for. The man could solve his problem of dependency by developing friendships, by becoming involved in work or hobbies or by enlisting the help of a professional person. You can try to urge, plead, beg, demand, threaten and manipulate him into broadening his horizons, but it's ultimately his choice whether to make use of the opportunities available. If he refuses to provide himself with the option of being less dependent on you, you'll need to decide where your responsibility to him will stop.

How Much Can You Help Him?

To clarify the limits of your obligations to your man, *make a list* of all the things you could do that might keep him from killing himself or cracking up. In order to broaden your perspective on what you can expect to accomplish, consider everything possible. If you stay with him day and night there's a good chance you can prevent his suicide. (Even then, he can probably do it if he's determined.) If you promise you'll never leave him, regardless of what he does and that you won't become involved with any friends or activities that don't include or center around him, will that prevent him from going crazy? Perhaps you're close to living that way now. If so, is his stability improving or deteriorating? What about yours?

What other less demanding, less dramatic action could you take to prevent him from self-destructive acts? Some, like helping him to find a counselor or make new friends may require his cooperation. Being available whenever he feels emotionally shaky or trying to build his self-esteem may necessitate lots of time and emotional involvement. If you decide to leave him, perhaps a daily phone call will be enough to help him stay in a fairly stable condition.

Activity 4   What Can You Do to Help Him?

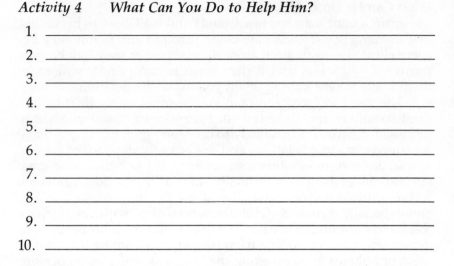

1. _____
2. _____
3. _____
4. _____
5. _____
6. _____
7. _____
8. _____
9. _____
10. _____

When you've made your list of possibilities, *underline* the ones you could do without danger to yourself. Allow for accidental, as well as intentional violence, especially if he abuses alcohol or drugs. Consider both psychological and physical danger. If being in regular contact with him saps your energy, lowers your self-esteem and increases your depression, that's a serious danger to your mental health.

If you're going to do something that requires his cooperation, *write down* how long you're willing to help, and what amount of cooperation you want from him. If after three months, he hasn't made a serious effort to make the change you agreed was important, it will be clear that no matter how helpful you are, he's not going to accept your assistance. And if you do decide to leave him you'll have a record of all the things you tried. It should minimize your guilt feelings and lessen the probability of your taking unfair blame for something you couldn't control. You'll be clear about the low probability of your being able to save him from suicide or a breakdown. You'll know that even had you been able to do it, it would have meant risking your own sanity or your life, on the slim chance you might have saved his. That is beyond any reasonable expectation.

WHAT ABOUT THE CHILDREN?

If you decide to leave and take the children, their father will very likely be hurt and angry. He may draw a dramatically bleak picture of total separation from his children from this day forth, even describing how they will gradually lose interest in him, or claiming you'll turn them against him.

At this point, your guilt feelings can do you in, especially if you're hoping the children *will* forget about him and won't want to see him. But there's no reason to buy the picture he's drawn. Neither of you can predict what it's going to be like, since each of you will change. The maturing process will have a great effect not only on the children, but on you two adults. In addition, as your individual lives develop in different ways and as you form new relationships with other people, your feelings toward each other will be modified.

Most of us find it hard to imagine feeling different about anyone from the way we feel right now. When we love, we can't remember how it was to hate. When we're angry, we can't imagine how we could have been calm. But people do change. What you do today is important, and will set the stage for future events, but it won't permanently set in concrete future relationships. There are many, many ways a father and his children can relate to each other whether they live in the same house or not.

A partial exception to this statement occurs when you feel your life or that of the children is so threatened that you have to sever the relationship entirely, and disappear to a place where the man can't find you. Even in that extreme situation, you may choose to resume contact in a year or two, or the children may exercise their right to spend time with their father when they're older. If you make the decision to cut all ties, it certainly shouldn't be done lightly. You're right to be concerned about its effect on the children. You'll probably want to consult not only a lawyer, but some friends or a counselor before you make the final decision. But be sure your consultants understand that both you and the children may be in very real danger if you maintain contact with the man.

Although it's your decision to take the children, the relationship the father maintains after the separation depends largely upon whether he's reliable and nonthreatening. In other words, he'll play a large part in whether he deprives himself of them.

What Does It Mean to Deprive the Man of His Children?
In order to evaluate just what "depriving" the father of his children means, ask yourself what he gets from them: Affection? Respect? Status? Attachment? A sense of continuity from one generation to another? An opportunity to nurture?

Pin down precisely what he gains now and how he gets it. Is there a way he can still get it, even if you separate? Status and continuity can exist whether he's a full-time father or not. Perhaps he limits his affection and nurturing to a few minutes before the children's bedtime each night, or to a half day on weekends when he feels good. If so, separation may mean the routine will change, but not necessarily that the children will be with their father less than before. Some divorced fathers become more fully involved with their children after a separation, because to have twenty-four-hour responsibility for them on a regular basis requires a more complex relationship.

It may be that the children's "respect" for their father is composed mainly of fear, and the more intimate relationship that develops from twenty-four-hour care (even for short periods) will result in a deeper or different kind of respect. The father may be surprised to find that what he loses in fearful respect is compensated for by an increase of trust and love.

Ways He Can Maintain Contact With the Children

If their father isn't abusive to the children, and if his expressed concern over losing a close connection with them is sincere, you can arrange for him to spend as much time as usual with them. However, it may take some time before you're able to work this out in a way that will guarantee your safety, both from his violence and from your own vulnerability to his persuasiveness. (See Chapter 14, "Protecting Yourself and the Children)".

If the father spends a good deal of time with his children in the evening and on weekends, then you may eventually consider shared custody. That is, if you leave and take the children with you, you might want to live close to his house so the children can have dinner with him several evenings a week, and spend half the weekends with him. But emphasize "eventually."

Shared custody will probably be much too dangerous to undertake until he's demonstrated for a full year that he's reliable in keeping appointments with the children, that he's not jealous of your new relationships, and that he fully understands your lifestyle is not his legitimate concern. He should demonstrate that he's neither violent nor emotionally abusive toward you or the children.

If you think you may want to consider such a plan later, let the man know it's a possibility. Discuss it with him one time, or write it out, and be sure he understands you won't even discuss it for a year. The reason for talking about it one time is so it will be clear to both of you that it's up to *him* whether he deprives himself of the children's company and affection. And that should help you keep in mind that he deprived himself of spending time with them; you didn't. If it's really important to him to spend time with the children he'll act in ways to make that happen.

Meanwhile, be clear about what you will and will not put up with during this interim period. It's your job to preserve your mental and physical health this first year by playing it safe. At the end of a year, you'll be in a better position to assess change and to distinguish progress from promises.

If your thinking becomes circular and repetitive, it's probably because you're determined to arrive at some solution that won't hurt anyone. You can't do it. Whether you go or stay, someone will be hurt, at least in the short run. The question is how to minimize it.

CHILD ABUSE

Children present special problems, since they haven't the power to control their own lives, and may be more vulnerable to rejection and feelings of abandonment than the adults involved. On the other hand, they're sometimes much more flexible and resilient than adults.

If their father is brutal to the children as well as to you, your decision should be easier to make, because of your obligation to protect them from physical or psychological abuse. You may be the only person very young children can count on to protect them from a violent father's dangerous miscalculations of his strength, which can easily result in permanent damage, or even death.

Child abuse takes many forms. It's easy to gloss over or not even recognize it, because there's such a fine line between the physical punishment of children that's acceptable to most adults and the abuse that's out of control.

We're horrified when we hear about an adult beating, burning or throwing a child. We wonder how an adult could do that to a small person. Yet many of us who've been confined for any period with a young child who continually cries or whines or who won't obey and is "into everything" can at least understand the urge.

When social isolation, poverty, feelings of inadequacy or worry are added to the ordinary stresses of life, it's easy to lash out at the least powerful creature available. For a man, that's often a woman and sometimes children. For a woman it's often the children, and for a child it may be other younger children or the dog or cat.

Violence against children, like violence against adults, is initially unthinkable. The first time a person allows himself or herself to lose control, there may be immediate horror and remorse, and promises that it will never happen again. Yet that first violation of the inhibition has made the act "thinkable" and therefore likely to occur again. Eventually it may begin to seem normal.

To get a perspective on child abuse, imagine for a moment you're in the sole care of an eight hundred pound giant who insists you do things that you don't like and don't understand, and who smacks you with a fifty-pound hand or huge board when you don't do as you're told or when you cry or complain. It's so acceptable for adult parents and teachers to physically assault little children that we easily lose the perspective that we are, comparatively, all-powerful giants. We also have more resources to use to solve problems since our intellect is more highly developed. We have more information and we're supposed to have a better handle on our emotions.

Even though violence against children is understandable, it's not acceptable. If it's the father who's violent to them, it's your responsibility to keep the children safely away from him. If he's also violent toward you, the only way you'll be able to protect your children is to get them away from him.

If you're afraid he'll get custody even though he abuses the children, be sure to take them to a doctor any time it happens, whether you believe they need treatment or not. If you ask the doctor to document the injuries, you'll be able to use the record if later there's a custody dispute. The doctor may report the injuries to child protection authorities, which may make your life more difficult in the short run, but help you to protect your children in the long run. (See Chapter 8 for more details on custody.)

If you're the one who's violent to the children, admitting that you have a problem is the first step in solving it. You may need help to stop the violence, and asking for it is the second step. Call Parents Anonymous, or the children's protection division of your state department of health or welfare services, a counselor or a crisis line. It will be hard to do, but once you have the support of people who understand your problem, and who can give practical help, you'll probably be very relieved to have your secret out. Not only can you learn to restrain your temper, but you can find better ways to discipline, play with, and enjoy your children. You can also get help in reducing your stress.

Each day that your child is in a household where violence occurs is a day that the child learns that physical brutality is acceptable. The child is learning from you — much more than from others — how to be an adult. If you want to improve the chances of the child avoiding a violent relationship later, you can set the example of saying "No more" now.

Sexual Abuse of Children

Until recently, incest has been a taboo subject, and even those of us who now understand how widespread it is find it hard to imagine that anyone we know could do such a thing. Yet it happens in families of all classes, races and lifestyles. It's not unusual for men who batter to sexually molest the woman's children, whether or not they're also his children. Don't shut your eyes to the possibility and don't depend on the child to tell you. If the man has molested your child, he very likely has also threatened her or him (yes, it happens to boys too) with dire consequences if they tell. The child may feel guilty and ashamed or afraid you'll blame her. This is likely to be so even though you've given no indication you would blame her, and even though she has no reason to feel guilty.

There are those who blame the "provocative" child for her own victimization and many adults claim that children even as young as five or six "asked for it" by their "sexy" behavior. But even a teenager feels powerless — with considerable justification — when faced with an adult's sexual demands. The authority of the adult, plus the teen's emotional turmoil about her sexuality may cause a confused reaction. It's the adult who must take responsibility even if the teenager walks around the house half-dressed. Rather than take advantage of her, the adult, whether he's her father, stepfather or your boyfriend, should tell her to put a robe on.

If you have even the slightest suspicion that any adult in your household has made sexual overtures to your child, find a quiet place where the two of you can be alone and won't be rushed. Bring up the topic, explain that you're concerned about it, and that you won't blame the child for whatever has happened. Then ask.

If the child says, "No, nothing has happened," explain that even though it seems shocking, it's something that does happen, and she has the right to say "No" to sex anytime she wants to, no matter who the person is who wants it. Tell her also that if she ever has anything she wants to talk over with an adult besides yourself, you'll arrange to have her see a counselor.

It is said these days by people who claim to be experts that a little incest between adults and children isn't harmful and may even be a good thing. Don't believe it. To be used as a sexual object by a trusted adult is a betrayal that produces in the victim a disturbing mix of anger, guilt and confusion and often results in sexual dysfunction when the child grows up. This doesn't mean the child will never recover, but that she'll need some help sorting out her feelings and rebuilding her self-esteem. If your child is molested by a man you've been involved with, a professional counselor may be the best person to help, especially if you're having difficulty with your own feelings of guilt or anger or jealousy.

Emotional Abuse

By now, you may be used to humiliation, severe ego damage, and unprovoked insults to the children as well as to yourself. You've lost the ability to distinguish them from kidding and minor incidents of rudeness. If you've given up hope of stopping the verbal abuse, you may try to persuade the children to simply tune it out. If the father bullies everyone, you may tell yourself the children understand, and don't take his emotional abuse personally. The children may, in fact, claim it doesn't bother them, either because they believe they're to blame or because they want to ease the family tension. Yet, while they silently nurse hurts and grievances their self-esteem is being chipped away with each insult, sarcastic verbal assault or outburst of temper.

Even if the man isn't cruel to the children, their witness of his brutal treatment of you is likely to damage their abilities to form satisfying intimate relationships as adults. This too is a kind of child abuse. Many women feel a deep sense of regret that they remained with the violent man because they had wanted to keep the family together for the children's sake. Some of them observe their grown sons beating their wives or their grown daughters being beaten, each following the most familiar pattern of an intimate relationship. "Why didn't somebody warn me about this?" they ask in despair.

Their father may threaten to abandon the children altogether if you leave with them: "I'm certainly not going to be a weekend father. They won't even know who I am after awhile. If you take them, I'll never see them again." If he makes such a threat, you're confronted not only with your self-blame for his "forced" abandonment of the children, but your own fears of having to care for them alone, which may be more than you bargained for. (Single parenting is discussed in Chapter 15.)

Kidnapping is usually an empty threat, born of the desperation of the moment. But it does happen, so it can't lightly be dismissed. If kidnapping seems to be a realistic possibility, you need legal advice, and perhaps a counselor to help you cope with your anxiety.

WHAT DO THE CHILDREN DESERVE?

What positive things do the children gain from their father? Love? Security? Affection? Respect? Money? Stability? Fun?

How much would they lose if they moved away with you? You can only guess, of course, but at least you shouldn't assume they'll lose it all. They might lose a good deal of security, stability, and money, though not absolutely. As for affection, respect, love and fun, there's no reason to assume those qualities will disappear. They'll just be available in different ways or at different times. Those times needn't be just every Sunday. There are many custody arrangements.

If you've had several intimate relationships with men, you may feel guilty about your children's attachments to them being broken when you separated. It *is* hard for children to separate from father figures, but it may not be nearly as hard in the long run as staying with an abusive man.

It's never enough to say "Children need a father." Consider what else they deserve, as well as your own rights. Do they deserve the right to be free of humiliating remarks? Free of physical abuse? Free of fear? Have they the right to an environment that promotes cooperation, mutual respect and protection? The right to nonviolent adult models? If you've rarely exercised those rights for yourself, you may need the help of a friend or counselor to gain a reasonable perspective on those questions.

A child who's reluctant to leave the father may present you with a difficult problem. This may happen even if the father is abusive to the child, and it will be particularly difficult if a child old enough to decide for him or herself makes that choice.

It may be tempting to stay with the man, either because you're unwilling to separate from the child, or because you hope you can protect him or her. You probably won't be able to provide adequate protection. In addition, you'll be continuing the example of an adult woman who's helpless in the face of violence. The message is, "When people brutalize you, there's nothing you can do but take it."

It may be extremely difficult to leave your child with the father, but if you do, at least you're saying — in the most powerful way possible — "I don't have to take it. I *can* get away." You're providing a choice for the child, if he or she decides in a few months, or a few years, to leave the father and go to a safe home. In any case, don't make assumptions about who will get child custody. Get some legal advice about what is most likely in your particular circumstances.

You don't owe your children a two-parent family. Although claims are made to the contrary, there's no persuasive evidence that children are happier or healthier in a two-parent than a one-parent home. There is no evidence that children whose fathers don't live with them suffer from lack of a male image. There *is* some evidence that males who have violent fathers tend to be violent men. You owe your children the safest environment you can provide, and the best opportunity to grow up to be responsible healthy adults.

Chapter 4

WHAT DO YOU OWE YOURSELF?

Try to read this section as if you felt free to make your own decisions. There will be a temptation to say to yourself, "That's all very well, but I'd be beaten to a pulp," or "That sounds great for two reasonable people, but he would kill me if I even suggested negotiation." Later, you'll want to consider whether it's safe to act on these ideas, and you might very well decide it would be too dangerous if you're going to continue to live with the man. But for the moment, consider only whether these ideas are just and reasonable. This chapter will help you to realize what rights you have and to remember that life wasn't always a kind of prison. If you're getting very few of the things that everyone has a right to, then you have no obligation to stay in the relationship.

Suggestions for asserting your rights are made to help you remember that it's possible to ask for what you want. Sometimes even unreasonable spouses surprise you, when you act as if you really believe in your rights.

ARE YOU SOMEBODY BESIDES WIFE, MOTHER OR GIRLFRIEND?

It's extremely easy for many women to fuse their identity with their children or their husbands, that is, to be unable to tell where the family leaves off and they themselves begin. When you lose sight of who you are, separate from your man and your children, it's easy to become confused about what you deserve and what you owe yourself.

Activity 5   Who Are You?

In a sentence or two *write* the answers to these questions:

1. What do you want? _____

_____

2. What do you want to do now? _____

_____

3. What do you like to do? _____

_____

4. Who do you like to spend time with? _____

_____

5. What do you like to wear? _____

_____

6. Where do you like to go? _____

_____

7. Where would you like to live? _____

_____

8. What do you want to be doing in five years? _____

_____

9. Ten years? _____

_____

10. Twenty? _____

_____

How many answers were something like, "I don't know, I haven't thought about it," or, "I want to live here because I wouldn't want to disrupt the kids' schooling," "My husband likes me to wear...," or, "There's not much point in thinking about it, because the kids are too young," "My husband wouldn't hear of it," "It costs too much," or, "I don't much care. I'm easy to please."

If you answered half or more along these lines, you've probably forgotten who you are. You stopped, somewhere along the line, being an individual person, separate from your family or your man. You either stopped considering what you wanted a long time ago, or you developed the habit of foreseeing obstacles almost before realizing what you wanted. Those obstacles are usually the things that others need or want. Or perhaps you've persuaded yourself that you have what you want, in order to avoid facing the reality that your husband and children wouldn't hear you even if you did ask for something.

Try answering the questions again, without regard to how anyone besides yourself would be affected. You may be reluctant to do it, because it seems selfish and wrong. Selfish means devoted to, or caring for, only yourself. That's not what I'm suggesting here. What I'm urging is that you become aware of what you want and like, so that — along with the other people you're close to — you can find your share of satisfaction and happiness. You have to know what each person wants before you can make decisions about what's good for a couple or a family as a whole and before you can arrive at reasonable compromises. You are a person, and your desires should be considered on their own merits, as much as anyone else's.

READING HIS FEELINGS, READING YOURS

Women are taught to anticipate the needs of others as part of their role, especially as mother and wife. Because young children are unable to articulate their needs, their caretakers — mostly women — develop the ability to interpret. Sometimes mothers forget that older children can speak for themselves. Those children learn that their mothers will know what they want sometimes even before they know it themselves.

But husbands, one might suppose, are quite able to articulate their needs and wants, so why does a wife expend psychic energy figuring out what they might be?

When we say that a man isn't supposed to be helpless or dependent, that's not meant to include his emotional life. It's considered appropriate for a man to be incapable of expressing certain emotions — tenderness, love, vulnerability, inadequacy, loneliness, dependency, fear — and yet, he must be given solace, somehow, when these feelings surface. Helpless in the face of these emotions, he's dependent on the woman he's close to to interpret them for him, and often to provide comfort, even when he doesn't know he needs it.

It is often essential to a wife's safety and health to be able to meet her husband's needs — even when he doesn't know what they are. If she isn't able to do that, his feelings of vulnerability, dependency or fear may emerge as enraged demands for sex, or a meal or some other form of attention. The woman who's busy with another task or sound asleep at 2 a.m. or lulled into inattention by the man's earlier good mood, will pay a high price for not being attuned to his wishes, whether he expressed them or not. (This doesn't mean even a perfect mind reader will be safe. Some violent men explode whether all their desires are being attended to or not.) You'll have to decide how much energy you're willing to put into mind-reading and whether it's really keeping you safe. However, even if you continue to do a great deal of it, it's time you start "reading" your own feelings as well. You may be such a stranger to them that you'll have to begin by making careful note of when you're tired, sad, or feeling hurt, rejected or used. Begin by noticing physical signs or overt behavior. When you're overly tired and sleepy, look for signs of hurt, rejection, sadness or depression. When you snap at the kids for no apparent reason, ask yourself if you're feeling unappreciated and used, or if you're angry at your spouse. When you can't eat, or when you stuff down sweets, or drink too much, what are you trying to compensate for? Loneliness? Lack of affection? When you become overly restrictive with the children, or resent other people's obvious good times, could it be that you're feeling your own confinement and lack of pleasure in life?

As you begin to recognize how you feel, you'll be able to explore what you want, and that's the beginning of a separate identity. Then you'll be on your way to answering the question: "What do I owe myself?" But there's another question that comes first.

"WHAT IF IT'S REALLY MY FAULT?"

If you believe you're responsible for the destructive aspects of the relationship, your awareness of your faults may keep you from even considering that you have a right to end it. This is an especially dangerous trap for you if you've lashed out at him verbally or physically at times. Perhaps you hit him back sometimes, or lost your temper and threw something at him, or even started the violence yourself. You may badger yourself with thoughts like, "Maybe I brought it on myself," "I shouldn't be so sloppy at housekeeping... cold in bed... selfish... demanding... bad-tempered," "He put up with a lot from me."

Think of the things you did, or failed to do, that may have "brought it on yourself." How did you know they did? Did you get hit every time you did those things? *Only* then? Be scrupulously honest. Often a woman is beaten for "reasons" she doesn't understand at all. In a desperate attempt to create order out of chaos, she reconstructs events and decides her own shortcomings "caused" the beatings. For awhile that may be a useful survival technique as it seems to place some responsibility and control in her hands if she can actually change herself, or cause the man to react differently. But with a man who batters, such control over behavior rarely exists.

In order to make a sound decision, different questions and more precise answers are in order. If there's someone you've confided in all along, you should ask her help now. She may have a more objective memory than yours about the certainty of cause and effect.

If some of your actions or attitudes are always followed by beatings, look at them closely and decide whether it's reasonable for the man to object to them. Suppose he becomes violent every time you spend time with a woman friend, or whenever you aren't home to answer his calls from work, or when you complain or when dinner is late.

Which of these "flaws" should you correct? Which do you want to change? It might well be worth your while to put time and effort into changing because you want to, and because it might please your man. But regardless of whether these are flaws that you both want changed, *your imperfections do not give your partner the right to "discipline" you with physical violence.*

Questions to Ask Yourself

Let's look at his objection to your spending time with women friends. If that always occasions his hitting or beating you, and if you're determined to stay with him, you might either stop seeing friends in order to protect yourself from his violence or you might decide to continue those relationships, but keep them secret.

If one day you give in to your loneliness and go off with a woman friend hoping to get away with it but he learns this and beats you, you may feel you asked for it. A friend or relative may tell you the same thing. "After all, you knew he would beat you if he found out, didn't you?"

The phrase implies you deserved it, which means either you behaved badly, so you deserve to be punished, or that you behaved stupidly, since you should have known the consequences that would follow your action.

Ask yourself whether meeting your friend was wrong, whether any adult has the right to punish another, and whether people who behave stupidly deserve bad things to happen to them.

Was meeting a friend wrong? Do you deserve to have friends, to be with people who give you some of the warmth and concern you seldom get from your husband? Isn't that a minimum of what *every* person deserves? If you agree, ask yourself again whether you really "brought it on yourself." At worst you may find that you didn't act in the safest way. But you were protecting another equally important aspect of yourself, that seed of independence and individuality, hungering to grow and needing warmth and nurturance in which to do it. You risked your physical being on the chance you could nourish your spirit. It's impossible to make a really good decision if the alternatives are either risking a beating or resigning yourself to isolation.

Does one adult have the right to punish another? If your man beats you, he's likely to explain that it was a last resort, a reminder that he's the authority over all aspects of your life. Whether he has that right has nothing to do with whether you have faults. He certainly has the right to point them out and to ask you to change, just as you have a similar right in regard to his flaws. But you're not his child, not his employee, not his property. He doesn't have the right to control your life. (For that matter, it's now recognized that even the rights of employers to discipline the employees and of parents to punish children are severely limited by law.)

No position of authority brings with it the power of judge, jailer and batterer. Certainly the institution of marriage, which is said to be based on love, respect and companionship should not foster such power. Nor should it grant the partner who has the most economic power and the greater physical strength the right to punish his spouse for either imagined or real faults.

Do people who behave stupidly deserve to have bad things happen to them? As discussed above, you took a calculated risk to get something you badly wanted. Just because you could have predicted you'd be beaten if caught doesn't mean either that you behaved stupidly or that you deserve a beating.

If you and your man each have serious faults, that doesn't necessarily mean you deserve each other. To the extent that you bring out the worst in each other, at least a temporary separation is indicated. This is especially true if you're both violent, alcoholic or addicted to drugs, which make you dangerous to each other. It can give you some space so that you can each learn more kind and constructive ways of treating each other. Then you can either come back together, or you might form new relationships that will be constructive and mutually supportive.

If you really do believe that you're very difficult to live with, you can start changing your ways now by practicing the exercises in the "Helping Yourself to Survival" section, especially Chapter 11, "A Courageous Act a Day."

WHAT DO YOU DESERVE?

For many people, to deserve something implies that it has been earned through work or suffering. Yet there are some things that everyone deserves, earned or not.

Freedom of speech is a fundamental right. Many a wife gives up this right soon after marriage, as she becomes aware of more and more things that upset or anger her husband. Perhaps the first statement to be eliminated is a comment about her past relationships, especially with men. Then she stops talking about her desires for the future, when he interprets that as a criticism of his ability to provide for the family. Next goes the expression of any negative feelings: depression, frustration, loneliness. She may no longer ask him questions about his work, where he's been or how he feels, lest she be accused of prying or nagging. Finally she may give up stating her own opinions, to avoid being called stupid.

A woman will often do this, at first out of consideration for her man's feelings, later to protect herself from his temper. He may directly demand her silence on many subjects and before long, she persuades herself she has no right to speak up. She thinks there's something wrong with her for even wanting to express herself.

The right to have some aspects of life remain private ought to be recognized by both partners. Many men who are violent toward their wives call them several times every day to check on whether they're home, insist on accompanying them to the grocery store and won't let them out of their sight unless it's absolutely necessary, which usually means when they're at work. They may closely question the woman about the smallest activities of her day and physically punish her if she refuses to respond to the cross-examination. Yet, if the woman asks questions related to their mutual concerns, such as whether they'll be going out Saturday night, or how much money is in the bank, she will be accused of invading male territory.

You may gradually have given up your rights without thinking much about them. How about the right to choose your friends? To decide how to spend money? How to use your time? What to eat, wear and how to look?

Take the matter of your appearance. Most of us like to look attractive to the people we're close to, but it's your right to dress and arrange your hair and makeup to please your family *or* to please yourself. If your husband thinks you look too flashy or wants you to look too obviously sexy, or your daughter accuses you of looking "old" or dowdy, you don't have to accommodate them by changing your appearance. One way to begin establishing your separate identity is to dress in the style that's comfortable for you, that feels like the real you.

As for money and time, some of it belongs to the family and is subject to family decisions. But there are two important qualifications. Only some of it belongs to the family; you have a right to use some money and some time just to please yourself, no questions asked. Secondly, what does belong to the family should not be distributed or decided upon only by the male, but at least by the two adults in the household.

Perhaps by now you're ready to consider what basic rights everyone is entitled to. *Place a check mark* in the first column, indicating each item that you believe everyone deserves.

Activity
6

Activity 6   *Rights List*

	I Everyone has the right.	II I exercise my right.
1. The right to privacy		
2. The right to express ideas, including unpopular ones		
3. The right to express feelings, even "negative" ones		
4. The right to choose work, religion, lifestyle,		
5. The right to be free of fear		
6. The right to have some time for yourself		
7. The right to spend some money as you please		
8. The right to emotional support from family and friends		
9. The right to be listened to by family and friends		
10. The right to cultivate friendships of your choice		
11. The right to do creative, challenging, absorbing, worthwhile work		
12. The right to decide whether to have sex or not		

All but two of the above are rights you can exercise now. (These exceptions are the right to satisfying work and the right to choose one's work. Most people are not fortunate enough to do that without careful planning, training and perhaps sacrifice of some immediate satisfactions.)

Put a check in the second column for each right you currently exercise.

If there are differences between columns 1 and 2, look closely at what's happened to your exercise of rights. Maybe you believe everyone except you has certain rights. Does that mean you're not quite a person? Does it mean that civil and human rights are suspended for women, or for wives — or for mothers until their children are grown?

In looking at these questions it's easy to be distracted by "Yes, but..." games. "Yes, but he's taking me out so I don't have any right to say where I'd like to go, or to refuse sex." "Yes, but I can't choose what to buy because he earns the money." "Yes, but none of us really has time or money to spare, so there aren't free choices to be made." "Yes, but he didn't choose his job and it's not satisfying at all, so I don't have any right..."

Money

Let's look at money. It can certainly seem as if there is nothing to decide, especially if it all goes for necessities. However, even when there's not enough to pay basic bills, some of it is always spent on discretionary items. If your grocery bag includes beer, sweets, packaged gravy, pop, frozen foods, magazines, or cigarettes, you've already made some decisions about "nonessentials." It's difficult to make mutual decisions about these matters because one person's necessity is another's luxury.

Even if it's a small amount, each person should exercise the right to have funds to spend with no questions asked. If you spend money that way already, that's a start. But perhaps you manage it by slipping a magazine into the groceries, or stashing small amounts of cash away until you have enough to take the kids to the circus, buy your teenaged son new jeans or purchase something you want for yourself. Or maybe you charge what you want, and then wait nervously for the blows when the bills come in.

In these ways you may get the things you want, but you pay a high price, and you don't establish any rights. If you have to be sneaky to get away with it, or to risk punishment, you're cast into the role of the irresponsible child who can't make her own decisions — a person who may only have what another person arbitrarily decides she deserves. A dangerous by-product is an increase of your guilt feelings and lowering of your self-esteem.

Time

The same principle applies to time of your own. How much time you can arrange to have to yourself depends upon your lifestyle: your housekeeping standards, the size of your garden, how much of your spouse's time is available for childcare (i.e., how much time he's not working at an outside job, how old your children are, etc.). As a minimum, each of you should have one half day and one evening a week to do as you please.

A problem may be that one or both of you doesn't want to take that time. Suppose you don't want the time, or you like the idea but you don't know what to do with it. It will be good for you to take it anyway. Use it to take a class, to shop, to walk in the park, to see a movie that doesn't interest your partner, to cultivate a friend in order to begin reestablishing your separate identity. You may spend a few hours being either bored or nervous until you get used to making decisions and participating in new activities, but it will be worth it in the long run.

It's good for your relationship if you each take some time for yourself, but if he insists that he doesn't need or want such time, you have little power to do anything about it. He might use the fact that he doesn't take his time to try to make you feel guilty for taking yours. In that case, you'll need to keep in mind that it's his choice. He's not making a sacrifice for you. He's doing what he wants, and you have the right to do what you want.

GETTING RESPECT IN THE WORKPLACE
(AT HOME AND ON THE JOB)

Often both husbands and wives consider the wife's earned income to be merely "pocket money." Both men and women want to believe the man is supporting the family, because that's part of the traditional myth of masculinity. However, as inflation spirals, more people are admitting that it takes two incomes for most families to live well. A woman's income is purchasing goods and services that are important to the family and it's no less important than her partner's income. Women can no longer afford to accept these traditional propositions:

- Women deserve less money in the market place, because their work is less important than men's.
- Since they're only earning "extras" their work isn't very important.
- Since their work outside the home isn't of much value, and women really should be at home anyway, they should still do the housework and childcare.

Those statements should be replaced with these:

- Work is of equal value, regardless of the worker's gender.
- Women need work and adequate pay as much as men do.
- If two people parent children, both should be responsible for home and childcare.

This doesn't necessarily mean that each partner must do precisely half of each job, but that the number of hours worked in and outside the home is near equal and is acceptable to the person doing the work. When this idea prevails in society, we will no longer find women doing the three unpaid jobs of wife, housekeeper and parent plus one underpaid job of waitress, secretary or nurse. Men and women will share and appreciate each other's contributions both in and out of the home.

If your role is that of the traditional wife or mother and your tasks of housekeeping and childcare are rarely finished for more than a short time, the lack of a sense of accomplishment may also contribute to the idea that you haven't done anything of value. This feeling is one of the aspects of homemaking that makes the job hard. According to recent surveys, women who have *no* children spend about five and a half hours a day on housework. So don't sell your labor short.

If your children are in school, or grown, you may not do much work at home. Some of us take housekeeping more seriously than others, and if you really want to make homemaking a full-time job even when your children are older, perhaps that's what you should do. But, if you can take care of it in two or three hours a day, consider getting a part-time or full-time job outside the home. Knowledge that you're pulling your share of the weight will help you make a better decision about leaving or staying with the man. Before you decide whether to take a job, make a careful count of the hours you spend at homemaking and childcare, being sure to include trips to the zoo and other child-centered activities on weekends and in the evening. Also consider your volunteer activities in the community and the church. They are work too. If your man wants you to stay home, yet looks down on the work you do at home, you need to change something. If you've begun to agree with him about the low value of what you do at home, you'll need to relearn respect for your work, or to start looking for employment outside. In other words, start respecting what you do or doing what you respect.

Look again at your responses to column II in Activity 6 and decide which rights you're going to begin claiming. Decide whether it's going to be safe to do it while you're still living with the man. Just in case, plan to tell him about it when you're someplace you'll be safe or where you can get away quickly if he becomes violent.

UNDERSTANDING WHAT YOU BOTH DESERVE

Perhaps you'd like to make changes in your life but are thinking to yourself, "He deserves things that he's not getting either," or, "There isn't any way I can get what I deserve." Let's consider both responses.

He's Not Getting What He Deserves Either.   A good place to start with this one is simply to ask him what he believes he deserves, and what he's not getting. He may refuse to participate in such a conversation. He may feel it's useless to think about such things since no one gets much in life anyway. Or he might react with suspicion, in which case you should be honest and tell him you have your own list that you want to share.

If he's willing to participate, you can begin to make some trade-offs for each of you to get something you want and deserve. Trade-offs won't work, though, unless there's at least a semblance of equality. If he believes he deserves peace and quiet when he gets home from work, does he recognize a time when you deserve peace and quiet? If he deserves not to be "nagged" about doing household chores on the weekend, will he agree not to nag you to sew buttons, serve meals, and so on during weekends? If not, you don't have grounds for negotiation.

If he flatly refuses to participate, there won't be much you can do. Maybe that will give you one more item for your own Rights List (Activity 6): "When I want to negotiate fair treatment for each of us, I deserve a response and some effort to work it out."

There Isn't Any Way I Can Get What I Deserve. If you've decided there isn't any way to get what you deserve, ask yourself why not, why won't it happen? It does to lots of people. It isn't always because they're lucky or smart either. Most people who get what they deserve have realized that it's up to them to make it happen. You can't control some parts of your life, but focus on those parts you can do something about.

You can lay the groundwork to leave your husband or to acquire work skills. You can make plans to overcome whatever obstacles stand in the way of getting what you deserve.

This is not to say it's easy. All the more reason to get started planning now. Remember the hardships and failures and disasters you envision if you get a job, go to school, or live without a man are frightening mainly because these choices are new to you. Your current way of life (having almost no freedom, being physically beaten and emotionally abused, feeling trapped and worthless) is probably much more dangerous and would be far more frightening to you if you weren't used to it. You can get used to the difficult aspects of a new way of life and the rewards will more than balance the hardship. Just give yourself a little time.

You owe it to yourself to begin getting the things you and every person deserve. No one is likely to give them to you unless you realize that it's your right to have them. You owe it to yourself to decide, to choose and to make of your life what you want it to be.

Chapter 5

"BUT I STILL LOVE HIM"

Friends and relatives may despair, hearing you say you still love the man who abused you, especially if the abuse was physical and seriously damaging. Perhaps you're bewildered yourself, or humiliated by the awareness that you still love the man who acts in a hateful way toward you.

WHAT DOES BEING IN LOVE MEAN?

Though we can't explain the condition of being in love, we recognize it when it happens to us, and usually we accept it on faith when someone tells us it has happened to her. Note that it "happens" to someone, like "a bolt from the blue." One helplessly "falls in love." These phrases indicate the passivity of Cupid's victim. Love, according to song and story and poem, is out of your control, not something you choose to do or work at doing. It causes symptoms that are similar to illness: palpitations, trembling, loss of appetite, weakness.

These symptoms, reflecting both the pain and exhilaration of being in love, probably originated with the Greeks, who invented the concept of Western love that — with important modifications — we cling to today. But, in contrast to modern Americans, the ancient Greeks considered love an amusing pastime, or distraction from more serious and important matters. They didn't view it as necessary to being a good person, nor as a lifetime commitment, nor did they associate it with the union of marriage.

Each age tends to view its concept of love as both the only way it could be and the way it's supposed to be. Patterns of love from past periods seem either comical or tragic. Morton Hunt, in *A Natural History of Love*, provides a useful modern perspective: "At no time in history has so large a proportion of humanity rated love so highly, thought about it so much, or displayed such an insatiable appetite for words about it."†

Most of us are appalled at the outmoded idea of loveless, un-

---

†Morton Hunt. *The Natural History of Love* (New York: Knopf, 1959), p. 341.

romantic, arranged marriages, but Hunt points out the absurdity of the contemporary idea that "the romantic attraction is considered to be adequate and indeed the only basis for choosing one's lifelong partner." He questions the commonly held idea that "...sex drives...must be completely and permanently satisfied within marriage... and that tenderness, mystery, and excitement are expected to coexist with household care, childraising problems, and the routine 15,000 nights together." †

Absurd or not, an impossible burden on marriage or not, to some extent we are stuck with these ideas. We're all shaped by films, novels and songs, law, economics and religion to believe that love properly takes only certain forms — and that all others are immoral, crazy, immature or just infatuation.

Romantic as this twentieth century age is, there are variations on the theme of love, and you can analyze your feelings (and his) to determine whether you're involved in a dangerously romantic or addictive relationship or whether you share a healthy, nurturing love that might even withstand 15,000 nights of routine.

To get a clearer perspective on the particular kind of love you and your man share, *put a check mark* in front of each of the following that seems true:

Activity 7   How Do You Love Each Other?

1. *I could never find another man to love the way I love him.*
2. *Without him, I have nothing to live for.*
3. *I know exactly what it is about him I love.*
4. *No one could ever understand him the way I do.*
5. *I suppose I should be interested in other people and activities, but I just want to be with him.*
6. *We help each other to explore new possibilities in life.*
7. *The idea of making love to another man is unthinkable.*
8. *Whenever I'm a few minutes late, or want to be alone, he thinks I'm with another man.*
9. *Loving him makes me feel more loving toward other people.*
10. *I try to keep on my "rose colored glasses" and see only the best in him.*
11. *I love him so much, I can't stand the thought of his being with anyone else.*
12. *I hope he never leaves me, but if it comes to that I'll be okay.*
13. *He would never love another woman the way he loves me.*

†*Natural History of Love*, p. 342.

14. *Often, I feel better when I'm away from him, yet I find myself calling him against my better judgment.*
15. *I feel good about myself when I'm with him.*
16. *I never let him see me without makeup, or with curlers in my hair. I want him always to see me at my best.*
17. *I feel that I'm nothing without him.*
18. *He brings out the best in me.*
19. *I don't know why I love him, I just do.*
20. *When things are going well with us, I don't need anyone but him.*
21. *He has many of the qualities I value, and that I'm trying to develop in myself.*
22. *He's so much smarter and more capable than I am, he seems to know everything about everything.*
23. *When I try to imagine never seeing him again, I feel empty.*
24. *It's wonderful to spend time with him at sports, work or having fun together with other people, and I enjoy being by myself or with women friends, too.*
25. *He's so special, I don't know why he's interested in an ordinary person like me.*
26. *Without me, he has nothing to live for.*
27. *He wants me to feel good whether I'm with him or not.*
28. *This time he means it. He's really going to change.*
29. *I know he loves me because he wants to know where I am every minute.*
30. *I like to hear about the good times he's had when he's been with other people.*

As part of your analysis of your responses look at three kinds of conjugal love that are common today. Romantic, addictive and nurturing love each have some overlapping characteristics, but they can also be looked at separately.

ROMANTIC LOVE

Romantic love grows out of the courtly tradition of the 11th and 12th century "knights in shining armor." It was noble, pure, sacrificial, often tragically destined to be unconsummated, yet the lovers might be faithful to death, enduring years of tragic suffering because the fates refused to allow them to come together. These lovers were often able to maintain their enchantment because they loved from afar, rarely coming into close enough contact to distinguish the real character flaws (and virtues) of the beloved. These romantic adventures were definitely not to be contaminated by the lustful sexuality of the marriage bed.

Today, of course, romantic love is supposed to lead to sexuality, married love, and happiness ever after. The lovers are by no means distant from each other. There are no long nights of sonnet writing or years of anonymous serenading under balconies today. Contemporary love relationships are likely to begin with the question, "What's your name?" on Monday, followed by "How about a date?" on Tuesday, and a few Saturday nights later "Let's go to bed," which may or may not be accompanied by promises to love faithfully, forever.

But the poetry remains, in however altered a form. Popular songs envelop the romantic couple with the magic, the madness, the otherworldliness, and sometimes the delicious tragedy of sexual love.

The "magic" aspect of love implies powerlessness in the face of an overwhelming force, insists that the feeling is not subject to rational analysis. Nor need there by any nameable qualities that cause you to love the specific person. It's "the touch of his hand," "the very thought of you," or other vaguely felt responses to the idea of him, more than his tangible qualities.

In order to see how romantic your relationship is, take another look at your responses to the statements about love in Activity 7. Note how many checks you had for numbers 1, 4, 7, 10, 13, 16, 19, 22, 25. The more checks, the more romantic your relationship is.

Questions 1, 4, 7 and 13 reflect the feeling that there's only one man for each woman in the world. Perhaps you reject that notion when it's stated so obviously, but check marks for those statements give away your lingering belief in it.

If you responded positively to questions 19, 22, 25 and 28, you're a victim of the romantic beliefs that your man is someone out of the ordinary realm of humans. Yet you can't even say which of his characteristics you value. You believe he'll turn from beast to beauty, from frog to prince. Regardless of the evidence to the contrary, he'll stop his cruelty and become tender and loving. Positive responses to statements 10 and 16 indicate you love your own idea of the person, rather than who he really is, and you want him to perceive you only at your best. This fosters illusions and psychological distance. If you don't allow yourself to see your lover's flaws, you'll be able to maintain the idea that he's not an ordinary human being at all, but a superperson, who for some mysterious reason chooses to love you. By virtue of his love, you're raised a bit closer to the world of superpersons. If you risk displeasing him, he may leave you, thrusting you squarely back in the world of ordinary persons — where you secretly fear you belong anyway. So it's easy to persuade yourself you'll fall apart without him.

This romantic relationship can be fun, exciting, all-absorbing, erotic, entertaining. It can keep you in a state of "delirious" happiness and plunge you into despair. It's a peak experience, a "high" unmatched by any other.

ADDICTIVE LOVE

There is a remarkable similarity between the effects of romantic love and of certain drugs, not only in the "high" state and the "low" of withdrawal, but in the potential for addiction. We've all been taught that certain drugs are dangerously addictive and that everyone should stay safely away from them, but there is a growing body of evidence that addiction lies as much in the person as in the substance.†

Many people have used cocaine, alcohol, cigarettes, sugar or other allegedly addictive substances with no difficulty. Others have become hooked, either quickly or slowly. At first, they're high — their minds and feelings are expanding. But addicts eventually find that they've become dull and that their worlds have shrunk. In addition to drugs, this might happen with an overdose of television, running, crafts, reading, housework — or love.

Addiction is often learned. The effects of drugs are often the result of what the user *expects* to happen. If the beginning cocaine, marijuana or alcohol user is coached to expect a "rush," or physical sensation, she is likely to experience what has been predicted to happen.

Having learned to anticipate it from an early age, a woman can experience romantic love as a special kind of high, in which the "oneness" of being a couple instantly banishes loneliness and the sense of alienation many of us suffer. If the woman has a good feeling about herself and some other solid connections through work or friends, she may realize she's in love with the idea of love rather than the actual person. If the man stops loving her, she will go through a period of mourning, but she won't let the break-up destroy her perceptions of herself. Nor will she imagine her lost love is the only man in the world for her.

But a woman who values herself less or needs love more will go a step beyond that romantic love into addiction. In addition to the characteristics of romantic love she'll be certain she can't survive without the man's love and that she wouldn't even want to, because there wouldn't be anything to live for. Her world has shrunk, and if the man stops loving her, she will feel abandoned and desolate. If he periodically neglects or abuses her, she'll allow

---

†Stanton Peele with Archie Brodsky, *Love and Addiction* (New York: New American Library, 1976).

herself to be persuaded each time that it didn't really happen, it was her fault, or it was a one-time aberration that will never happen again.

The degree to which she's vulnerable to this script depends upon how suggestible she is and the extent to which society — her friends, family, advertisements, songs and movies — have coached her into expecting that being in love will bring ecstasy and that being abandoned by her lover must be a tragedy.

The man who believes he can't survive without love often fears that his woman will become involved with someone else if she goes to the grocery store alone or may work himself into a jealous rage if she happens to be away from the telephone when he calls. He wants to exercise total control over her life; if she refuses, or seems to refuse it, his fear of being abandoned may lead to psychological or physical abuse of the woman he loves, and to the extent she's addicted to him, she'll be unable or unwilling to escape that abuse.

When this happens, the woman becomes helpless and dependent. Her life may be reduced to the addictive cycle: the overpowering need for him, the "high" of momentary fulfillment, and then the "downer" when the "supply" is removed. If he removes himself — emotionally or physically — often, or for long periods, she'll become absorbed in her loneliness and grief. Paradoxically, if he's always available, her dependency on him will only grow.

The more her world becomes centered on the addiction, the more narrow it becomes; and the more narrow her world, the more it centers on her addiction. When a couple is mutually addicted, they can sometimes work out a tolerable relationship, though it makes for very confined lives. When one person is a batterer, it is a deadly, dangerous relationship, and often more difficult to break away from than other forms of addiction.

You can tell whether you're involved in addictive love by reviewing your answers to questions 2, 5, 8, 11, 14, 17, 20, 23, 26, 28 and 29. Positive responses to numbers 8, 26, and 29 indicate that the man is addicted to you. Check marks for numbers 2, 5, 11, 14, 17, 20, 23 and 28 reflect your addiction to him. In a two-way "habit" you both believe that without each other you have nothing to live for. When you're addicted you're sure you can fulfill all of the other's needs and that your demand for total, exclusive possession of each other proves your love. If there's some specific quality you value in him, it may be something you believe you lack. If you've convinced yourself you're not very smart or capable, you may feel a need to associate with a man who seems to have those qualities. If your self-esteem is very low, your need to be associated with a man who seems competent may be so great that you grossly overestimate his desirable qualities. You depend on him to be capable for both of you, so that you don't have to develop your own capabilities. Meanwhile, your inflated view of his abilities may help him from moment to moment to deny his feelings of inadequacy, and the need to overcome them. He won't grow either, and you'll each become helpless and dependent on each other.

NURTURING LOVE

Nurturing love is the opposite of addictive love. It sustains life, promotes growth, and increases energy. It is not possessive, and it grows out of a realistic appreciation of the loved one's attractive qualities, without a need to minimize his flaws.

Nurturing love is based on what each partner *wants*, rather than needs. If the loved one has important qualities that the lover lacks, she'll want to develop them in herself rather than simply basking in the reflected light of the loved one's admired characteristics. This type of love allows for the expansion of abilities, knowledge and experience rather than the shrinkage of relationships and activities. To find out if this is the kind of love you feel for the man in your relationship, check the number of your responses to questions 3, 6, 9, 12, 15, 18, 21, 24, 27 and 30. The more checks you have, the more nurturing your love is likely to be. If you have a healthy, mutually respectful relationship, one partner may lose his or her temper from time to time, but the result will not be battering. The man in a nurturing relationship can be expected not to hit his spouse but in the event he does lose control, he will immediately find a way to regain it, or will find professional help, and at the very least arrange for the woman's safety if a similar situation is likely to occur.

REASONS FOR LEAVING SOMEONE YOU LOVE

When abused women say "I know I should leave, but I love him," they suggest "Because I love him, I can't leave him." But that doesn't necessarily follow. Loving an abusive man will make it hard to leave, but not impossible. Loving him may make you want to stay with him, but in the long run the most loving thing you can do for each other is to separate, at least temporarily. No one wants their loved one to continue a round of violence and remorse. If you separate, you'll at least interrupt that pattern. If you're involved in an addictive relationship that's abusive, you'll have to cut the relationship off immediately and totally. In either case, you'll have to get rid of the romantic ideas that he is the only one who can provide you with what you need, that you'll never find another man to love, and that life isn't worth living without love.

By now you should have a pretty clear idea of what kind of love you're involved in and the extent of the problem you'll be faced with if you decide that for your safety you must leave. But for many women, it's a long step between that realization and taking action on it.

Chapter 6

MAKING THE DECISION

So here you are, thinking about separating from your man and dreading the thought of no one's voice to fill the silence when you come home from work. Perhaps you'll have one or more children to support and discipline, teach and love on your own. You may be thinking about a job you'll have to keep for many years, whether you like it or not, or worrying about responsibility for all decisions: where to live, what to buy, who to get to fix the toilet, how to do the income tax yourself. In short, whenever there's a question about what is to be done, you'll have to make the decision.

If you've been going around and around on a mental treadmill for some time, unable to decide whether to leave or stay, now is the time to take your first decisive step. It's time for action.

HOW SERIOUS ARE YOU?

Some people use self-help books to clarify their thoughts or to start changing their lives. Others read one after the other without ever helping themselves. They use the books as a way to avoid making changes, while persuading themselves that they're "trying." Similarly, some abused women read everything that's published about women in their situation in hopes of finding a solution that will neither require them to leave the man nor take risks nor endure pain. That isn't going to happen. If you decide to change your life, it may be challenging, exciting, and rewarding, but it will also probably be difficult, lonely, and frightening at first.

As a check on how seriously you've been considering the content of this book, look back and see how many of the questionnaires you answered with pen or pencil rather than simply reading through them. The more active a reader you've been, the more serious you probably are about making a decision that you can live with and stick to.

If you've been just a passive reader, go back now and complete the questionnaires. They're designed to help you clarify your thoughts and feelings. Your participation is a message to yourself that you're taking your survival seriously.

WHAT'S THE WORST THAT CAN HAPPEN IF YOU LEAVE?

Do you imagine that if you're totally responsible for yourself or for the family, the day might come when you're faced with someone's judgment that you've been a colossal failure? One of society's rejects? Incapable of making it on your own or of being a competent single parent? Perhaps your fears take the form of vaguely felt apprehensions or maybe they're clearly visualized tragedies. You become so depressed you take an overdose of pills. You lose custody of the children because you can't support them and take care of them at the same time; your son becomes an alcoholic; child protective services are called in because your children are reported to be neglected.

Your concerns may not be as acutely dramatic as that. Maybe they're along the lines of the children's daily discipline problems or the constant colds and years of runny noses that seem to be ahead. Or you imagine years of boring factory or office work, poverty and sameness with little hope of either romance or security. Or the continual emptiness of knowing there's no one special who cares, no one to understand in-jokes or to share responsibility, blame and triumphs with you. The thought of starting over with someone else seems impossibly burdensome.

Perhaps your greatest fears are of boredom, lack of excitement, romance and companionship. Try to make the frightening notion of being alone specific. Is it sex you'll miss? Or companionship? Someone to go places with, or to share the worries and pleasures of childraising? All of the above, plus someone to lean on and be needed by?

Activity 8   Worst Fears List

WORST FEAR: Losing the home and garden that I've worked for twenty-two years.

Reasons It's Likely	Reasons It's Unlikely
I can't afford the payments	*I'll probably get house, because*
Bob probably won't pay house	*I'll probably get custody*
maintainence	*Child support might include*
I'm too old to get a better job	*enough for payments*
	Could have kids double up and
	rent two rooms
	Might be able to refinance

Do this exercise for yourself now.

Worst Fear: _____

Reasons It's Likely   Reasons It's Unlikely

_____   _____

_____   _____

_____   _____

_____   _____

_____   _____

You may be able to fill in some of the blanks with certainty. But other tentative answers may simply raise more questions. This is important. In some situations you may only be able to make guesses, and you'll need to find specialists in certain fields to answer your concerns. The questions may be about property settlement, custody, employment or public assistance, and the people you turn to may be lawyers, job counselors, battered women's shelter staff, or social workers.

Getting expert advice can be costly. Call a shelter or women's center, legal services or the American Bar Association, or crisis line information and referral service to find out if there are any low-cost services for people in your circumstances. Be sure to say that you've been battered, in case there are special services for battered women. (If you haven't talked about it, this may be hard to do, but it's a good time to start. Saying out loud that you've been battered is a good way to remind yourself that you have nothing to be ashamed of.)

If there are no special services for battered women in your community, you may have to travel to find them. If you have to pay high fees, it will probably be worthwhile in the long run, but first ask several people for referrals so you have a better chance of finding someone worth all that money. (See the next section for ideas on how to deal with doctors, lawyers and counselors.) Your alternative is to spend more years worrying about events that may be extremely unlikely, and possibly to make some bad decisions on the basis of your miscalculations.

When you've gathered as much information as possible, modify your answers to the questions about the likelihood of your fears coming true. Share your new information with friends or relatives who you're sure understand you and have your best interests at heart. Be wary of advice that's too easy. ("Oh, you won't have any trouble getting a good job just because you're fifty years old.") But if most people you trust believe your fears aren't justified — and if they're standing by to help — you may want to reconsider your negative judgments.

WHAT'S THE WORST THAT CAN HAPPEN IF YOU STAY WITH THE MAN?

Many a woman who is involved with an abusive man describes herself as fearful, unwilling to take risks, or even cowardly. But those of us on the outside looking in see that such a woman takes enormous risks every day of her life. People have a remarkable ability to get used to almost anything and then to define their way of life as normal or even rewarding.

If you consider yourself a generally fearful person, you probably don't realize how many risks you take every day. *Make a list* of all the chances you took during the last few days, including risks of succeeding or failing, being hurt or being safe, of feeling accepted or rejected, or making your life better or worse.

Activity 9   Risk List

1. _____
2. _____
3. _____
4. _____
5. _____
6. _____
7. _____
8. _____
9. _____
10. _____

What's the most *likely* bad thing to happen if you stay? Consider the physical and psychological damage, both long-range and short-range, to you and your children. *List the things* you're afraid of. If they don't seem so bad, think back to the last time you were abused. Remember what you were afraid of then, and *write down everything* you were afraid would happen to you during the few minutes or few hours following the crisis. Do it even if it's very painful, and *compare that list* with the list of of things you're afraid of now. If there's a big difference, the chances are that you're letting the memory of the real dangers of your situation fade away, so you won't have to think about leaving — and facing the unknown experience of being alone. Ask yourself, "If I stay, what are the odds of each danger happening?" Ninety percent likely? Seventy-five percent? If you're afraid of being killed, even a twenty, or a five percent chance is too high.

Activity 10   Comparing the Dangers

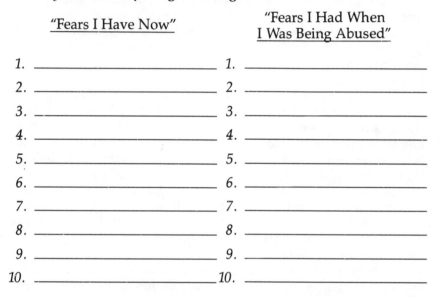

"Fears I Have Now"	"Fears I Had When I Was Being Abused"
1.	1.
2.	2.
3.	3.
4.	4.
5.	5.
6.	6.
7.	7.
8.	8.
9.	9.
10.	10.

Try to make yourself imagine what it would be like to die. Then force yourself to imagine what it would be like to kill the man, as many women have done after years of abuse. Think about what it would be like to be paralyzed or deaf from his brutal injury. Don't just shudder and shrug it away. Stay with the thought. Visualize yourself, your man, your family, the police, your relatives. Feel what you would feel if each of these actions were really happening.

Do you get enough from the relationship to risk all that?

If you do decide to separate from the man, you'll probably look back with amazement at the dangerous situation you lived in and at your low level of awareness of the danger. It's shocking how many women are able to endure such situations. Yet it's not altogether surprising that a woman in seemingly inescapable danger will use whatever psychological means she can to keep fear at a tolerable level. Denial is one of those methods, and it's quite useful at certain times. But if you want to get out of the situation, you'll have to break through that denial and admit just how much risk you face every day.

BALANCING THE SCALES

If you did Activity 3 in Chapter 2, you have a list of disadvantages of marriage in general and of the relationship with the man who abuses you in particular. Look at the lists again and add to them if you can think of other disadvantages. Now list the disadvantages of *leaving* this relationship.

Even though it's a bit repetitious, it will probably turn up new information. You might find that items you normally think of as disadvantages of leaving show up also on the "Disadvantages of Staying" list. "Fear of inability to cope" may appear on both lists, even though you normally focus on it only when you think of leaving.

Without, perhaps, stating it in so many words, you've probably been assuming or hoping or wishing that you could overcome the disadvantages of staying — that you would somehow eventually find a way to please your man so that he won't become violent. Now is the time to make your last serious attempt to do anything that might overcome a disadvantage of staying.

The same can be said for your hopes and dreams about overcoming the disadvantages of leaving. If you haven't been able to overcome them by this time, it won't change unless you make some very specific plans to deal with those obstacles and start carrying them out now.

Loneliness and financial insecurity often loom as very important disadvantages of leaving, because there's an assumption that you can't tolerate either situation and that you won't find love or security with anyone else, nor as a single person. List the ways you might overcome these disadvantages. Solutions may range from methods of accepting the lack of love or security in your life, developing other satisfactions so that they're not missed so much, or finding people, places or activities that will meet those needs in different ways.

Once you've listed the possible methods of overcoming the disadvantages, *underline* the ones you're seriously interested in trying soon. Then put down your "Plan for Action," the time when you'll start it and a time for completion of it. Your paper might look something like this:

Activity 11   Plan of Action

Disadvantages of Leaving	Plan of Action	Start	Complete Plan
Loneliness	Make new friends	This week	Two friends, 3 months,
	Learn to like my own company	Today	One year?
	Enroll in class	Next quarter	Four months
No sex life	Be sensual by myself	Today	Three months to get used to it
	Talk to myself about not needing sex	Today	Six months to convince myself?
	Eventually meet a new man	One year?	Two years to be sure
Not enough money	Take computer course	Next quarter	Two years

Disadvantages of Staying	Plan of Action	Start	Complete Plan
Broken bones, internal injuries	Hide money and keys, for escape	Today	Today
Bad example to kids	Talk to kids about how wrong it is	Today	Continue indefinitely
Depression	Talk to old friend 2X week on phone	Tomorrow	Three months to get habit back
	Talk to self more positively	Today	Three months to form habit
No friends	Call Sally	Tomorrow	Three months
	Talk to neighbors even if Tom gets mad	Next week	Three months to form habit

Disadvantages of Leaving	Plan of Action	Start	Complete Plan

Disadvantages of Staying	Plan of Action	Start	Complete Plan

Trying Out Your Plans

It's important to stick to the plan for a particular period of time, so that you'll know you've tried hard to make things change. You may not succeed in making those changes, but it's important for you to know you made a serious, well-thought-out effort.

If you realize some time before your deadline for completing the plan that you're not following it, try not to feel guilty. Instead, figure out what's wrong with the plan and revise it, so that it becomes something you can really do. If you get to the deadline and find that you haven't really tried, don't immediately assume there's something wrong with you and that you have to keep pretending to yourself that you're going to follow the plan eventually. Accept the fact that it's not a plan you're ready to follow and that you haven't a way to overcome that particular disadvantage right now.

When you've made a reasonable attempt to change for a specified amount of time, *list* the advantages and disadvantages of leaving and staying one more time. If you still can't decide what to do, score each item on a scale from one to ten, with ten indicating the most important item. Make your decision on the basis of the highest score. If it makes you feel better, decide to do one thing or the other, not forever, but for a specific trial period. That period shouldn't be less than six months, though, because you'll need at least that much time to test the results. And just because it's a trial doesn't mean there is no commitment.

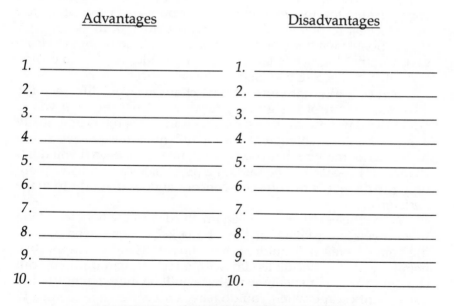

Activity 12   *Leaving and Staying: Advantages and Disadvantages*

Advantages	Disadvantages
1. _____	1. _____
2. _____	2. _____
3. _____	3. _____
4. _____	4. _____
5. _____	5. _____
6. _____	6. _____
7. _____	7. _____
8. _____	8. _____
9. _____	9. _____
10. _____	10. _____

MAKING A COMMITMENT TO STAY

It's not enough to say, "Well, I guess I can't leave, so I'll just have to stay with him for now." That isn't a real commitment. The next time you're hurt or scared or angry, you'll probably begin the fantasies of leaving again. A commitment goes more like this:

"The disadvantages of staying are not as bad as the disadvantages of leaving, so I'll stay with Tom for six months and carry out my plans to make changes in a very serious way. I won't even consider leaving until I've done all that I can think of for six months." If your man has made some concessions to you, a variation might be, "I'll stay with him and be serious about carrying out my plan of action, as long as he goes to AA...or to counseling...or as long as he doesn't humiliate me."

If you indulge yourself in fantasies of leaving the man even though you know you're not really going to, you're encouraging a dangerous self-delusion. But that doesn't mean you shouldn't have a plan to leave as a temporary emergency measure to protect yourself when you sense he is building up to violence.

What Can You Do If You Stay?

It may be possible to gain some freedom if you stay. Sometimes women think their husbands won't "let" them go to work, make friends or hire a babysitter, but if they just go ahead and do it, they're surprised to find that the men either don't notice, don't mind or grudgingly put up with it. Many women who get beaten are those who ask for nothing and are extremely compliant. If you're beaten for no apparent reason or punished even when you do your best to please, it may be worth the risk to assert your rights. Some men bully only those who are afraid of them. However, it's still a big risk to take, so it's a good idea to plan an escape to a safe place before you take any new chances.

Another alternative is to start changing your life secretly. Save money out of the grocery fund, don't tell the man you're going to a day-time class or support group. This too is potentially dangerous. An involvement with a violent man is always a very high risk, no matter what you try to change — or even if you don't change. (The same can be said for a psychologically abusive man, only the danger is to your self-concept and your ability to make decisions.)

Nevertheless, if you've been involved with the man for a long time, if you're unskilled for the job market, unemployed outside the home, have small children, have no real friends or supportive people, you may decide to stay with a violent man until you can change your life in such a way that you'll be more committed to permanent escape when you do leave and better able to stick to your commitment. Acquiring job skills, getting your children into school, making friends, joining a support group — all will help, though all of them can be begun after you leave too, and in some respects will be easier to do then.

If you don't succeed in averting his violence and after he

beats you he's remorseful, take advantage of that phase to begin going out with women friends, to join a support group or enroll in community college, or to otherwise branch out and begin a life for yourself. By the time he's recovered from his guilt, he may be used to your new habits. It will be difficult to go out and meet new people if you have a black eye or a missing tooth. Try to make yourself do it anyway, because if you let too much time go by he may be into the violent part of the cycle again. As soon as your wounds become invisible it's easy for both of you to act as if it never happened.

Learning the Signs of Coming Violence

If you pay careful attention you may be able to see the man's rage building at quite an early stage. Perhaps you already know the signs. Does he drink more, find many petty things to complain about, want to go out every night, or sit morosely in front of the TV more than usual? If you feel it coming on but can't name the actual changes in him, work on sharpening your observations. It's important for your own self-confidence to be able to state clearly that his tone of voice, what he says, his habits, his behavior towards you and the children change before he goes into a violent rage. It's important to be as certain as you can, whether these changes take place weeks or merely hours or minutes before he becomes violent. Writing them down will help you get a clearer sense of the pattern and make you more self-confident of what you observe.

If yours is the sort of violent man who is terribly sorry after he abuses you and who promises never to raise a hand again, or says he'll do anything you ask if you'll just stay and help him lick his problem, you may have a chance of developing an escape plan. It's during this "honeymoon" phase that you should point out that there are certain things he does that let you know he's building toward violence. If you can get him to agree with you that you should temporarily leave, or that he will leave at those times, so much the better. Probably, though, he will try to persuade you that it won't be necessary because he won't let those things happen next time.

Whether he agrees or not, you can tell him you're going to go to a safe place the next time you see the signs of violence beginning.

LEAVING TO PROTECT YOURSELF

When he gets into another violent phase, he probably won't remember or care that he's agreed you should find safety. But you will, and that will make it easier for you to take action. Once you've said out loud to him that a particular set of actions usually leads to violence, when you see it happen again, it won't be so easy to say to yourself, "Maybe this time it won't happen," or "I must be imagining it after all."

The important question is what you can do to protect yourself. The best choice is to go to a good friend's or relative's house — a place where there's plenty of room for you with people who care about you. A danger is that in order not to impose on others you'll wait until it's too late. If you've gone to them or to other people after you've been beaten in the past, try to keep in mind that most people would rather help you protect yourself than to mop up after the damage is done.

You should stay in that safe place until the man's rage is spent. The trouble, of course, is that you might find it hard to know when that time has come. If you can get a third party to speak to him periodically, you might get more reliable information, and you'll avoid the possibility of being talked into going home too soon. There are two problems with this plan. The man may be so used to releasing tension by using you as a punching bag that he has no other outlet and will hang on until you return. The other is that — even though he is about to lose control — he may be adept at persuading you or your intermediary that his rage is all over and that he's prepared to be both loving and calm. And then, when you get home, you'll find that he's determined to punish you for leaving. You can probably remember times when he's manipulated you by temporarily controlling his violence, so that you have believed the danger was over.

Planning for the Emergency

At the very least you should have enough money to pay a cab to take you to a safe place, and if you're in a strange community, enough to pay one or more nights' rent in a motel. You should also have an extra key to your car and the house, and a list of telephone numbers to call in case of emergency. You may also want to stash a change of clothes for yourself and/or your children. Ideally, you'll keep these items at a neighbor's house, at your job, or someplace else away from your home. If you need to leave in a hurry, you may not have time to take them from the house.

Even if you have no place to go except a motel, you should know which one and how to get there, and you should go from your house to it several times so that in a time of high stress you'll realize it's a nonthreatening and familiar alternative to staying with a dangerous man. Your fear can very easily paralyze you, but that's not so likely to happen if you've rehearsed an escape plan ahead of time.

Rehearsing for Departure

Be sure not to tell the man that you're leaving to protect yourself. He'll almost certainly become even more enraged and controlling and will try to stop you. Try to anticipate his violence early enough so that you can slip away when he's at work, but if that's not possible, say you have to go get some milk for the baby, or offer to get beer for him or say you promised a neighbor to bring her a recipe. Rehearse this ahead of time also. Have several plausible reasons to leave for different times of day or night. If his rages build late at night, plan to have a reason to go outside. Develop a habit of forgetting to take part of the laundry in until late at night or walking the dog or throwing out the garbage at midnight. Once outside the door, just keep going. Get into the car and drive as quickly and quietly as possible or keep walking until you get to a telephone.

How and Why to Take the Children

You may want to leave by yourself in order not to upset the children, especially if you imagine them sleeping blissfully in the middle of the night. Chances are, however, they're lying awake terrified by the current of coming violence. They may be less frightened at getting up and being rushed away from a threatening father than finding out in the morning that you've disappeared without saying good-bye. Another thing to remember is that even if the father has never battered the children, you can't be sure he won't start now, especially when he discovers you've left the house.

Making your escape with children is more complicated than making it alone, but it can also be prepared for. Talk to them periodically about the importance of safety. Teach older children to call a relative, a friend or the police when they hear or see violence. If a child or neighbor that the child runs to can call the police, officers may help you leave with the children.

If it's a baby you're concerned about, tell the man you hear her crying, take her out of her crib and go out a back door or window before your partner realizes what's happening. Keep going until you're in a safe place.

When events happen so fast that you do have to leave without the children, arrange to go back for them as soon as possible. Either pick them up at school or return to the house with a police officer. You'll need to ensure the children's physical safety, let them know you haven't abandoned them and protect your right to custody.

In custody cases there's a strong tendency to leave children with the parent who has them at the time the court becomes involved. If they're with you, your chances of gaining permanent custody are far better than if you leave them with their father, regardless of the reasons.

PREPARING TO LEAVE PERMANENTLY

Sometimes women who have left their partners suddenly or with a minimum of emergency planning never go back. Sometimes they follow a pattern of leaving and returning when the man's violence is spent. And sometimes they stay with him forever.

You may not be willing to make a decision to leave until you are physically injured. You'll have all the problems then of sudden escape and the crisis feeling that accompanies instant change. If you weigh the advantages and disadvantages of leaving in a calmer moment, your decision will probably be more reliable and less emotionally disturbing to you and your children. At the very least, planning ahead will give you some financial security.

Although it's unusual, difficult and often dangerous, some abused women stay with a man for months or years while planning a separation. For some it means going to school, getting a job or job training in order to have an independent income when they finally leave. For others it entails saving small amounts of money for a ticket across the country. Or waiting another painful and high-risk year or two until the children are in school or old enough to take care of themselves.

Leaving in an emergency and returning after it's over because you aren't prepared to be on your own is an understandable pattern. But it doesn't mean you have to follow it the rest of your life. The previous chapters should have given you some ideas about gathering information and deciding how and when to take action. Here are some other practical matters to consider if you're going to leave permanently.

Protect Your Money and Property

Property rights in marriage differ from state to state, and are even more uncertain for cohabitants, so you'll need the advice of a lawyer to get an idea of what you'll probably be awarded by the court and what you can legally take with you. (See Chapter 8, "Making Legal Decisions.") Then plan how you will get the items you're entitled to.

Take as many (as possible) of your personal belongings out of the house beforehand, especially things of sentimental or financial value or those your partner knows you especially like. If you're going to risk staying with him a few more months you can take important items for safe-keeping with a friend. Tell him, if necessary, that it's clothing to be cleaned, family photographs to be framed, jewelry to be reset. However, if the man is very observant and suspicious, it might not be safe. It's important that you know your man and whether he'll notice how long it takes for things to come back after cleaning, etc. before you take this risk.

If he is suspicious, you'll do better to make a list of the important items, gradually move as many as you can to two or three places in the house, and plan what suitcases, boxes or bags they'll go into so when you do leave you can pack them quickly. Include items important to your children, too. Try not to leave anything behind that will cause you misgivings if he threatened to seize or destroy it.

Find out if community service officers in your police department or another agency will stand by while you remove your personal possessions. Take care of it while your partner is safely away from the house, but have a friend go with you in case he comes back sooner than anticipated. Even if he's never destroyed your property before, once you've left him, he's likely to use any tools at hand to threaten or punish you.

Unless you have different legal advice, take half the money in checking and savings accounts and any other assets, such as charge card accounts, that can be quickly redeemed. If you believe you're entitled to more, ask a lawyer about it. Be sure not to leave your share of the money in joint accounts to take out later. After he learns you've left him your partner may withdraw all the money from the accounts, take your name off credit cards or change all the locks on the doors. Many women have refused to believe their partners would do that, only to find themselves with no resources twenty-four hours after they left. If you have little knowledge of what assets you and your partner jointly own, spend some time looking around for papers that indicate what stocks, property, insurance pensions or other assets there are, as well as loans. Write down all the information or, if you can safely do it, xerox the papers. If necessary, put all papers and lists in the safe hands of a friend. It isn't mean or cruel to take what is yours, so don't deprive yourself or your children because of unwarranted guilt feelings.

Plan Where To Go

If possible find a place to live before you leave, whether it's a temporary shelter or Safe Home for battered women, the home of a friend or relative, or a new apartment. Try to decide where you'll settle permanently, whether it's in a different neighborhood or a new city (in which case a shelter may be able to arrange for temporary shelter there.) Check the papers for housing ads so you'll know what to expect in your price range. This will make your later search for a permanent place easier.

   ˙ If you think you may need welfare assistance or public housing, get all the information you can before you leave. Find out what papers you'll need and get them together to take with you.

   Many of the practical problems you'll encounter by leaving are discussed in detail in Section IV. That information may help you make effective plans now. By learning to look squarely at what you can and can't do to make a new life for yourself and your children you can form a realistic picture of your options.

   If, at each suggestion, you've been saying something like, "Yes, but I can't do that..." because of no car, no money, no friends or other problems, look at what these answers mean. You're saying there is no way to protect yourself from abuse and the fear that accompanies it. You're saying, "I accept a life of periodic violence. I'm not going to try and change it." Are you willing to accept that? If not, you'd better make plans to leave.

SECTION II

Getting Professional Help

THE PROBLEM OF SEXISM

Professionals can heal your bruised body, increase your safety, guide you through the legal system, advocate for your rights and assist you in reorganizing your life. The special skills and knowledge of doctors, police, lawyers and counselors — and the community's recognition of them — can make a great difference in whether your crisis has a permanent and damaging effect or is the motivator to start constructing a new and satisfying life.

Professionals can also make things worse for you. Some of them are not competent in their work, regardless of formal training. Others are competent, but their social attitudes and ways of relating to clients have damaging effects that sometimes outweigh the good they do in the operating room, courthouse or counselor's office.

You can maximize benefits and minimize harm from professionals by knowing as much as possible about what the law or professional ethics require of them, or prohibit them from doing, by carefully choosing the people you hire, respecting your own responses to them and knowing your rights. In this section I'll present some guidelines on when to hire a professional, how to choose one and how to evaluate services.

Sexism, in its extreme form, is the belief that males and females have completely different characteristics, inherent rather than learned, that males are superior to females and that males have the right to make decisions and laws that govern women's lives. "Men's work" is defined as more important and more difficult than "women's work" and therefore higher paid. This fits into the sexist idea that men are the providers for families, and thus not only deserve higher pay, but need it more. Women are viewed as inherently attuned to emotions, relationships and intuition. The belief that those inherent qualities make women superior to men is a form of "reverse sexism." Because sexist ideas have been threaded into all our institutions and absorbed by us all, it's impossible to divide people neatly into categories of those who are and who are not sexist. We can only talk about those who are more and less so. As a shorthand I'll use the terms "sexist" and "nonsexist" to mean more sexist and more nearly nonsexist. It's important to understand the sexist biases of many professional people from whom you'll be seeking help.

Awareness of institutional sexism developed during the 1960s and by the early 70s important changes had begun in schools, churches, the law, medicine and other institutions. Nevertheless, many people, including professionals, cling to the ideas that women are biologically limited in what they can accomplish intellectually, artistically, physically and financially. They believe men are therefore destined to take care of and protect women and that, since men are limited in expressing their emotions and handling domestic and personal problems, women are obliged to take care of men's emotional and personal needs.

No one can deny the strong tendency for women and men to fall into those styles of relating to the world and each other. The question is whether those traits are inherent or acquired. Sexist people believe traditional sex-roles can't be changed, in spite of recent extensive evidence that women do hard physical work and make important intellectual and artistic contributions to society, and that men can be nurturing and emotionally expressive. Nonsexist people believe many of the sex-stereotyped characteristics are a result of women learning roles society identifies as sex-appropriate, and defining other traits as unacceptable or unthinkable. ("Girls don't fight," "Big boys don't cry.") Nonsexist people believe each individual should be encouraged to develop the traits, learn the skills and choose the occupations she or he wants and is personally most suited to. Males can be daycare workers and females can be firefighters. Males can also still be mechanics and females can be nurses.

To a large extent, institutional sexism still determines the jobs that men and women work at. The highest paid and highest status jobs — often incorrectly assumed to require higher risks and greater stamina than "women's work" — have historically been reserved for males. Although some women have been admitted to all professions in recent years, you're likely to find mostly men working as doctors, police officers and lawyers, especially outside big cities. Among counselors, there is more of a possibility of finding women, though most psychiatrists and psychologists are still men. (More social workers are women.)

Women can be just as sexist as men, but the sexist roles we've all been taught are more likely to be played out by male professionals in relation to female clients. A male attorney who believes he, as a male, is more capable than women will tend to take over much more than is necessary, making decisions that should be yours. If you feel helpless, share his ideas about male and female roles, or are intimidated by his masculine power, you may let him take over. These reactions are not as likely to occur in relationship to a female attorney — or other professional — even if she's quite sexist. A female professional may be condescending, patronizing or downright insulting to your intelligence, each of which may be an aspect of sexism. But the impact won't be nearly as powerful as when such treatment comes from a male in authority. To the extent you're victimized by your own sexism — as we all are in some degree — you'll interpret the male professional's attitudes as indicating something wrong with you, and you'll begin to doubt your own judgment.

It's not unusual for professionals to use their position and the client's vulnerability to take advantage of clients sexually. This unethical and often illegal practice is nearly always perpetrated by males who exploit their women clients. It's often presented as something good for the client, and her loneliness, mixed with sexual need and the status of the professional man, places the woman client in a vulnerable position. She is nearly always hurt by such a relationship.

For these reasons, it's safer for you to hire a female professional, assuming you can find one who is sensitive, relatively nonsexist, competent to solve your specific problem — and within your budget. Each of these characteristics is important. If your choices are limited by time, money or the community you live in, it's important at least to recognize the person's inadequacies so you can guard against them. The following chapters will help you through the process of finding, hiring and evaluating professional workers.

Chapter 7

EMERGENCY HELP FROM DOCTORS, POLICE AND PROSECUTORS

Even if you're not ready to leave your partner, professionals can provide important services that will make your situation more bearable and that may help you prepare to end the relationship. Once you've made the break, they can contribute to your safety and help you start a new and satisfying life.

This chapter will help you decide what you want from doctors and police and give you ideas on what to do if you're not getting the services you want.

MEDICAL HELP

The Emergency Room

If you need immediate medical treatment, it's likely to be in the middle of the night or on a weekend, and you'll go to the nearest hospital emergency room and take whoever is assigned to you. Try to get someone to go with you, as it may be a long wait. Tell the receptionist or nurse you've been assaulted by your husband or lover. Then describe your pain and injuries as accurately as possible. At this point, the staff will only know how much pain you're in if you tell them.

Ask for an estimate of how long you'll have to wait for an examination. It may not be accurate, because in an emergency room those in most severe danger are treated first, regardless of who arrived first. But knowing how long you'll be waiting will allow you to relax without feeling you're being purposely ignored or neglected. Now is the time to ask if there's a special program to help victims of domestic assault. If there is, a social worker may be able to give you a referral to a shelter or other service, as well as some comfort, while you wait for medical treatment. If your condition worsens, tell the person at the desk right away.

The Family Doctor — Pros and Cons

If it's not an emergency, you may decide to see your family physician. A family doctor can be particularly useful if she or he knows you well, cares about your welfare and respects you. You may have good reason, though, to avoid your usual doctor.

Perhaps she or he is so close to your spouse you don't think you'll be believed, or you might feel embarrassed or want to protect the man. (Try to keep in mind it's the violent man who should feel ashamed or embarrassed, but if you'd feel better talking to a doctor who's a stranger, go ahead and do it.) Or perhaps you know from past experience that she or he will pressure you to either report to the police or separate from the man before you're ready, or *not* to prosecute, even though that's what you want to do. The doctor may have a sexist attitude toward you, implying you deserve to be hurt or asked for it because you've continued to stay with the batterer.

You're likely to feel at the time you get medical treatment that you'll never go back to the man. When a doctor or nurse advises you to stay away from your partner, you may agree with enthusiasm. They'll believe you and when you come back the next month with another injury they'll feel disappointed, discouraged and afraid for you. A feeling of hopelessness might turn to resentment or thinly disguised hostility as they realize their careful medical treatment may have to be repeated the next time you're beaten. They only see the results of the man's worst treatment and the evidence of his destructive character. It's hard for them to imagine that there are some needs being met in the relationship.

If you do want to try a new doctor, put some effort into finding one who's sensitive, who respects women and who understands the problems of women victims of violence. Ask at a shelter, women's clinic or other service for abused women, or try a rape crisis line for a referral. Even if they don't have an official list of doctors sensitive to women's issues and battering, you may get an informal recommendation from a staff person.

What to Tell the Doctor

Many women are ambivalent about telling the doctor what happened. You may want the doctor to know, but be embarrassed to blurt out, "My husband beat me." You wait for the doctor or nurse to coax it out of you, and wonder why they don't at least ask when you appear month after month with unexplained bruises. When you explain that you just bruise easily, you may half hope the doctor will call you on it, but some doctors don't want to know what happened. They may find it embarrassing, might be afraid of your feelings spilling over if you start talking about it or they may be afraid they'll have to appear in court. So if you want the doctor to know, you'll have to tell. Get the physician's attention by saying, "I want you to know how I got these injuries." Once started, you'll probably find it fairly easy to go on, and a great relief to have it off your chest.

Not telling the doctor what happened may relieve you of a few awkward moments, but you may be sorry later. There's a good chance the medical record will be admitted as evidence in an assault charge and will impress the judge with the seriousness of your situation. If you have a custody dispute, the record of the father's violence can be an important factor in your favor and in some states it can help you get a better divorce settlement. You may hope to avoid any such court actions but there's a possibility you'll be involved in them whether you like it or not. If you never have to make use of the medical record you can just ignore it and nothing will be lost.

When you've found a cooperative doctor say at the outset that you'll want a full description of each injury included in the record and that you'll want to see the record when it's completed so you can have important information added if necessary. It will be useful to have a friend or advocate handy when you make these requests. You needn't feel guilty for taking extra time. It's the doctor's job to give you respectful and competent treatment—at public health agencies as well as at private clinics.

If you're very timid in the face of medical authority, take a friend with you and ask her to back you up in exercising your rights. You can tell the doctor you want her to come right into the examining room with you. And stick to that plan, regardless of whether the doctor objects. Keep in mind that you are hiring the doctor and if you don't like her or his treatment or attitude, you can take your business elsewhere. The mere presence of another person sometimes makes a difference in a physician's attitude.

Depending upon your relationship with the doctor, your emotional condition and whether or not you have other people to ask for advice and help, you might want to listen to a doctor's counseling. If you think the doctor has your best interests at heart and understands the situation, get what you can from the counseling. But keep in mind you're there for medical care. The doctor shouldn't continue to give advice about your relationship if you don't want it. You have a right to say you don't want to explain what happened beyond medical necessity and that you don't want to discuss your plans for the future.

POLICE INTERVENTION

In some communities, police are extremely slow to answer domestic violence calls, and many calls are not responded to at all. Their reasons range from fear of being killed (not surprising, since about one-fifth of police homicides occur when they respond to domestic violence calls), to discouragement when they answer the same call month after month and nothing seems to change, to pure and simple sexism ("If she's getting beaten up by her old man, she must deserve it.").

On the other hand, some police are protective in the best sense of the word and will take victims to a shelter or hospital, refer them to special services for battered women, and give careful, precise advice about how to follow through with the case.

Should You Call the Police?

Decide ahead of time, if you can, whether you'll call the police the next time you're assaulted or the man trespasses on your property. Think about what result you'll be looking for. Will you want an officer to stop the man from immediate attack and calm him down, arrest him, remove him from the scene or take you to a safe place? When you've answered those questions, call a shelter for battered women, a women's rights group or the County Bar Association to find out what you can reasonably expect from police and prosecutors in your community.

You may feel it's not worth it to call the police if there's little likelihood of arrest or jail time for the batterer. He may reinforce that feeling by making a show of nonchalance, but few people are casual about being confronted by police, even when they're not taken to jail.

You may be reluctant to call the police because you feel sorry for the man who battered you and don't want him punished by being sent to jail. Your fears about him being jailed are probably unfounded, unless he's already in trouble with the law. If he has a criminal record and is on probation or parole, fears related to his serving time may be more realistic. But, if you blame yourself for that, remember it's his own actions that result in jail time. Or you may fear that a jail term will make him angry at you and that when he gets out, you'll be confronted with more violence than you face now. To protect yourself from his anger, you might have to find a secret place to stay while he's out of jail on bail. It may be months before the case comes to court, so find out from the prosecutor whether you can get a "no contact" order (see page 84).

Even when it's extremely hard to do, pressing charges may be worth it. Taking legal action and following through regardless of the consequences may be the only way you and other women can persuade batterers and justice system personnel you won't tolerate men's abuse. If the man doesn't have a criminal record he might be sentenced to alcoholics' or batterers' counseling and that might be the best thing for him as well as you.

If you decide to call the police, be as calm as possible. It's extremely hard to do that in an emergency, but if you practice saying a few sentences beforehand, you may be able to say them automatically when the emergency arises. The main things you want to do are to get your address across clearly and accurately and make sure the police know it's an emergency. One or two short sentences should be enough. "I'm being beaten up. I'm at 628 Borden Street, East." Don't say it's your husband or boyfriend who's attacking you.

HOW TO GET THE MOST EFFECTIVE POLICE RESPONSE

1. Be as calm as you possibly can be.
2. Don't be afraid to ask the police to make a report.
3. Tell them about the assault in detail.
4. Show them any injuries or bruises or damaged property.
5. Let them know if there were witnesses.
6. Tell them about other violent incidents.
7. Show them any court documents you have such as "no contact" or "restraining" orders.
8. Ask them for community resources such as shelters, hot lines, counseling and advocacy.
9. Ask for the case number of the report and a phone number if you want to follow up on the case.

WHEN WILL POLICE MAKE AN ARREST?

Police may legally make an arrest if they have "probable cause" to believe that a crime has been committed which involved injury to a person. "Probable cause" means there is some evidence of the crime, such as a bloody nose, or other obvious injury. However, they will probably not make an arrest unless:

1. There is a *warrant* out for the abuser. Tell the police if you know about any outstanding warrants.
2. The assault was very serious, involving a weapon or major injury.
3. The abuser attacks the police or attacks you in their presence.

From "Legal Issues in Domestic Violence," Washington State Department of Social and Health Services

PRESSING CHARGES FOR ASSAULT

You don't need to decide about pressing charges the moment the police arrive. Just see that they note the evidence of violence and help ensure your physical safety. You can decide in the next day or two if pressing charges is a good idea in your case.

If you press charges and the man is convicted, there can be some advantages for you and for him. The court can order the man to have no contact with you for the duration of the sentence (six months to a year), to get batterers' counseling or alcoholic treatment and to pay for your medical treatment or replace stolen property. Some batterers are concerned enough about what will happen in court that they stop threatening and attacking the women while the case is pending. If the man does assault you again while the case is pending, police are more likely to arrest him. If he assaults or threatens you, call the police to get additional charges reported and let the prosecutor know right away.

Once you've decided to cooperate with the prosecutor in pressing charges, it's important to follow through. It's a way of making a strong statement that the man must change. It's a way of saying to both of you that you're taking care of yourself.

If you reconcile with the batterer before he's brought to court, you'll probably feel under a lot of pressure to drop the charges. Only the prosecutor or the judge can do that for you. That can be an advantage for you, since you can honestly tell the man it's out of your hands.

What Do You Want to Happen?

When you've gotten some ideas from a shelter or women's organization about how police and prosecutors in your community are likely to interpret the law and how they'll treat you, ask yourself more questions. Consider what you'll want to happen and how you'll probably feel about various results.

- *In addition to the possible results mentioned above, what are your own personal reasons for pressing charges?* Do you want punishment, revenge, to have the man taken away or ordered to have counseling? Do you want your action to stand as a public statement that men will no longer be permitted to batter women without some legal consequences?

- *Have you pressed charges before and did you follow through?* How did the outcome affect you? Did you feel let down or betrayed by the system? It may be that the courts weren't as responsive to battered women as they are now. Find out from women's groups or Legal Services whether there have been important changes in your district.

Perhaps you decided you still loved the man after all and

didn't want him to suffer. Or maybe you felt guilty for "putting him in jail," even though it was only for a few hours. He and family members may have persuaded you it was your fault; perhaps you were afraid of even greater violence; the continual stress wore you down or you believed he had changed.

• *Which of your previous situations are different now?* If nothing much happened as the result of your action before, is there reason to think the judge will make a different decision on a second charge? Is there better evidence? Might the prosecutor take your case more seriously, now that you've gone through it once?

How can you be sure you don't still love him, even though you feel hatred or indifference right now? Or are you willing to go through with it, even though you still love him? Do you have reason to believe you handle guilt and emotional turmoil better now, and that you can't be persuaded to change your mind? Is there a reason you won't be afraid of worse violence or can rise above those fears enough to follow through this time?

• *Where can you get emotional support and practical aid?* Is there a special project at the prosecutor's office or a shelter? Will a friend go through the whole process with you, accompanying you to interviews with the prosecutor and court proceedings? Will you have access to one particular prosecutor who will answer your questions as they come up? Is there a safe place to stay, in case the man does become violent?

Enlist a friend's help in going over these questions. Have her pretend to be a persuasive or threatening person — your partner, a relative or the prosecutor — who plays on your guilt feelings and ambivalence. Try to respond honestly, as if she were really that person, so you'll get an idea of how vulnerable to persuasion you are. You may decide you don't want to press charges after all or you might decide to keep practicing your responses so you'll be able to resist whatever pressures you face in the future.

You might believe you don't need such help. Maybe you pressed charges before, but dropped them when the man pleaded with you to come back. If you're persuading yourself there's no point in testing out how you'd respond to his pleading because this time he definitely doesn't want the relationship, consider it again. Even if he's acting hateful or ignoring you and has a new woman, the moment he believes you're serious about taking action, he's likely to come back to threaten or sweet-talk you, or both. Even if you believe there's no chance he'll ask, a little practice in resisting both his threats and promises will make you stronger.

WHAT THE PROSECUTOR CAN AND CAN'T DO

Many women are confused when they discover how little power they have over whether the violent man will be prosecuted. They expect the prosecutor to be mainly concerned about the victim's safety. But the prosecutor's job is to preserve the peace and order of the state, rather than to protect the individual; it's to redress public wrongs, not private ones.

Because prosecutors are authoritative figures, it's easy to imagine they have more power than they do. You may feel you're getting the run-around when they tell you court dates are unknown or delayed and that the prosecutor hasn't taken you seriously if the man doesn't get jail time. Whether the case is successfully prosecuted depends upon a great many factors including how good the evidence is, the man's history of violence, the attitudes of the community and judge and how hard the prosecutor was willing and able to work on it.

The man who battered you can be prosecuted whether or not you're married to him, but because it's technically the state's case, it's the state's decision what to do about it. Jennifer Baker Fleming, in *Stopping Wife Abuse*,† describes the situation this way:

...Prosecutors have a great deal of latitude in deciding which accusations will become the subject of a formal charge and which will not. There is virtually no review of this decision and virtually no guidelines, so prosecutors tend to exercise this power of "prosecutorial discretion" on the basis of their own values, their perception of society's view of the crime charged, and the likelihood of success in getting a conviction. Their calculation of these factors and their decision to prosecute or not is final...

Usually the decision about whether to prosecute is made on a case-by-case basis, after considering four or five basic issues: the extent of the injuries and their seriousness, the defendant's apparent intent, the victim's desire to prosecute, the defendant's history of similar or other violent conduct — especially whether he has a criminal record — and the prosecutor's own estimate (based, among other things, on the existence of tangible evidence and other witnesses) of the likelihood of success at trial.

†Jennifer Baker Fleming, *Stopping Wife Abuse* (New York: Anchor Books/Doubleday, 1979), pp. 198-99, p. 200.

The decision is complicated by the fact that prosecutors often don't realize how much their personal values, including sexist attitudes, affect their judgments about matters that are supposedly factual and objective.

DEALING WITH THE PROSECUTOR

Nevertheless, you may be able to influence the decision. Your enthusiasm for going ahead with the case and understanding of just what it involves for you will help. If you've filed charges before and dropped them, that doesn't mean you shouldn't press them now. If that's the message you're getting from the prosecutor, try especially hard to have someone with you to help you state your case. Carefully list the reasons things are different this time, so if you forget to mention some of them, your advocate can help out during the interview with the prosecutor. If you pressed charges before and got no support or information from the prosecutor's office, explain what happened as thoroughly as possible. Use statements like: "When you insinuated I asked him into my house, and that's why I got beaten up, I thought you didn't believe me and weren't interested in my case," and "If your office can tell me what's happening as we go along and give me some encouragement and emotional support, it will be easy for me to follow through."

If the prosecutor tells you the office is understaffed and can't give you the support you want by keeping you informed and helping you understand the legal process, give yourself time to consider whether it will be worth the struggle. While you're rethinking the situation, talk to women's organizations (National Organization for Women, YWCAs, a city, county or state office of women's rights) as well as a shelter to enlist help. One of them may be able to pressure the prosecutor to take your case seriously or give you the support and information you'll need to get through the ordeal. They may be able to put you in touch with other women who've been through the court process. It's easy, under these circumstances, to feel isolated and in the wrong. Knowing that women in similar situations successfully used the system will help you gain a healthy perspective.

In any case, if you get vague answers from the prosecutor, or your telephone calls aren't returned and it looks as if no action is taking place, keep politely, but firmly, asking questions. Sometimes the case is going along as it should, but nothing much can be done until a court date is assigned. In that case the prosecutor is doing an adequate job, but is insensitive to your feelings or hasn't time to call back.

When you're angry and hurt it's hard to realize that a prosecutor has numerous other cases that are just as pressing as yours. It may seem you're being ignored, but the prosecutor may know she or he can't get to your case until a few days before the court date, because other cases are demanding a similar amount of work. Nevertheless, let the prosecutor know how you feel. You might want to add that the better informed you are, the more confident you feel about following through and being a good witness. The prosecutor wants to win the case and must have a good witness to do it.

If you're convinced you're not being taken seriously or if the prosecutor is blatantly sexist, ask for a different prosecutor or to speak to her or his supervisor. In some communities you might be assigned to someone more compatible, sensitive and nonsexist. In others, you will get nowhere with your request. It may be that there are no prosecutors in a particular office who are sensitive to the problems of battered women. An additional problem is that there is frequent re-assigning of cases in some offices. If you just wait it out, you may get someone better by the time you go to court. You might want to consult with knowledgeable women's groups before you decide how far you'll go in fighting the system.

HOW CAN YOU KEEP THE BATTERER AWAY?

There are many legal methods of ordering a violent person to stay away and stop abusing or threatening you. But you don't need any special methods unless you have a legal relationship with the man such as marriage or a child in common. If a boyfriend, former lover or husband from whom you're legally divorced enters your house without permission, forces you to have sex with him, threatens or assaults you, you have all the rights you'd have if he were a stranger. In some states, you can charge him with trespassing, rape or whatever would be appropriate if you had never had a relationship with him. Call the district court to find out what charge you can legally make.

If you do have a legal relationship with the man, you may need a legal order to keep him away. The type of order and what it's called varies from one jurisdiction to another. It may be a temporary restraining order, no contact order, or order of protection. For some of these orders you don't have to consult a private lawyer or a prosecutor. Call your County Bar Association or district court to find out what the proper order is called, whether you need a lawyer to get it, and how to go about getting it.

The order in itself probably won't keep the man away from you. But the combined action of consistently calling the police whenever it's violated and following through with calls to the prosecutor may frighten the man into staying away.

These ways of using the criminal law system will help you in certain ways, but they don't cover everything. You might have other legal problems that don't have to do with crime. They are the subject of the next chapter.

Chapter 8

MAKING LEGAL DECISIONS

For most of us, the law is a mysterious set of rules and regulations, a system of reasoning that's often confusing or intimidating. When we're faced with legal problems and have only a hazy understanding of the system, we may not know when to go to a prosecutor, how to find a trustworthy private lawyer, what to ask them or how to evaluate them. Some of those lessons will be learned by experience, but I'll try in this chapter to make suggestions that will spare you the most expensive lessons.

WHEN SHOULD YOU HIRE A LAWYER?

Although a prosecutor will take cases in which there's a crime against the state, which means also one against another citizen and there are many legal actions you can take without a lawyer, there are also situations in which you'll want the special knowledge of a private attorney. In the 1960s and 70s, public agencies provided legal services to poor people accused of crimes, and sometimes special services for abused women. Many of these programs have been cut back, but if there are some in your community, try to use them. See if your local Legal Services, County Bar Association, City or County Prosecutor's office or women's organization has a legal advocacy service. Sometimes workers in public agencies are so overworked they can't give enough attention to each client, but often that problem is balanced by the highly developed expertise of the lawyer or paralegal worker in a special area of law which private lawyers may not know much about.

If you're ending a marriage or separating from the father of your child, you'll have important legal questions to settle. These are civil cases; that is, cases between private parties, in which the state has no interest because no crime has been committed.

If you're acutely aware of the crimes your husband has committed against you or your children, it might seem outrageous that the state is indifferent. (As discussed in the last chapter, the state can become involved if you press charges against the man for a particular crime.) Evidence of abuse may help you in some states, but in "no fault" states it has nothing to do with your divorce, property or custody settlement.

Some states have "no fault" divorces, which means neither partner has to be blamed for the failure of the marriage. Instead, the couple is assumed to have the right to dissolve the marriage and the reasons for it are not the business of the state. This change has had the beneficial effect of allowing for a friendly parting of the couple, but it also has effectively eliminated alimony in those states. It also means that the abuse isn't taken into account in the settlement.

DIVORCE

You'll save a lot of money if you get a divorce by yourself, without an attorney. If you can agree with your husband on custody, child support and property division, a do-it-yourself divorce might be for you. However, if you have large amounts of real estate or personal property, if your husband has been able to manipulate you in the past and has hidden his and your assets or makes vague promises about what he'll do for you in the future, be careful. Not many batterers are willing to talk reasonably about these difficult problems and to be honest and fair in arriving at decisions. If your husband is the exception by all means consider the possibility. For details on the do-it-yourself process ask your local County Bar Association or women's organizations about kits that tell how to get a divorce without a lawyer. The availability of self-help legal materials varies in different localities.

If you decide to hire an attorney, ask a number of friends for recommendations or call those organizations mentioned above for suggestions of someone who's particularly experienced in and concerned about wife beating cases.

When you call for an appointment, say you want to discuss the possibility of hiring the lawyer and ask if there's a charge for the initial interview. Try to find a lawyer who doesn't charge for the exploratory interview.

Before your first appointment, try to make decisions about exactly what you want. You may have mixed feelings about what to do, because you both love and hate your husband. A private lawyer has little time or ability to help you with your emotional see-saw, and will charge a great deal of money to listen to you or discuss it. If you can't sort out your feelings by yourself, a counselor can help. But first, try answering these questions:

Do you want a divorce? This is usually an agonizing decision, and to think it through you may want to review Section I. It's essential to examine your fears and obligations, as well as the roles of love and loneliness in your life.

If you do get a divorce, is this the right time? Will the degree of stress and anger you feel give you the strength to go through with it or will it create such a feeling of helplessness that you'll back out before it's completed and be left at square one, with a large lawyer's bill?

If it isn't the right time, what do you need to do first? What changes can you begin that will prepare you to make the break? Do you need to make friends, consult a counselor, get a job or go to school? What can you do to begin those changes right now?

CHILD CUSTODY

Arranging custody of the children is one of the most difficult of legal problems and even more so when the father is violent. This subject will be discussed further in Chapter 15, but meanwhile it may be helpful to continue asking questions, this time about how you feel about custody.

Do you want custody of the children? Are there some reasons to fear you'll lose custody? If your husband is an influential person in a small community, if you have a history of mental illness, emotional disturbance, drug, alcohol or child abuse or a criminal record, you may have good reason to be concerned. But don't assume it's hopeless. The father may only be using the threat of winning custody to keep you in line, and if you resist, he may give in quickly. You have no way of knowing whether you'll have a problem getting the custody arrangement you want until you consult with someone who knows the law, the community and its judges and the details of your situation. He or she can discuss with you what you might expect under various circumstances as well as what you can do to make a good case for yourself. The lawyer can make a more educated guess about the outcome, but no one can be sure of it until the case has gone to court.

If you believe you haven't been a responsible parent, now is a good time to begin changes. Enroll in parenting classes, join AA or do community volunteer work — whatever is appropriate to establish yourself as a good parent and citizen. Maybe you don't want custody, but you're feeling guilty about it.

If you give up custody, how often will you be able to see the child? How will the child react and how will that affect you? Will the child be physically safe? Emotionally cared for? What if you change your mind later? Try to be clear about what's good for the child and what's good for you and explore ways you can make compromises between the two.

It may seem to you now that you can barely take care of yourself. In a few months you may feel much better and want the children with you, yet not be able to get them from their father. Think about what help you might get from counselors, nursery schools, friends, family and agencies such as child protective services. Maintaining custody doesn't necessarily mean you have to do everything all by yourself all the time. Whatever decision you make, it will be a better one if you make it after you've weathered the crisis.

PROPERTY DIVISION, ALIMONY AND CHILD SUPPORT

If you shared property with the man who battered you, it would be wonderfully simple to divide it in half and each go your separate ways. That doesn't often happen, especially among people who aren't rich. If you were married, your husband may have earned between ten and thirty thousand dollars a year and you've either stayed home with your children or earned between five and sixteen thousand dollars a year; you own part of a house, car and some household goods, have a good-sized mortgage and some hefty monthly bills. Perhaps you have some small savings and investments and if you're like most Americans, you live pretty much from paycheck to paycheck. Items of significant value, like a house or car, don't lend themselves to being divided in half. If you sell one to divide the profit you'll each feel you have to buy another, and at today's interest rates, you probably can't afford it.

In some states the property of married couples is considered "community property." That is, most of the property acquired during the marriage is owned jointly by the two people who have equal rights to dispose of it or use it. In most of these states only inheritances and property acquired before marriage or after legal separation or divorce is considered separate property. Debts of either party are a joint liability too.

In other "common law" states, the property jointly used by the couple may belong to one of them. When marriage goes well, everything seems like "ours," but that can change quickly when the relationship changes. If your husband made the payments on all your major purchases, he may be considered the owner. If you've worked hard and contributed your share of expenses either by unpaid work at home or by purchasing many small items, it will naturally seem an unfair system. You can't tell how the property will actually be divided until you begin negotiating. If you can't agree, you may have to take the case to court for a judge to decide. Avoid it if possible, because it will be an emotional strain and extremely expensive. Keep working at negotiations through your lawyer even when it's tiresome. Many women lose what's rightfully theirs because they just want the relationship and disagreements to end, regardless of the cost.

Although laws and judges' attitudes are changing along with social customs, it's still common for women to be awarded custody of children, especially young ones, and for the custodial parent to be awarded the family home until the children are grown. But situations and communities are so varied one can't be sure what a particular judge will decide.

Alimony and Maintenance

Money will very likely continue to be an important tie to — and a problem with — the man. If you've been married a long time and own a home, if you haven't worked much outside the home, or you have custody of young children, you'll probably be awarded the house and perhaps your former partner will have to make payments on it for a period of time. He may also have to pay you temporary maintenance (until your divorce is final and the property divided or until you've had time to complete an educational or job training program) or alimony if you live in one of the states that allows for it.

Alimony can be a great help to women who have few job skills, but even in states that still assign fault to one party or the other less than five percent of divorced men are ordered to pay support to their ex-wives. Of those who are ordered to pay, a very small number pay anything.

If you've shared living quarters, property or expenses with a man you're not married to, your legal situation is uncertain. It presents new legal questions that are just beginning to be settled in courts. Even if you decide not to take your case to court, a lawyer who has experience in such cases might be useful in negotiating a property settlement.

Child Support

Both parents are obliged to support their children, so even if you're not married to the father of your child, he should contribute. A judge may order either one of you to pay child support, but less than twenty-five percent of divorced or unmarried fathers pay child support and of those who do pay, only about half pay the full amount ordered by court. There's a tendency for those men who make regular payments during the first year or so after the divorce or separation to then stop or taper off.

Sometimes a man's reluctance to pay is the result of his second marriage, more children and more expenses. Sometimes it stems from an absent father's belief that it's unfair for him to pay child support when he's deprived of living with his child. He may be particularly resentful if the woman lives with another man who seems to play a more meaningful role in the child's life. If the father doesn't pay, you may be tempted to withdraw visitation rights, but legally you have no right to do it. Child support is legally unrelated to visitation rights.

COSTS AND BENEFITS OF SUPPORT FROM THE MAN

When you finally break free after months or years of financial and emotional dependence, it would ease the pain if you never had to look back and had no strings or qualifications on your freedom. Continued financial dependency will be hard on you and very likely be used by your former partner to threaten or cajole you into going back to him.

Whether you exercise your right to ask for support from your ex-partner for yourself or your child will depend on how dangerous the man is and whether you think a continued financial relationship will put you in danger. You might also consider whether he's been generally financially responsible. If not, there may be little point in your taking any risks at all, unless you're willing to carry out a lengthy fight for your rights, as a matter of principle.

Even men who are generous with money and dedicated to their children are likely to be much less dependable after separation than before. You'll be in a better position if you can get your share of the property or a lump sum of money right away. Even if it's less than the total you'd receive if he actually paid monthly support over a period of years you'll have it in your hands. You won't have to wonder each month if your payment will arrive early, late or not at all.

If you do ask for support, keep in mind it's your right and the children's right. Their father is not doing you a favor, regardless of whether he thinks he is. If you have custody, it costs you money to support the children. You're putting in many hours of childcare labor worth hundreds of dollars and may be paying for additional care while you're at a paid job. (If he has custody and you have a job, you may want to pay child support whether the court orders it or not.)

Find out if payments can be made through the court or automatically taken out of his paycheck and put into your credit union or bank account. That will ensure that it's there on time, and you won't have to speak to him about it each month. Whether such arrangements can be made depends on your state law, his employer and in some instances, his willingness to comply.

OTHER LEGAL PROBLEMS

Is there something else you want that doesn't fit neatly into any of these categories? There are other legal procedures and goals that may help you. You may want to sue for damages to you or your property, have your husband ordered out of the house, restrained from destroying property, harassing you or even coming near your house or workplace. You may also want something to happen that can't be done through legal procedures. The only way to find out whether your goals can be accomplished through the law is to ask a lawyer who specializes in domestic relations and who's experienced in wife abuse cases.

If you're not going to get a divorce or permanent separation, what you can do is increase your safety. Can you stay away long enough to get your partner well started on counseling, AA or other constructive action? Is there any way you can protect your children from witnessing at least the worst of his abuse?

Considering each of these legal options and your questions about them with the aid of a friend should help you make some decisions. Write the answer to each question, including partial answers like "don't know," "probably yes" or "ask lawyer about this one." If you have many vague responses go back to the beginning and review each question. When you can't answer any more of them, list the questions you will have to ask an attorney. When you know the possible legal consequences of certain actions, you'll be able to answer the questions you're uncertain about now.

INTERVIEWING THE LAWYER

If possible, take a friend with you to the lawyer's office to act as your advocate; that is, to help you speak up for your rights. You may find it difficult to understand and remember the attorney's advice and explanations. Your friend can take the notes that you might be too nervous, confused or distracted to take down. If you're embarrassed to ask questions and admit your ignorance, your friend can help by asking for clarification. She can also give some objective feedback when you leave the office. She must, of course, be someone you trust. If you can't find an advocate, don't hesitate to take notes yourself and, when necessary, to say, "Please go more slowly so I can write down what you're saying."

Questions to Ask the Lawyer

Going into the office with a clear idea of what you want, what you don't want, what you're not sure of and questions for the lawyer to answer will put you on a more even footing. Don't be embarrassed at having your lists of questions in hand to check off.

The attorney will probably be pleased at your businesslike attitude, and the efficient use of the lawyer's time will save you money. Give her or him a duplicate of the questions so you don't get rushed out of the office before they're all answered.

Begin by asking the lawyer these questions:

1. What is your fee?
2. Does the fee include time spent on telephone consultation? What else? Are filing fees included in the initial fee?
3. Will you send an itemized bill at least once a month?
4. Will you estimate for me the time you expect to spend on specific tasks as they come up?
5. Will you answer my questions even when they seem unimportant or difficult?
6. What period of time will be required to complete my case?
7. What role will I have in decision making? (Then state whether you want to be an active participant or leave it up to the lawyer to decide questions about the case.)
8. Will you let me know what problems and plans you're making as you go along?

Lawyers' fees range from thirty to over a hundred dollars an hour, depending on where you live and the experience and status of the firm. A few lawyers charge on a sliding scale according to income. Most lawyers won't take certain cases until they're paid money in advance (a "retaining fee"), which might be five hundred dollars or more. If you have no access to money but your husband has a good income, you may find a lawyer to take your case at no charge to you, on the assumption the settlement will include payment of your attorney's fees by your husband.

Most lawyers charge for any time they talk to you on the telephone as well as for time in court and working on your case in the office. Clients usually underestimate charges because they don't remember that three twenty-minute telephone calls may add up to a seventy-five dollar charge, and they don't realize paper work takes many unseen hours. The attorney's agreement to keep you informed of charges, as you go along, will save you from the shock of unexpected large bills at the end of the services.

If the attorney doesn't give specific answers to questions about fees, if you think the fees are too high or if you're not satisfied with answers to your other questions, don't feel you're obliged to continue with that person. Say you'll let her or him know your decision later or state your objections. You might find there's a misunderstanding. If necessary renew your search for a lawyer you can feel confident in working with.

What To Do If You Don't Understand the Lawyer

Some legal ideas are hard to translate into layperson's language, but it can be done. Some lawyers are thoughtless about speaking the language of law, which is foreign to most of us. Some of them purposely speak more "legalese" than is necessary, to increase their authority.

Make it clear from the beginning that you want the lawyer to speak plainly and you want to understand everything. When the lawyer uses vaguely familiar legal phrases, you may tell yourself you should know what they mean or that you'll look them up later rather than appear stupid by asking for clarification. There's no reason why you should know legal terminology, so ask.

If you ask for clear explanations and the lawyer ignores your request or says not to worry about legal details ("Just leave it to me"), this may be a form of sexism and is certainly disrespectful. Say, "Thank you for your time, but it's important to me to understand what's happening, so I'll find another lawyer." Then do it. Shopping for a lawyer can be stressful, but so can hiring someone who doesn't respect you.

EVALUATING THE LAWYER

As with all professionals, keep in mind that you're the one who's hiring the services and you have a right to ask for what you want. Continually review what you want, weigh it against what the lawyer advises, consult with friends and advocates at shelters or other women's organizations and then make up your own mind what's best for you and what's best for your children. If you believe your attorney isn't taking your case seriously enough, say what you think and insist on an explanation. If it doesn't seem adequate, let the lawyer know you'll have a hard time following through with action unless something changes, or that you're thinking of hiring someone else.

It's difficult to start over with someone new, but it may be even worse to continue with a person who's doing an inadequate job. Many lawyers are competent in some kinds of cases but not others, so if you're not satisfied, give notice and don't feel guilty about leaving the lawyer. Your business now is to take care of yourelf in the best way you know how. You need a lawyer you can count on to help you do that, and there are many of them who will, so keep on looking until you find the right one. Then let the lawyer do a lot of the worrying for you.

The Attorney Doesn't Know Everything

Like doctors, lawyers are often asked by clients under stress to help them make decisions on matters other than their area of expertise. Eventually, some of these professionals begin to believe they're experts in a great many areas, for instance, finance, politics, or human relations. Sometimes their work does afford them an opportunity to develop expertise in these fields, but often their alleged understanding of human relations is little more than the sum of their accumulated biases.

If you've answered carefully the questions on previous pages about your legal options, you'll be clearer about what you want to do and whether your doubts are related to positive feelings for the man, fear of him or of other things, considerations of what's right and wrong, or lack of sufficient knowledge. This self-awareness will enable you to weigh whether your attorney's advice is based on personal feelings or politics, or on strictly legal issues.

Let's suppose you're one of the fortunate people who earns enough money to support your child without help from the father. You understand you don't have to contact the father to get child support. But you also know yourself well enough to realize if he owes you money every month, you'll use the situation as an excuse to contact him. Even though the children have a right to support, and he has the obligation to pay, you may decide not to ask for support. That decision might be safest for you, and in the long run for your child.

If your lawyer tries to change your mind about it, listen carefully to the reasons. There may be a number of facts you don't know, and if you're in crisis you won't have the broad perspective your attorney has on your own and your children's rights. It's appropriate for your lawyer to tell you what rights you have, and what you might expect to happen if you exercise them. Then it's appropriate for you to decide whether you'll exercise them.

Any time you're in doubt about a lawyer's advice or plan of action, ask why she or he considers it the best one. "Is that strictly a legal decision, or are you considering other things, too?" Or, "What will be the effects if we do something different from what you're suggesting?"

Many male attorneys have sexist attitudes and are paternalistic toward women in distress. You may get an answer like, "Well, we wouldn't want a pretty girl like you to go without, would we?" Or, "You don't want him to get away with this," or "Later on you'll wish you'd gotten a divorce." Don't let an attorney treat you like a child or define for you what you want or how you feel. What may seem like welcome protectiveness may just be another form of sexism. (He or she might legitimately tell you how most women in similar situations feel, and then you can decide whether you're enough like most women to make that information useful.)

If you find you're being persuaded to change your mind about an action you were pretty sure of when you started out, be a little suspicious. Are you changing your mind because of legal considerations you weren't aware of? Or have you, because of your feelings of helplessness and confusion, developed the idea that the attorney knows best even about your personal choices like whether you will divorce or press charges? If you've been persuaded to change your mind about one of those major questions, it might feel wonderful to let someone else be in charge. But when you leave the lawyer's office, you might gradually return to your original position. Then you may feel too embarrassed to explain your changed mind to the lawyer. It's your right to change your mind, but to save yourself from that awkward situation, whenever you have any doubts about taking an action, say you'd like a day to think it over.

Legal Advice Doesn't Include Emotional Support

Your attorney may be so emotionally supportive while you're consulting in the office that when you're in stress you'll be tempted to call her or him rather than a friend, counselor or support group member. This can result in disappointment, since your attorney will probably be busy with other clients, often in court all day, and unlikely to return your call unless there's something specifically legal that it's necessary to talk to you about.

If the attorney does call and listens to your troubles for twenty minutes, you may later be surprised by a bill for twenty dollars. It's important to distinguish the roles of each person who can give you advice or treatment and to rely on attorneys for legal help only.

If you find yourself frequently crying on the shoulders of your lawyer or friends, and thinking continually about your troubles yet not able to make headway in resolving them, you may want to seek professional counseling. The next chapter tells you how to go about doing that.

Chapter 9

GETTING HELP FROM A COUNSELOR

You don't have to be "crazy," "sick" or "neurotic" to seek help from a counselor and the fact that you've been abused doesn't mean there's something wrong with you that a counselor can "fix." But living in a violent situation — or leaving it — creates practical and emotional problems difficult to sort out alone. As you'll see in the next chapters there's a great deal you can do for yourself or with the help of relatives and friends. But if you're depressed or isolated, or there is no one you want to talk to who can be counted on to be sympathetic, consider a professional counselor. She or he can help you decide whether or not to leave your partner and give you courage to carry out your decision. After a separation you might discover long-standing problems you want resolved before you become involved in another relationship, or you might just want short term counseling to ease your way through the crisis period.

WHAT DO YOU WANT FROM A COUNSELOR?

Finding and choosing a counselor who is right for you may be difficult. Perhaps you're vaguely unhappy, fearful, tense, confused, and unsure of what you want or could reasonably expect from a counselor. Will she tell you what to do, help you make decisions, make you feel better? She may do most of those things and more, though you'll need to be wary of a counselor who tells you what you should do.

The following sets of questions are designed to help you decide what you want. *Check* the appropriate spaces, keeping in mind there are no right, wrong or best answers.

Activity 13A   What I Want From a Counselor

1. *I want to know*
   what I'm feeling ....——
   why I'm feeling it ....——
   other ....——

2. *I want to stop feeling*
   confused .... ——
   trapped .... ——
   angry .... ——
   sad .... ——
   lonely .... ——
   afraid .... ——
   other .... ——

3. *I want to learn to express*
   anger .... ——
   fear .... ——
   sadness .... ——
   joy .... ——
   other .... ——

4. *I want help in making decisions* .... ——
5. *I want help in solving problems* .... ——
6. *I want help in becoming more confident* .... ——
7. *I want to become more employable* .... ——
8. *I want to know what I want* .... ——
9. *I want to be able to ask for what I want* .... ——
10. *I want to be able to say "No" to unfair requests* .... ——
11. *I want to get along better with people, which includes*
    knowing why I have trouble getting along with people .... ——
    ending involvements with destructive men .... ——
    having better sexual relationships .... ——
    finding men who treat me with respect .... ——
    making better friends .... ——
    coping better with children .... ——
    being a better parent .... ——
12. *I want to*
    gain more control over my life .... ——
    be more disciplined .... ——
    make better plans .... ——
    stick to my plans .... ——
    learn to take better care of myself .... ——
    other .... ——

If you checked a number of items, you have a good start on knowing how to ask for the right counselor for you. But other questions will help too. *Check* these desired counselor traits as honestly as you can, even if you think you shouldn't care about them.

Activity
13B

Activity 13B   *What Kind of Counselor Do I Want?*

I want to see a counselor who:
1. *is objective and unemotional* ....____
2. *is friendly, warm and casual* ....____
3. *is younger than I am* ....____
4. *is older than I am* ....____
5. *is about my age* ....____
6. *is a woman* ....____
7. *is a man* ....____
8. *has experience with abused women* ....____
9. *won't say it's my fault I got hit* ....____
10. *believes women should have as many choices as men* ....____
11. *believes in traditional marriage relationships* ....____
12. *shares my values:* ....____
    political ....____
    religious ....____
    sexual orientation ....____
    ethnic, racial, cultural traditions ....____
    other ....____
13. *is a parent* ....____
14. *other* ....____

From the answers to the two sets of questions, *circle* the counselor's characteristics that are most important to you, and what you want her to help you do. *Underline* the things that are definitely unacceptable. Perhaps you'll compromise on the desirable age or parenting experience but not on values or counseling experience. As you read the next part of this chapter, you may want to add to those lists, and you can refer to them when you're ready to call or see a prospective counselor.

FINDING A COUNSELOR

Ask friends and co-workers if they know of good counselors. Try to find out what they liked about them, what problems they were useful with and whether they seem to have the qualities you're looking for. If they're willing to answer your questions, friends can be the best referral source.

If you're living in a big city, you may find therapy referral services or counseling services that are specifically directed to women, or to abused women. There may also be agencies that charge according to income. Look in the telephone book yellow section under "Social Services," "Social Work," "Psychology," or "Therapy." Check in the white section under "Abuse," "Battering," "Women," "Feminist," "Rape Counseling," and "Child

Abuse." You may find agencies which have expertise in domestic violence or who can refer you to the best person.

Settle down for an hour or two of phone calls. You'll probably get a mix of answering services, receptionists who have little information, receptionists who have a great deal of information, recorders, and people who say so-and-so will call back in thirty minutes or who refer you to four other numbers. It will help if you think of this as an exploration to find the best counselor for you, rather than making one quick call to make an appointment.

If you continually postpone making these calls, consider the possibility that you're scared. Most people are nervous about their first contact with a prospective counselor, so give yourself permission to feel what you feel.

Have pencil and paper with you when you call, so you can note the fee, address, and other pertinent information. When you call, tell the counselor right away that you have a number of questions to ask so she'll know she has to allot more than a couple of minutes for you. If she says she hasn't time to answer your questions, ask when would be a good time to call back.

Interviewing the Counselor By Telephone

Your first questions might be, "What are your fees?" and "Do you have a sliding scale?" If you don't have much money, you won't want to waste your time interviewing someone you can't afford to see anyway.

If transportation or time is a problem for you, get that settled right away by asking where the office is, and whether the counselor is available at the times when you're free.

Before you ask more questions, give a general idea of what your goals in counseling will be. Use your answers to the questionnaires as a guide. Then ask "How would you approach that kind of problem?" The counselor might say she has to know more before answering and then you'll have to decide whether to take a chance on an exploratory interview to answer that question. Some counselors will be willing to give you a very clear answer to how they would work with you.

If you've never talked to a counselor before, your nervousness about her specialized language may cause you to have trouble understanding her. Don't assume it's your fault. Tell her you don't know much about counseling and ask her to explain what she means.

Sometimes it's hard to understand professional people, so don't expect to get a perfectly clear picture right away, even when you've asked for clarification. But you should expect the counselor to try to help you understand and to use ordinary language rather than the special jargon of therapy. After a couple of questions are answered, you should have an idea of whether you can expect counseling that's mostly talk or that includes a good deal of direction from the therapist, or activities designed to help you relax, express your feelings or explore your potential. Take notes on what the counselor says.

You might want to ask the following questions also, either on the telephone or at your first interview when you can get a clearer impression face to face.

About how many battered women have you counseled, and have you had any special training in working with battered women? Your counselor should be experienced in counseling battered women, and have attended at least one workshop or class that dealt specifically with the issue.

What do you think is the main reason men batter women? There's room for a variety of opinions on this, but the counselor's opinion should have some reference to the sex stereotyping and socialization of men and women; that is, she should understand that women are taught men are boss and men are given permission to control women and to express their anger in violent ways. She should put the responsibility for violence squarely on the shoulders of the person who does it.

Deciding On a Counselor

At this point you might have a definite impression and be ready to hang up or to make an appointment. If not, feel free to ask more questions. Some of the people you talk to might be gracious about answering them at length, others will be brusque, and still others willing, but too busy at the moment. You'll have to decide how important it is to you to get the information you want before making an appointment.

After each call, write your impressions, beginning with both pleasant and uncomfortable feelings you had as you talked or just after you hung up. Your first response might be "ugh" or "I feel awful" or something equally vague. Try to remember what was said or what attitudes were subtly expressed that caused the feeling. For instance, you might note "seemed hurried" or "laughed when I was funny." Then write other comments or information about fees, neighborhood, and so on, and rate each counselor as "No," "Possible" or "Yes." Note any questions you'll want to follow up on in your first session, and be sure to take them with you at that time.

If your telephone interviews give you two or three people that seem like good prospects, make an appointment with the one who sounds the best: the one who undersands what you want, is easy for you to understand, is open to answering questions and has considerable experience in counseling abused women. Beyond these criteria, each woman's opinion will vary. Explain that you want your first visit to be a mutual interview to see if you want to work together.

THE FIRST COUNSELING SESSION

Each of the previous steps will increase your sense of control over the initial interview, though if you've never talked to a counselor, you may still have some nervousness. The best way to dissipate it is to simply state that you're nervous, have never been to a counselor before and don't quite know what's expected of you. The counselor will probably say something reassuring and then ask you to say why you're there or what's troubling you.

If you have more questions to ask, say so. If you ask them at the beginning of the hour you'll be sure not to run out of time before you get to them. Additional questions may arise during the session. Ask when the interview is scheduled to end so you'll be sure to have time to say what you want. Have your written questions in front of you and don't feel embarrassed about making notes as they're answered. The more nervous you are, the more you're likely to forget what was said, unless you take notes.

Here are more questions you might want to ask:

How long have you been counseling and what kind of degree do you have?

Psychiatrists and most psychoanalysts have medical degrees as well as training in psychotherapy. Their fees are generally the highest, unless they're in public agencies that charge according to income, or you're receiving public assistance. A psychiatrist may be willing to accept medical coupons for payment. Their training tends toward upholding traditional sex roles and they're more likely to be interested in why you're involved with a violent man than in how you can change your life.

A psychologist usually has a Ph.D. degree from a university and often is trained in research on the behavior of animals and humans, knows how to do diagnostic testing of intelligence and other factors and has some training in psychotherapy.

Social workers have a Masters or Ph.D. degree from a university and are trained in research, community organization or counseling. A social worker may have more concerns than other therapists about public policy and social services.

Counselors have degrees in counseling and often degrees in many other fields. Their backgrounds may include formal training in institutions of higher learning or therapy institutes, private training with other therapists or on-the-job training and community sponsored workshops. Each profession has its competent and not-so-competent members, and it's impossible to say that one group is better than another. It's the individual who counts.

Paraprofessionals often counsel battered women, especially at shelters. They don't have degrees in counseling, but have on-the-job training and much more experience in handling the problems you're faced with than have most professionals. If you have severe problems aside from those directly related to the battering you may want to see a professional person. But for the crisis period or for problems related specifically to battering, you may get the best help possible from a paraprofessional. Whoever you choose, experience with and knowledge about the problem of battering is essential.

Will you expect me to talk most of the time and what other methods will you use to help me change?

There isn't one correct answer to this question. The therapist may expect you to spend most of the sessions talking while she makes only occasional remarks, both of you might talk, or she'll ask you to do relaxation exercises or to play roles in specific situations in order to understand or handle them better. Or she might ask you to do certain physical movements to help you express emotions.

You'll have to be the judge of whether the methods make sense to you, or whether you have a good enough feeling about the counselor to take a chance they'll work for you.

Is this session, in general, about the same as I can expect from other sessions?

Some counselors gather extensive information at the first interview. In some agencies, this "Intake" interview is done by a special person, and will not be the same person you see for counseling. The "Intake Worker" may even assign you to a counselor and if you want to see a particular person or type of person, you may have to be very assertive to get the person you want.

If the counselor indicates the other sessions will be quite different from the first, ask for an explanation. You may want to wait until the end of the second session to make your decision.

You have the right, also, to ask about the counselor's marital status, lifestyle and other questions about her personal life and personal values. She has the right to decline to answer and may or may not have good reasons for it. If she does decline you'll have to decide how important it is to you to have answers to those questions. If it is important, you have a right to find someone who will answer them for you.

What to Expect from the First Session

The first interview may provide you with clarification of your problems, plans to resolve them or increased awareness of your feelings. Or it may take the whole session to relate your story and get your questions answered. How it goes depends on the counselor's skill and methods, on how upset you are, and whether you're well-organized about presenting your problem and clear about what you want. If you have many interconnected problems, one session may not be enough to give the counselor a clear picture. Aim to finish the session with agreement on whether you'll come back, how often, what you'll pay, and on the goals you want accomplished.

Sometimes in an initial interview a client becomes so immersed in her emotions or her story that she forgets to ask questions, has trouble saying what the problem is, and leaves with only a vague idea of what the counselor is like. If that happens to you, continue to follow the suggestions for the first interview in the second one. If by the end of the second session you don't have agreement about what you'll work on and how the counselor intends to help you, something is probably wrong.

Once you've invested an hour of your time in an interview and discussed troublesome and personal aspects of your life, it's difficult to conclude you don't want to continue seeing the person, even when you have misgivings about her. But if you have any doubts about whether you and she can work together, don't make a permanent commitment. If you're clear about what your reservations are, explain them. The problem may be just a misunderstanding. If not, the counselor's response may reinforce your negative feelings, so you'll be able to make a more definite decision. Remember there are other counselors available who may be much more satisfactory for you.

THE SPECIAL CASE OF A SEXIST COUNSELOR

It's difficult to say exactly what the counselor should do for you because the goals are hard to measure and it's not always easy to separate what you can expect of the counselor from what you must accomplish yourself. At a minimum, insist on respect. Among other things, that means sexist attitudes are not acceptable.

In the Broverman study referred to in Chapter 1, it was discovered that both female and male therapists believed it appropriate for men to be more confident, dominant, worldly and emotionally reserved than women, and for women to be submissive, passive and dependent. Counselors who accept traditional sex stereotypes such as these can have a powerful and damaging effect, especially on women. A woman may have just begun to gain a sense of what she wants from life, to make independent judgments, or to exercise her rights when she sees a counselor for the first time. If the counselor defines the woman's role for her in a narrow way, the woman may decide she was "crazy" to think she could be independent or make her own decisions. She may retreat from a newly developed determination to get a professional job or training in a trade, or to define her own sexuality.

You'll experience special problems if you contract for the services of a sexist therapist. She or he is likely to reinforce your self-blame. If you're already blaming yourself for the abuse, it may not take much for your guilt feelings to lead you right back to the man. You may persuade yourself, or be persuaded by the counselor, that by becoming a better person yourself you can control the man's violence. Sexist therapists often ask battered women, "What did you do to provoke him?" and imply that it's the women's responsibility to change, so the man won't have a "reason" to beat her up again.

Whether they admit it or not, many men (and some women) believe it's the man's responsibility to control his women, especially his wife. Counselors are among the people who believe that, and it may take you quite a while to discover what your prospective counselor's attitudes are unless you ask pointed questions early on, at the first session or even before, over the telephone. Try these:

• How do you feel about how women's and men's roles have been changing?
• Do you think mothers of small children should work outside the home?
• Do you think the one who earns the money should make most of the decisions in the household?

Answers to these questions won't tell the whole story, but they'll give you an idea of how similar or different your values are from those of the counselor's and whether she or he is rigid or flexible about sex roles, or leans toward traditional or contemporary definitions of what it means to be male and female.

ADVANTAGES OF A WOMAN COUNSELOR

We've all grown up believing males are the people in authority, are knowledgeable and can tell us what to do, whether they're doctors, husbands, or TV repairmen. That means you're particularly vulnerable to a male counselor, because of his double authority as a counselor and a male, and you'll probably be cautious about confronting him on his sex bias and speaking up for your own ideas.

A woman counselor is more likely than a man to understand and empathize with your feelings about the violent man, and also want to help you protect yourself. She may be more likely to help you get in touch with supportive women's groups in the community that many male counselors won't know about. In addition, she'll be a good role model for you. But many female therapists identify with male values, so don't assume if a female therapist implies you're in the wrong, she must be right.

Not all counselors realize it's the batterer who must change, his victim is not to blame and her obligation to keep herself safe is more important than an obligation to continue the relationship. You're more likely to find a female counselor than a male who's developed that awareness, but you'll need to ask questions to be sure. Ask, "Do you think one partner can be the only one at fault when there's battering, or is it always both partners that contribute and are equally responsible?"

If the counselor believes the problem is caused by the way the two parties interact and that they have equal responsibility for the battering, you had better look further. Keep looking until you find someone who recognizes that only the person who does the battering can stop it or start it and only he is responsible. (Assuming you also behave in destructive ways sometimes, you're responsible for those actions, for what you do.)

HOW TO EVALUATE THE COUNSELOR

The goals you and the counselor agreed upon at the first or second session give you criteria for judgment. For instance, after two months of counseling you may still feel unhappy, but if you remember that the goal is to gain insight or express your emotions, you'll realize it might be necessary to experience more pain as a by-product of growth. On the other hand, if your goal is to receive support and validation of your feelings and ideas, and yet you emerge from each counseling session feeling worse than when you went into it, something is definitely wrong.

When sessions aren't going well, allow for the fact that the fault may lie either with you, the counselor or the relationship between you. Don't assume you're a failure and beyond anyone's help. And don't expect magic of the counselor or blame her when you're not immediately "cured." Perhaps one or both of you is not working hard enough or well enough, or you're not working together well. Don't give up until you've considered each factor.

Express your dissatisfaction to the counselor in terms of the agreed upon goals and the length of time you've been meeting together. "We agreed that I should work on becoming more self-confident, and after three months I don't feel any different." "I was supposed to be able to express my anger, but after four months I don't even know how I feel."

An open, ethical counselor will explore the reasons, trying to reach a balance of responsibility between you and her, and, most importantly, a satisfactory way to proceed. It might be you've said you'd do suggested exercises but haven't followed through; the exercises haven't been appropriate for you; the counselor hasn't been consistent in her expectation, has stated one goal but then drifted toward another; or you've continually redefined your goals without beginning work on any. Maybe there's nothing wrong with either of you, but you just don't like her much. That's important too.

Reevaluating the Process

The counselor, ideally, will admit to some questions about her methods, and will accept your criticism as possibly valid. The result of such a discussion should be a new plan with a clearly defined goal and an agreed upon time and method of evaluation. An alternative is to recognize that it's time to end the relationship, either because the counselor isn't acceptable to you, or because of a personality or values clash or, for reasons only dimly understood, it's just not working. Together you can discuss alternative counselors. You may find that your counselor knows several others and their methods of working, and by now knows you well enough to make a good referral.

And what if she isn't that sort of ideal counselor? Suppose you tell her you don't feel any changes are taking place and she says it isn't so, or you should let her worry about that, or the problem is your hostility toward her, or any number of non-direct responses? You should be very careful to state what it is you want ("I'd like you to tell me now what changes you see, and why you feel that's significant progress"), or what she does that you don't like and find out if she's willing to change ("When I get stuck and don't talk, it makes me uncomfortable for you to just sit in silence. Would you be willing to help me get started?").

She may point out a number of changes that you've lost sight of or don't count as important. It's very hard to discriminate between the validity of a counselor's evaluation and your own, especially if you've been depressed for a long time, or if one of your problems is holding on to unrealistically high standards. If the counselor can remind you of how you were when you first came in ("Remember when just a couple of months ago you wouldn't even get out of bed for days?"), if she can give concrete examples of positive steps you've taken ("You've stood up for your rights three times this week, found an apartment, started making a friend"), you may have to put your trust in her.

On the other hand, if she's vague about what progress you've been making, and thinks the changes she wants you to make are more important than ones you're interested in, it may very well be time to stop seeing her.

Deciding to Leave or Change Counselors

It's extremely hard for most clients to tell a counselor they want to end the sessions, so they find excuses for not coming to appointments, hoping to gradually slip away unnoticed. This is not the most useful method for either party. Your absence *will* be noticed.

Try to screw up your courage to tell the counselor exactly why it is you want to stop. If she disagrees with your reasons, try honestly to listen to her and weigh her comments against your ideas. Be as frank as you can about your reasons, and don't back down just because of her power and authority. She may try to talk you out of leaving, or she may disagree with your reasons but encourage you to act on your own beliefs, or she might come around to agreeing with you. In any case, acknowledged or not, you will have done her a favor by letting her know why you're choosing to leave. And you will have done yourself a favor by standing up for your rights and taking full responsibility for your decisions.

As you choose, work with, and evaluate a counselor, keep in mind that you're purchasing services. If you're not getting what you want, you have every right to buy them someplace else or to negotiate until you get what you want. After three visits to one counselor, don't let yourself off the hook by saying, "I tried counseling but it didn't help." Keep on looking until you find a person you can work well with.

If you're lucky, you'll find a counselor who shows you how to help yourself. Regardless of what you get from formal counseling sessions, in the end it's up to you.

SECTION III

Helping Yourself to Survival

Chapter 10

YOU CAN BE YOUR OWN COUNSELOR

Professionals of various sorts can be lifesavers at times, but ultimately you have to save your own life and create your own destiny — even if you feel you're the last person you can count on right now.

You want to get out. You want to stay. You feel dependent on your partner, yet you know he can't be depended on. You want a job, but do nothing about getting one. You're sad and depressed. There's an angry monster that pops out when you least expect it. You love him, you hate him. You say you couldn't tolerate the loneliness of leaving him, but you're lonely when you're with him. All those contradictions make you feel like you're going crazy, and they may paralyze your will to act.

But you *can* help yourself. The contradictions don't mean you're crazy, though many abused women do wonder about their stability. When the most important adult in your life regularly gives you negative feedback about the kind of person you are, you're in a "crazy-making" situation: a situation which continuously causes you to question your judgment on things you previously felt secure about; a relationship that causes confused thinking, a mass of contradictions, and a frequent feeling that nothing makes sense anymore. It's especially so if you've been isolated and get no balancing positive messages from other people.

It's true that some women stay in the situation long enough to go a little crazy. But it needn't be a permanent condition. Changing your situation, either by leaving the man, or by expanding options and activities within the relationship, can begin important changes in the way you think and feel about yourself, enabling you to start believing in your sanity.

You can begin to recapture the will to act, even when you're still feeling confused. You've already started by reading this book. This section will help you learn how to be a good counselor to yourself.

CHANGING HOW YOU TALK TO YOURSELF

Any woman involved with an abusive man hears a great deal

113

of verbal abuse directed against her. Few women can take it for long without beginning to agree. Often, unknown to the man, his woman begins to talk silently to herself the same way he does. After a while, he doesn't have to give the negative messages any more to keep her in line. She does it for him.

If she has friends or relatives who give emotional support and believe she's a good person, she may eventually begin to trust their judgment. But if she feels her man is far more important or knows her much better than they do, she won't hear the supportive, positive messages that come her way. If she spends little time with people other than her man — a common situation — there won't be other messages to hear.

All of us counsel, or coach, ourselves in ways that are either useful or damaging. It's easy to get into the habit of coaching for failure, but that can be changed. You can begin by modifying your "self-statements," the things you say to yourself, about yourself. If you give yourself messages to the effect that "You don't deserve to eat well or dress well because you're too fat and ugly," "You're helpless and stupid and can't take care of yourself," or "Nothing is ever going to turn out right for you," your life probably won't get better. You may make dozens of promises, weekly, or even daily. "Tomorrow I'm going to look for a part-time job, learn to type, clean the house from top to bottom, enroll in a class, be a better wife, a more patient mother." You won't be able to fulfill any of these promises if you constantly tell yourself you're hopeless and incapable of change.

The next series of exercises is designed to combat the hostile messages that are probably coming from you as well as the man who abuses you. You may not be able to change his behavior, but at least you can stop verbally abusing yourself.

The Importance of Writing
Many of the activities below require writing, and some people resist them because they don't like to write. They think the writing is "just a gimmick." No one but you will see what you write, so it doesn't have to be correct. Writing is a gimmick, but it has a purpose. In fact, several purposes.

Writing things makes them concrete. If you're of two minds (you want to leave, you want to stay; you have rights, you deserve nothing), your conflicting ideas can be confusing and discouraging. Writing can help clarify them. It can also make you more aware of your unconscious thoughts. Because you don't always hear the things you tell yourself, saying them out loud helps; writing them down helps even more. If you try to repeat back exactly what someone said two or three minutes ago, you'll realize how easily the spoken word drifts away. (A tape recorder will help too, if you really hate to write, but there are important advantages to writing that I think will become apparent as you do the exercises.)

You may be afraid of the changes necessary to get out of your painful situation, and you may rather stay hurt and bewildered than face a frightening unknown. But if you don't do the written exercises to give yourself an opportunity to see your thoughts more clearly and to understand the changes that *can* be made, there's a good chance you'll remain confused and unable to take action. If you continue making excuses for several months, you may need professional counseling to get started.

WHAT DID YOU DO RIGHT TODAY?

Make a list of all the things you did right today. You'll have to decide what "right" means to you, according to your own values, but here are some questions you can ask yourself, and some ideas about what you can take credit for. Even if they don't seem like a big deal, they're still things you can feel good about.

What did you do to try to make things better for other people? Perhaps you prepared a meal, comforted a child, controlled your temper, shopped for a sick friend, taught a neighbor to crochet, listened to someone's troubles, smiled at the letter carrier.

This question is placed first, not because it's the most important kind of thing to do, but because you're likely to do things for others and value them more readily than what you do for yourself.

What have you done to begin getting more control over your life? Have you made a decision, tried something new, enrolled in a class, started learning to drive, made a phone call to get information, stayed away from a destructive person?

Any action, no matter how small, that moves you a little further in the direction you want to go, is "right."

What have you done to make yourself feel better? Luxuriating in a long bubble bath, walking for the joy of it, taking the time to look at the sunset, going out to listen to music, playing cards with a good friend.

Notice I haven't listed activities that can be done without much conscious choice, or time-passers that seem pleasant at the moment but later leave you feeling you've wasted your time. In this category are alcohol, drugs, watching whatever happens to be on television, looking through magazines you aren't interested in, and passively talking with people you didn't choose to be with.

Women who've been abused often find it extremely hard to

think of anything they've done right. When they do remember it, they're afraid to say it out loud. Writing about your activities helps you to be honest and precise, so when you read what you've accomplished, you're confronted with the fact that you're not hopeless, not a total failure.

If you want to gain some control over your life, you have to start giving yourself credit for things well done, which doesn't necessarily mean you succeeded in exactly what you wanted to accomplish. If you've been sitting around in a depressed funk for a few months or years and then decide to take up jogging, you may not get farther than one block. What you did well was to make a change. You made a decision, got up off your chair, got some exercise, and started moving in a different direction. As you increase your awareness that you've done some worthwhile things already, you'll gain courage to try more activities and a greater sense of what's possible.

Note whether you've added any negative qualifiers to your positive statements. When women are asked to make positive statements about themselves, they often qualify the self-compliment with a criticism, or by discounting its importance. "I have a good disposition — except I get mean when I'm depressed." "I'm a good mother — but anybody could do that." *Draw a line* through the qualifiers.

Activity 14   Do Right List

	Day 1	Day 2	Day 3
HELPED OTHERS FEEL GOOD	Listened to elderly, lonely neighbor		

	Day 1	Day 2	Day 3

GAINED CONTROL OVER PART OF MY LIFE

Called for info on class

DID WHAT FELT GOOD

Went shopping

Go back over your list one more time. What have you left out? Did you fix the children a nutritious meal? Get to work on time? Do the laundry? Are you telling yourself those accomplishments don't count, because "It's something any responsible mother/employee would do"? Of course it counts. The way you're feeling, you could have thrown together jelly sandwiches and coco-puffs to keep the children happy and off your back. You could get to work late, take long breaks and leave early. What else did you do that you didn't list because you thought, "It had to be done, so why give credit for it?"

Sometimes you have to get out of bed but it takes a gigantic effort, and perhaps there have been days when you've just refused to cope and stayed in bed or stared at the television all day. If you felt like that but got up and went on with your day, give yourself credit for it.

Remember that "doing right" means doing the best you can at the moment. Look again to see if you omitted anything you tried to accomplish but didn't work out well. There might be times when you take hours (or days) to work up your courage to make a phone call, and the person you call is out of town. That can be a letdown. But at least take credit for making the call, which you could control, and don't blame yourself for the result, which you couldn't do anything about. You ought to have at least thirty items on the credit list for the first three days. Keep listing them every day.

WHAT ARE YOU TELLING YOURSELF?

List your self-criticisms exactly as you say them: "Dummy!" "Oh my god, you screwed up again." Some may be single words: "fat," "ugly," "gross," "stupid," "hopeless." Others may be whole sentences or paragraphs that demolish your ego. *"You dimwit! You really are a hopeless fool. Everything you touch, you ruin. You never learn. You keep saying you're going to reform, but you never get better. You're ugly and fat, too, because you don't have any willpower."*

Activity 15   Self-Criticism List

1. _____

2. _____

3. _____

4. _____

5. _____

6. _____

7. _____

8. _____

9. _____

10. _____

     This kind of inner monologue may be nearly constant and such a familiar part of your being you're no longer aware of it. In order to appreciate how damaging this slanderous self-talk can be, consider how you would feel if someone else continually insulted you that way. Perhaps you heard something like it from a parent or spouse, and can remember how small and helpless it made you feel.

     However bad that may have been, what you say to yourself can be much worse. No one else can equal the many opportunities you have to hurl insults at yourself all day, every day. Another important difference is that other people's insults are verbalized aloud, so that however hurtful they may be, it's possible to fight back. Your own criticisms, in contrast, are often silent; so you may be unconscious of them and unable to contradict them. If you continue to be unaware of what your self-criticisms are, they can make you a very effective one-woman demolition squad, chipping away at your self-esteem a little more each day.

     You may find it difficult, at first, to notice what you're saying, but just making the decision to record the statements will improve your awareness. If nothing comes to mind the first day, don't give up. Get a nice drink, settle into a comfortable chair, and recall the last twenty-four hours in detail. Form a picture in your mind of each event, recapture the mood, try to experience again what you felt at the time, and pay special attention to what you said to yourself when you were bored, angry, disappointed; when you forgot something or failed to follow through on a plan. If even one slightly self-critical word comes to mind, write it down.

     If you can recapture a negative mood but can't recall any specific statements, ask yourself what you might have said if you had chosen to put the mood into words. Never mind whether the words are rational or accurate. You're not trying to find the absolute truth, you're getting a process started. Putting these imaginary statements on your list will help you form the habit of listening to yourself.

THE DIFFERENCE BETWEEN
THE GENERAL AND THE SPECIFIC

Generalizations have a very different effect from statements that only criticize particular acts or single aspects of your character. ("You were selfish about going out to dinner." "You're not good at gardening.") The general statements speak of who you *are*, the others describe a specific behavior or failure in a particular area. It's easy to forget that sometimes smart people do dumb things and good people do bad things.

For instance, the generalization, "You're so stupid!" leaves no room for change or improvement. In contrast, "That sure was a stupid thing to do," allows for the possibility that you're not generally a stupid person and can correct your action. In the following example, the woman: 1) accuses herself of being a stupid person, 2) writes it down, 3) analyzes the self-accusation and realizes that she was referring to one action that seemed stupid, and 4) states what happened: she burned the toast.

Activity 16   *Substitution List*

Self-critical Statement   What Happened

1. *You're sure stupid!*   *burned the toast*

2. *Oh, my god, you're never*   *ate double ice cream cone*
   going to change; you'll always
   be a fat useless slob.

3. _____

_____

_____

4. _____

_____

_____

5. _____

_____

_____

This exercise is a modified version of Sharon Berlin's model of self-criticism reduction. See "Resources" list at end of book.

A simple statement of what you did takes the comment out of the realm of blame and praise. No intellectual or moral evaluation is made of the act of burning toast. If you do this exercise regularly, you'll avoid the guilt, depression, and anxiety that often follow self-blame, and you'll be free to consider how you can change the behavior. Blaming won't improve your life, but changing what you don't like will.

Self-criticism can be useful, but not if it implies that you're destined to remain lazy, idiotic, and ugly until you die. It can be put to use only if it's specific and not so constant that you become overwhelmed with the number of things to be changed.

Substituting the Specific for the General

Continue to take the steps of (1) Increasing awareness of self-criticisms, especially general or total characterizations, (2) Recording, (3) Analysis, (4) Restating. Do it every day. It may take several weeks to progress to (5) Developing the habit of automatically substituting a statement about a specific action for a generalized insult.

First, work on corrections, noting each day how many times you remembered to correct each general criticism as soon as you made it. Soon you'll be able to substitute the more specific, rational statement for the general criticism. Your inner monologue may go something like this: "Well, fatty you did it again!.. Whoops! I mean...let's see, what did I do? Correction: I had potatoes and gravy." After several weeks of these kinds of corrections, you'll find yourself skipping over the, "Well, fatty" remarks entirely and substituting a factual statement about what was eaten.

The ability to skip over the general self-criticism to the substituted specific statement isn't necessarily a continually improving path. There will be setbacks, but gradually there will be more items in the substitution column than in the correction column. Sometimes it takes weeks for that to happen.

EVALUATE YOUR RULES

Take another look at your self-criticism list. How many criticisms imply rules about what you should do, or what you should be like? If you're confused about what the rules are, try writing them. *Write* one criticism at a time, then *write* the rule you seem to be trying to obey. Rules usually demand that you must never do something (lose your temper, be late for work) or must always do something (remember to call mother, stick to your diet, be nice, be sensible, etc.).

Where do your rules come from? Your mother? Your father?

Your husband? Your children? School? Friends? Who said you should have a complete hot dinner and dessert on the table at six p.m. every night? Who insists you be clever, competent, and unruffled? Who said you should be smart? A good housekeeper? Able to handle money well? *Write* the name of the rule-giver beside the rule.

Activity 17   Whose Rule?

<u>Self-Criticism</u>	<u>Rule</u>	<u>Whose Rule</u>
I'm just a slob. The house is always a mess.	*The house must be clean and uncluttered at all times after ten a.m.*	*Mother*

You may have trouble deciding where the rule came from. Perhaps you're thinking it doesn't come from anyplace special. "Everyone knows you shouldn't leave dishes in the sink," or "That's just the way people are supposed to be." If so, shut your eyes, and try to visualize a house that "looks the way it should." If it's your mother's house, the rule probably came from her, whether or not it was stated in so many words. If you still don't have a clue, ask yourself what person could drop in unexpectedly — however unlikely — and cause you embarrassment at the condition of your house? A neighbor? The minister? That person may never have made any sort of rule, yet you may be trying to live up to a standard you think the person demands.

What Are Your Rules?
You'll do better if you try to live up to your own standards.

Suppose no one except you ever saw your house? Would you still try to abide by that rule? If not, what would *your* rule be? Maybe only part of it suits your lifestyle. Perhaps you like the kitchen clean because you don't like the looks of kitchen mess, but you'd rather keep the bedroom doors closed than make the beds. Maybe you'd prefer to clear away the clutter at the end of the day than at nine-thirty in the morning.

Give some thought to what it feels like to try to live up to other people's rules. Does it make you nervous? Bad-tempered? Defensive? Do you feel guilty? Inadequate? If you experience some of those feelings, consider whether the rule itself might be at fault, rather than you.

Write your own rules now, noting it's your own decision this time whether you'll follow each one or change it when it seems unreasonable.

Activity 18   *Your Own Rules*

New Rules   Whose Rule?

Wash dishes after each meal.   *Mine*
Pick up general clutter between ten a.m. and noon.   *Mine*

_____

_____

_____

_____

_____

_____

_____

All the activities in this chapter work together: giving yourself credit for what you do right, reducing self-criticism and establishing rules that are your own. The next chapter tells you how to begin making changes, one at a time, even when you don't want to take action at all.

Chapter 11

A COURAGEOUS ACT A DAY

Perhaps your picture of a courageous act is restricted to the drama of saving people from a burning building, leading a platoon into battle, or donating a kidney. If so, you'll need to broaden your definition. Any worthwhile activity you do in spite of the fact that it causes you nervousness, anxiety, pain or insecurity is a courageous act. Worthwhile simply means an activity worth doing. The range might be from asking a friend to come for dinner to job or house-hunting or to asking a social worker to help you stop abusing your child.

You can probably see that the last example takes courage, but you may argue that the other two are nothing to be nervous about.

THE USES OF DENIAL

It's natural to deny feelings of insecurity or anxiety, because you feel there's something shameful about them or they're painful to live with. You deny their existence, hoping if you ignore them they'll go away.

Denial does work that way sometimes for some people; more often, however, it has an opposite effect that goes something like this: "I shouldn't be nervous about a little thing like apartment hunting. So I'm *not* nervous about it. It's just that I don't want to do it today, because I think I'm getting a cold. I'll wait till tomorrow." And when tomorrow comes: "I'd better stay home and mend this dress so I'll look nice when I go apartment hunting tomorrow." And tomorrow and tomorrow.

Flimsy excuses will increase your confusion and sense of helplessness. "I couldn't call emergency housing, because the line was busy," won't wash. Nor will "I couldn't look for work because I missed the bus." Those are excuses, not reasons. Excuses may explain why it was hard to do something (going out in the rain when you have a cold, getting up early even though you didn't sleep well). They don't explain why you didn't do the difficult task.

When you reorganize your life, you may have to talk to many

people with whom you've had nothing to do before (lawyers, crisis counselors, rental agents, welfare workers, employment interviewers, plumbers). Most people are anxious, in varying degrees, when faced with unfamiliar contacts and new roles. So don't be surprised if "just" talking to a plumber makes you nervous. If you were once accustomed to handling money and making business contacts, but your partner has "protected" you from all that for several years, it may be especially difficult to accept the fact that you are now uncertain and scared. Admitting it would make you feel as though you'd regressed, and that might be humiliating.

Are You Denying Your Feelings?

If you make a decision to do something that seems right for you, and postpone doing it several times, that may be a clue that you're playing a denial game. Listen carefully to the explanations you give yourself and determine whether they're really excuses.

Suppose you're asking yourself why you put off house hunting. "Well, without a car it's hard, and Monday it was raining." Note that the lack of a car and the rain make it hard, but they don't say why you didn't put on your raincoat and get on a bus. "Tuesday I thought the baby was sick. It turned out she wasn't, but by then it was too late." Perhaps you really couldn't go if she was sick, but did you take her temperature or take her to the doctor as early as you could? Did you try every way you could think of to find a baby sitter? Could you have gone to one or two places after you learned she was all right, even though it was later than you wanted it to be? A second postponement is cause for suspicion, even when the reason seems valid.

"Wednesday my friend came by and I didn't want to hurt her feelings by leaving." Did you think of asking her to come with you? Did you have any special reason to think she'd be hurt? The third postponement in three days almost certainly indicates you're not being honest with yourself.

One way to catch yourself at that game is to ask if you really mean "couldn't." Usually "couldn't" means "I didn't want to" or "I was too scared, but I didn't want to admit it." Reasons are honest. Excuses are partly true (you really did miss the bus), but they don't explain much and may even turn the truth upside down (maybe you missed the bus so you'd have an excuse not to job hunt).

UNCOVERING YOUR FEARS

When you suspect yourself of denying your feelings, some further questions are in order.

- What are the feelings I most dislike experiencing?
- What kinds of situations usually cause me to feel that way?
- If I *were* feeling that way about this situation, why would I feel that way?
- What's the worst thing that could happen in this situation?
- What's the best thing that could happen?

Suppose your husband has done the shopping for the past ten years, including all the groceries. Now he's gone and it's up to you. You postpone going to the supermarket and get by with what the children pick up at the corner mini-market, but you're concerned because it's so expensive to shop there. The first few times you put off shopping, you give yourself excuses. Finally you admit you just don't want to do it. Then you get to the questions above and answer them like this:

- I most dislike feeling inadequate or confused or stupid when out in public.
- I feel inadequate when I don't know how to do something and when people expect me to know certain things that I don't.
- Maybe I'd feel this way because of not knowing what are reasonable prices, not remembering how to pick out good meat or fruit, some young customer or clerk asking my "expert" opinion.
- The worst thing that could happen is I wouldn't be able to answer, or I'd start crying, or would wander around, feeling so anxious that I wouldn't be able to find anything, make a fool of myself, be carted off to a mental hospital.
- The best thing that could happen is I'd remember it all and just start doing it again like I used to.

Now you can be pretty sure it's your fear of feeling inadequate, foolish, or crazy that's keeping you from the supermarket. "But that's ridiculous," you may think. "I used to handle everything, I even gave public speeches and terrific dinner parties until he took over everything and we stopped seeing anybody. I can't be putting off shopping because I feel like some dumb little kid when I think about trying to find my way around the supermarket." But apparently that's the reality, and now that you know what it is, you can deal with it.

Suppose you have to look for a new place to live. Maybe you've been staying with friends or at a shelter and now it's time to move out on your own. "Anybody," you say, "should be able to look for an apartment, right?" Maybe you've put it off because it's boring and you'd rather sit in the sun. That's probably true as far as it goes, but it's not far enough. If you ask those same questions, you might realize that you most hate feeling poor, and you feel poor when you live in dingy places or have to admit you can't afford to live where you want. You're afraid you'll only be able to find a place that's cramped and depressing. So boredom is only part of the picture. If you thought your hunt would reward you with a wonderful place, you'd gladly suffer the boredom of looking.

Answering the last question, "What's the best thing that could happen?" may surprise you. If the best thing that could happen is finding a place to live by yourself, and the feeling you hate most is loneliness, it might be you're afraid you'll succeed in finding a place. When you move into that wonderful place by yourself, you'll miss the people you're staying with now. Perhaps you're not quite ready to be on your own but you haven't wanted to admit it.

As long as you continue to deny your fears, you can postpone action indefinitely with a series of excuses which hide the real reason even from yourself. But when you recognize the fears you can force yourself to rise above them and that's what takes courage. As you'll see in the following pages, there are things you can do that make it easier to be courageous.

The days you force yourself to get out of your chair and go to the supermarket, regardless of your feelings of anxiety, confusion, and frustration, the days you pound the pavement for a new place to live, even though you dread moving, those are the days you act with courage. If you didn't have those feelings about the tasks, they wouldn't be remarkable at all. It's the feelings, together with your willingness to rise above them, that make those acts courageous.

REDEFINE THE TASK

If you're promising yourself you'll go out to get a job, rent an apartment or make a new friend, you may be afraid you'll be even more depressed if it doesn't work out. You need to reword your intention so that it states only what you know you can do: "I'm going to *look* for a job or apartment." "I'm going to *invite* someone out for coffee." Perhaps these seem small distinctions, but they're important. Although you can't control other people's responses, you can take responsibility for your part of the interaction. If you don't get the job or the house, you needn't be depressed over failing. You can give yourself credit for working hard and intelligently, even though you couldn't control the result.

Choose your task carefully. Make it one you're willing and able to carry out, and then hold yourself accountable. That does not mean building up a lot of anxiety over failure to succeed. Nor does it mean putting yourself down if you don't carry out your plan. It means you're clear about your intention, and clear about whether you carried it out. It may mean figuring out why you didn't do it.

Once you establish the reason you haven't acted, you can begin to work on changes. Not by telling yourself you should be brave or should want to do it, but by choosing a task that's the least threatening to begin with and getting help from a friend in carrying it out.

Suppose you've been telling yourself you'll enroll in a community college and learn to be a computer programmer. After you postpone applying for admission several times, your self-questioning tells you you're afraid you can't do the work. Maybe you've been at home with several children for ten years and feel your brain is frozen.

Stop thinking of your task as getting through one or two years of schooling without flunking out or making a fool of yourself in comparison to all those bright young students.

Start thinking about the first step. You'll need to talk to a counselor at the college about requirements, how you can prepare ahead of time, how other people in your circumstances manage, and so forth.

If you postpone doing that two or three times, choose another step for an easier task. It might be just walking through the campus a few times to make it familiar and noticing how many older students there are. Maybe it's talking to a friend who's a student or looking up the number you'll need to call for an appointment. Or each one of these, one each day.

"The longest journey begins with a single step" is a saying with much truth. Your job is to concentrate on that first step.

TAKE CREDIT FOR EACH COURAGEOUS ACT

You probably accept the idea that it's right to be good to other people, especially those you care about most: your children, your husband, parents, friends. Yet you may object to being good to yourself, insisting "That's just selfish. I don't deserve it."

Women have a way of copping out when credit is due. If husbands, lovers, children, or friends come to us saying, "I'm a failure, I didn't do well at all," we quickly run to their defense, attempting to rescue them from despair with words of comfort and reassurance, reminders of things done well, and efforts made. Why don't we do that for ourselves? It doesn't seem appropriate to toot our own horn or to promote ourselves.

If you care about yourself, you'll treat yourself well. If you have hostile, punitive, disapproving attitudes towards yourself, then you'll see to it that one way or another, you're deprived of things that make you feel good. Make up your mind to behave as if you like yourself and deserve to feel good. If you're willing to change your actions for awhile, you'll find before long you're beginning to believe you're as deserving of respectful and nurturing treatment as anyone else.

Often you're the only one who knows what task you've assigned yourself, and you're certainly the only one who knows just how much courage and energy goes into goading yourself to get started at it and follow through. So you're the best one to assign credit. (Review the Do Right exercise in the last chapter.) Your own encouragement is the only response you can control, so make the most of it. When you appreciate yourself, you'll appreciate others. When you value yourself, others will value you. Start now taking credit and giving yourself specific rewards.

BE GOOD TO YOURSELF

Being good to yourself may mean rewarding yourself for courageous or other worthwhile acts, or it may mean allowing yourself pleasures for no special reason. Either way, you have to know what things make you feel good. Does listening to your favorite music cheer you up? How about going to a fashionable restaurant for lunch? Or seeing a good movie, walking in the park, lingering over a letter from a friend? See how many pleasures you can find or invent, especially things that aren't expensive, fattening, illegal or potentially dangerous.

If you've been in a brutal, restrictive relationship for a long time, you may have trouble thinking of something you enjoy. If you married or had a child shortly after you finished school, you may never have had the opportunity to explore what you want. If you haven't known many people, read many books, had many jobs, or tried many sports or arts, you may think you don't want much of anything, or feel it's impossible to find out what interests you.

Think about the people you like or admire or envy, men or women, old or young, in fiction and history, or real and alive. What is it about their characters, abilities or lifestyles you find attractive? If the excitement of a TV detective's life or a mountain climber's opportunity for bravery and risk-taking are what appeal to you, don't assume you could never do anything like that. Consider less dramatic, more available activities that provide opportunities to learn skills and experience similar feelings. Imagine yourself learning to ski or mountain climb, with the long-range goal of becoming an instructor or part of a rescue crew. Never mind that it could take years to become proficient, that skiing can be quite costly, and that in real life you think of yourself as "chicken." You don't know exactly how chicken you are until you try some slightly risky activities and give yourself a chance to overcome your fear gradually. Start with a low-risk sport to get in shape and gain more confidence in your body. When you find you're becoming a little braver, you'll be motivated to consider how you can earn or save money for skiing or climbing lessons. The point is, there's no need to give up any dreams or fantasies until you've thoroughly explored how they can be made real, and what you'll need, to begin the process.

Suppose you want a long vacation by yourself or with another adult. If you are tied to children for a number of years, that may very well be an impossible dream for the near future. But with some imagination, and careful planning, you may be able to get away for a weekend or a day, or arrange to have a few free hours each week.

Be wary of sentences that begin with, "Yes, but..." and finish with all the reasons you can't give yourself pleasure: "I'll never have time, energy, money or opportunity to do what I want." When you have few opportunities, it's certainly painful to be aware of all the things you'd like to have and do. But suppressing awareness of what you might want dulls the senses and increases depression. It also almost guarantees the depression will last longer, because if you don't know what you want, you can't begin to get it.

Find Out What Would Give You Pleasure

Make three lists: 1) pleasures you enjoy and want more of, 2) pleasures you used to have (at any stage in your life), and 3) things you might like but have never tried (caviar, gardening, black satin sheets, bowling). Be sure to include small pleasures like reading in bed, watching a plant flourish, putting up a shelf, browsing in a book store.

Activity 19A   *Pleasure List*

Pleasures I Enjoy	Pleasures I Used to Have	Pleasures I Might Like
Watering plants *Visiting*	*Roller skating* *Crocheting*	*Riding river rapids* *Writing poetry*

_____

_____

_____

_____

Put a check next to each of the pleasures you might have in the next week. Include those that require you to give up something else, plan ahead, or get some information. If you haven't at least ten activities that are possible to do almost immediately, go back and see what you can add to the list.

Make a list of pleasant events you can look forward to early in the morning, sometime in the afternoon, and in the evening:

Activity 19B   *Daily Pleasures*

Morning	Afternoon	Evening
Lingering over newspaper	*Read mail*	*Telephone (Sue)*
Water plants	*Crochet*	*Write poetry*

_____

_____

_____

_____

_____

_____

_____

You now have the possibility of waking up each morning with something to look forward to immediately and again later in the day and of finishing off the day with the knowledge you can have some pleasures in life if you'll take them. Make it a reality by giving yourself some joy at least three times a day.

BE PHYSICALLY SELF-SUPPORTIVE

When you're depressed or worried, frightened or over-worked, it takes special effort to remember that your body is as much a part of your self as your mind and your feelings. It's affected by the way you think and feel, and its condition will, in turn, dramatically affect your thoughts and emotions.

Eat Well

Don't let yourself forget meals, and don't eat junk food. If you must have a sweet, take the time to go to a special store or restaurant where you can get something really worth spending extra money on, and worth gaining the extra pound. Or fix something delectable at home. Allow yourself to plan and thoroughly enjoy it without guilt. Otherwise, eat what's good for you: fruit, fresh vegetables, protein. Prepare them so they taste wonderful. Set the table and sit down to eat in a leisurely way. Don't grab food on the run.

It's easy when you're feeling down to form the habit of eating food that's neither delicious nor good for you, nor even the right price. Make up your mind that anything you eat should have at least two of those characteristics.

Sleep Well

If at all possible, get somewhere near eight hours of sleep each night. If you have trouble getting sleep, pay attention to what you can do that's relaxing. Anything that calms rather than stirs your emotions and that doesn't fill your head with disturbing ideas is good to do during the hour before bedtime. A warm bath and milk will help, but if you can't shut your mind off from worry, anger, or confusion right away, accept the fact that it may take a while to learn how. Meanwhile, rather than tossing and turning and gnashing your teeth, try to turn that time into an enjoyable period. Turn on the radio and just let yourself listen without purpose. Read something light and entertaining. Without becoming restless and irritable, use the time to stretch and rest without trying to sleep. Learning relaxation techniques or meditation will help.

Recognize that although a regular good night's sleep will help you to feel your best, you won't collapse from lack of sleep. Don't dramatize the situation. Avoid talking to yourself (or others) with phrases like, "I hardly slept last night," or "I was awake all night." You and your friends will both become bored by it, and continually thinking about it will make you more aware of the negative aspect of your life.

If you become desperate, and threaten yourself with messages like, "I've got to sleep tonight or I'll fall apart," you'll find it even harder to relax and sleep. If you begin to feel pretty ragged because you're really sleeping just a few hours a night over a long period of time, get medical advice. If your doctor prescribes tranquilizers or sleeping pills, you may want to use them during the crisis period, but stop taking them after a few weeks. You may be surprised to find you don't need them after all. You can't necessarily count on the doctor to tell you whether the pills are addictive or have side effects that are dangerous if taken for a long time. This is a time when you may be tempted to overuse pills or alcohol, so pay close attention to any new habits you're forming now.

Even if you feel like you "just got to sleep" at eight a.m., don't sleep past ten in the morning and don't take sick leave unless you're really sick or are planning a pleasure-filled day. Get up and get some tasks accomplished and then, if you must, take a short nap later in the afternoon. Plan it for a time when you're certain to be awakened within thirty minutes. If you sleep until noon, or nap for several hours, you'll easily fall into a demoralizing cycle of feeling half awake at night and half asleep all day and "never getting anything done." Forcing yourself to be up during the day will help you get back on a schedule that helps you feel good.

Exercise

Many forms of exercise help you feel optimistic and invigorated. Running and swimming have the advantage of being available whether you do them by yourself or with others. If you like to compete, you can join with a team or enter a marathon, but if you'd rather keep it noncompetitive, that's easy too.

Running is available to almost anyone, almost anywhere. The exercise is good for you, but that doesn't mean that the more you suffer, the better off you'll be. If you're out of shape, begin by walking a mile or two, then running a short distance. Concentrate on the pleasure of being in motion, and continue running only as long as it feels good, even if it's only a few yards. If you stop while you're still enjoying it, you'll probably do it again.

Follow the same principle whether you swim, do calisthenics or join a soccer team. It's no longer strange for a woman to jog alone, or to play team sports. Take advantage of the times and do something for yourself.

Look Well

The way you look affects the way you feel. Start the day by getting fully dressed, arranging your hair, and putting on whatever make-up you're accustomed to wearing, whether or not you're going to leave the house or see anyone. This is one way to banish the demoralizing habit of glowering at the mirror and saying, "Ugh! See? On top of everything else, I'm ugly too."

Looking well doesn't have to take a lot of time, so don't use that as an excuse. Clean, combed hair, clean jeans and no-iron shirts are minimal. Add a bit of bright color somewhere and splash cold water on your face. You'll feel better. People will react positively to you too. But do it first of all for yourself.

If you find it difficult to ask for what you want, if you believe you must always be nurturing, sensitive and giving, and are quick to label yourself "selfish," it will take courage to follow the advice in this chapter. Giving yourself rewards for tasks and pleasures for no reason at all and treating yourself well physically may make you nervous at first. So those turn out to be courageous acts, too.

In addition to treating yourself well, find people who will distract you from your troubles, entertain you, and who have the potentiality to become good friends. The next chapter is about how to start that process.

Chapter 12

AN END TO ISOLATION

If you've been involved with an abusive man for a long time, it's likely you have few, if any, friends. A man who abuses a woman often senses, correctly, that the fewer relationships she has, the more easily he can control her. Over a period of months or years he'll demand that she be more and more available to him and less available to friends and relatives.

When you've been beaten and humiliated by the one special person who says he loves you, before long you'll probably feel pretty worthless and unlovable. Even if you know you've let your friendships go because of his demands, you may reinterpret events so it now seems it's your own fault you lack friends.

Some women are certain that friends can never provide the security and degree of caring nor the stimulation that a lover relationship brings with it. It's true that there's a great difference between the kinds of relationships, but some of the differences exist only because we place arbitrary limitations on our friendships, because we believe we can find intimacy only in sexual relationships. We can change those attitudes if we choose.

To begin that process of change, you can become more discriminating about a potential new lover and less critical of potential friends.

HOW CRITICAL OF OTHERS ARE YOU?

People who are overly self-critical often have similar attitudes toward other people. This is especially likely if they have few friends. The self-loathing is turned defensively onto others, sometimes toward those acquaintances and colleagues who are potential friends. It's as if the lonely, friendless person says, "I'm so uninteresting that no one would want me for a friend; but that's too painful to accept completely, so I'll keep reminding myself that there's something wrong with everybody I know. I'll reject them before they have a chance to reject me." And so begins a habit of criticizing and blaming other people.

To find out if this is something you habitually do, *make a list* of at least ten people you know or see frequently, no matter how

137

casual or fleeting the contact is. Ask yourself these questions about each one:
- Is this a good friend?
- Is she sometimes a friend but sometimes not?
- Is this someone I've wished were my friend?
- Is it a relative who might become a friend?
- Is this an acquaintance — someone I work with, see in the neighborhood, at church, school, or where I do business — but who I've never considered as a potential friend?
- Is this an acquaintance or relative who I'm sure could never become a friend?

Activity 20   *Why Aren't Acquaintances Friends?*

1. *Mary*   *sister-in-law; lives in San Diego*

2. *Betty*   *neighbor; gossips too much*

3. _____

4. _____

5. _____

6. _____

7. _____

8. _____

9. _____

10. _____

If there are quite a few acquaintances who are potential friends you'll have a good pool to draw from. If you dismissed many as impossible to develop friendships with, you have a problem.

Think about those people who you indicated are not potential friends and *complete this sentence* for each one: "She or he hasn't become my friend because..."

Your sentence completions might include anything from descriptions of the person's faults ("mean," "flighty," "stupid") to reflections of your own sense of inadequacy ("not interested in me," "she's too popular") to an assumption that certain differences make friendship impossible (age, income, educational level, marriage, parenthood).

Perhaps you haven't pursued relationships among many of these people because of what you perceive as their faults and inadequacies. You're either so critical of others that no one seems quite good enough to be your friend, and you haven't made enough effort to find people who share your interests and values, or you're so anxious to spare yourself rejection that you've persuaded yourself they're impossible.

If you've made critical judgements of quite a few people, notice whether they're generalized criticisms like "she's crazy" or "she's stupid." If so, you're discarding the possibility of any kind of relationship, even a limited one. You can use the same techniques you learned for reducing self-criticism in Chapter 10 to develop a more balanced attitude toward other people.

Give careful attention to what you say about other people. Change generalized criticisms to specific descriptions of behavior. "She's a fool" will become "She giggles when she's nervous" or "She's too loud." After a little practice, you'll be able to substitute the description before the generalized put-down even comes to mind.

While you're practicing, you can also begin to look for positive aspects of the people you know. Begin with potential friends who've sometimes seemed friendly to you. *List* all the positive qualities of five of these people. If you have trouble thinking of anything desirable about them, try looking at the way they relate to people other than yourself. How do they treat their children, neighbors, parents, husbands, bosses? *List* anything they've done that you approved or liked. *List* the skills and abilities they have, whether they're pertinent to your relationship with them or not.

Activity 21   *What Can You Appreciate About the People You Know?*

1. _____

_____

2. _____

_____

3. _____

_____

4. _____

_____

5. _____

_____

This doesn't mean you have to like everybody. If someone is a fine parent or hard worker, she still may not be someone you want to be with much. The point of looking for positive traits is to counteract the tendency to see everything and everyone in negative terms. When you break that habit you'll be able to make better judgments about potential friends.

START WITH THE PEOPLE YOU KNOW

Consider again whether each person on your list of acquaintances has enough positive qualities for you to spend even a little time with them. A woman who's tiring for an entire evening may provide an entertaining half hour over tea every week or so.

If an acquaintance is interesting but is a non-stop talker, enjoy brief conversations before or after a movie with her. Maybe there's a pleasant person who's so shy she makes you nervous. Go to a sports event or the zoo, so the structure of your activity will reduce some of the nervousness and give you both something to talk about. If there's a tennis partner in the neighborhood whom you don't like well enough for a long conversation, play with her, and limit your after-game visits to a half hour.

Many people are pleasant to be with on the job or in the neighborhood. If you never thought of associating with those people outside of the situation where you regularly see them, think about it now.

Perhaps there's someone you once liked, but later became bored with. Why not revive the relationship now, but plan to keep it on a once-a-month basis? What about someone you poured out your troubles to and then avoided because you regretted imposing on her? When you're feeling very positive, call and make a point of listening to her and saying some cheerful things about your life.

Look for people who can momentarily give you some pleasure, help you feel less lonely, and expand your interests, rather than waiting until you meet someone who looks like she'll be the perfect intimate, long-term friend. Casual relationships may begin in surprising places, and may take years to develop, flourish and become solid friendships.

If you don't want to risk placing all your emotional needs in the hands of one person, on whom you'll become increasingly dependent, you have to take the risks that go with creating friendships. When several acquaintances have become good friends, you'll enter relationships with a man from a position of strength rather than vulnerability, knowing that romance is something you *want*, rather than something you'll die without. You'll then be able to make clearer judgments about the men you become involved with, and the decisions you make in regard to them.

MEETING NEW PEOPLE

Learn to look at all the people you meet as potential friends. Rather than assuming none of those relationships will grow into friendships, consider that they might. Take a fresh look at the drug store clerk you've passed the time of day with for years. You know her pretty well and enjoy your periodic short conversations. Is it possible you'd enjoy more of her company? Ask her to have coffee with you during her break.

How about the secretary in the next office, the one you had a delightful conversation with when you accidentally shared a lunch table in the cafeteria? Why not invite her to join you for lunch? See how many old acquaintanceships you can revive or develop into friendships. Virtually none of us are so isolated that we know no one. Even if you moved to town yesterday and you have two small children who make it difficult to get around, you have to go to the grocery store or laundromat at least. Eventually, one of the children will get you to a doctor's waiting room and the drug store. You may have to wait in a welfare or foodstamp or public housing office. With a little energy, you can turn these situations into opportunities to socialize and to learn more about the city or neighborhood.

Perhaps it sounds unrealistic to think you'd connect with someone you'd like while standing in a Safeway line or riding the city bus. Have you ever known anyone who met an exciting man in that sort of situation? Why not an interesting woman, then? It's especially likely to happen if you have small children, since strangers often talk to and about them and if you meet another woman with a baby or child the age of yours, you already have something to talk about.

In addition to considering all the people you meet as potential friends, go to the places where the kinds of people you'd like to know are likely to be. Picture the people you like to be with, or if you've never been around many people that you liked, what they *might* be like. How would such people spend their time, and where would they be?

CHOOSING JOBS, CLASSES, ORGANIZATIONS

Although you can make friends almost anywhere you go, some places are easier than others. Classes and volunteer organizations are two of the best. Social clubs you find through your church or in your neighborhood are also good possibilities. Paid employment is another.

Paid Employment

Not many people evaluate job opportunities in terms of social contacts. The rate of pay, chance for advancement, opportunity to learn and the satisfaction or stimulation of the work are most important.

But there are other considerations as well. You may be looking for a challenging, absorbing and well-paid career, or a stopgap job to pay this month's rent. Of course, whether the salary will pay your expenses is the first requirement, but in pursuing any of those goals, you can also consider the social possibilities of employment.

Whether you work as a fast-food cook, administrative assistant, store manager, nurse, or receptionist, think about the neighborhood you'll work in. It might determine the type of clientele you'll serve, the size of the company, the lifestyles of your co-workers and even, perhaps, the type of management. In a downtown financial district, dress will be high style, speed and efficiency greatly valued. A university district, tourist area, or neighborhood shopping mall may offer informality and flexibility in a slower-paced atmosphere. When you apply for work, notice the social atmosphere as much as possible. If it isn't visible, ask for a tour of the work place. If your job would be joining workers at rows and rows of desks with telephones constantly ringing, it may be an unpleasantly noisy atmosphere, yet there ought to be someone among so many workers that you'll find compatible. On the other hand, if you would be the only non-professional person in a five-person office, or if you're forty years old and everyone looks twenty-one, you're likely to feel socially isolated.

If you're able to find a job that's interesting, challenging, pays well or allows you the opportunity for advancement, you may very well decide to take it even if there are few opportunities for developing friendships. In that case, keep in mind that you'll need to make more than the usual effort to make friends outside of work, since you won't have that potential during the bulk of every day. For example, you can reduce the loneliness by finding friends who work or live nearby to have coffee or lunch with every day. That's especially important if you work alone, if you have a nontraditional job which until recently have been available to men only, or if the male workers are hostile to you because of your sex.

Classes

Long range goals are most important in determining what classes will be most useful in developing skills and planning or changing a career. But consider other opportunities besides the value of learning the skill. One major consideration should be whether you're likely to make friends in the class.

Although it's certainly possible to develop male friends in a class, friendships with other women are easier to make and maintain because they're less subject to the unpredictable whims of romance and sexuality. Look for women's classes first. Neither you nor the others in the class will be distracted by the pressure of trying to impress male classmates, and you can assume some of the women are there partly to make friends. In a mixed class, you can be sure some of the women are there partly to meet men. That doesn't preclude their responding to a friendly gesture from you, but if you're feeling shy and insecure, you'll want to be among people more interested in you than a man.

It's stimulating to break out of old habits and meet new kinds of people, but it's also frightening. You may want, at first, to try to find a class where the members share some of your values and lifestyle. You can't be sure you have a true image of the women who attend particular classes at a church, YWCA or community college until you've attended for awhile. But you can get an idea of how you'll fit into the group by asking direct questions of the agency or the teacher. You might want to explain your particular concerns, whether they're about being shy, being with people of a different age or economic class, or who are too feminist, or not feminist enough.

Ask the instructor whether the class is formal or informal, large or small, includes activities and discussions or mostly lectures. You'll have more opportunity to get to know people if the group is small, informal and active than if it's large, formal and academic. You may, for instance, decide to begin with a rap group at the YWCA or the local chapter of the National Organization for Women or a small church-related group. Later, you can enroll in assertion training or social skills classes, where you can develop friendship skills while you practice them.

You should get the information you want, as well as a feeling about the teacher's willingness to explain her technique and outlook and about her warmth and attitudes toward the women she teaches. If you don't have a good feeling while talking to her, try to figure out why, so you can get more information on the spot. If it isn't clear what bothers you and you have alternatives, follow your hunches. But if you live in a small community where the choices are few, take a chance. It's better to go *somewhere* than nowhere, better to know *someone* than no one. Above all, don't sit twiddling your thumbs waiting for the perfect situation to come your way.

If you decide that your most immediate need is for the kind of formal education that can only be found at a community college or university, you can still plan your first quarter program along these same lines. Check out the Women's Center, now a fixture at many colleges. There you'll be able to meet other women in an informal atmosphere, and get information about which teachers are good and which classes are likely to be useful for you. The centers usually provide a lounge for informal interchanges, as well as structured activities.

If you plan to take classes for a couple of years, you'll have plenty of time later for the difficult ones, the large lecture courses and those that seem intimidating. What you need to begin with are courses that are fairly easy and have plenty of opportunity for interaction. Once you've started a support system and have proved to yourself you can manage in an academic setting, you'll have a base from which to take more challenging classes.

Volunteer Work

If you're able to work without pay, there are a great number of challenging and educational jobs available. To find out what's right for you, use roughly the same criteria that you used in finding the best classes. Of course, it's important that you do something worthwhile and meaningful to you, and you should also weigh the experience in terms of your career goals.

But these shouldn't be your only considerations. Think, too, about what organizations and what kind of work will bring you into contact with potential friends. For instance, working as a volunteer coordinator or assistant program developer at a women's center or YWCA will provide dozens of contacts with many women in a context where you can get to know them fairly well rather quickly.

If you're a low-key person who likes to take things slowly and form relationships in a structured environment, you might join a library group or club and learn to maintain and care for books with other people who have similar interests. If you like dramatic personalities, try helping out with the scenery or fundraising events at a local theatre. If you crave intellectual conversation with friends, see if there is some unpaid work you can do for a department of a graduate school or a museum. In any case, choose a place and a particular kind of volunteer work in which you are likely to meet compatible people. Watch the newspaper for notices of where volunteers are needed, or call the local United Way for lists of such organizations.

To recapitulate: consider everyone you're in contact with as a potential friend. Analyze what you like and don't like about each. If you're overly critical, use Activities 15 and 16 in Chapter 10 to make your criticisms more rational and precise. Spend limited time with people who make you feel bad. But if they're somewhat interesting or pleasant, find out what you can do together that will maximize their assets. Choose classes, volunteer and paid work partly on the basis of whether you can find potential friends there.

Chapter 13

REACHING OUT

So there you are, on the job, at the laundromat or a ceramics class. How do you make a new friend?

First, you must think well enough of yourself to realize that people will want you as a friend. If you're still full of self-blame and convinced you're too dull to interest anyone, it will be hard to reach out to other people, or even to recognize and accept their friendly gestures. To paraphrase Woody Allen, "Why would I want a friend who would talk to a person like me?"

RISKING THE FIRST STEPS

There are risks involved in initiating friendly gestures, and there's no point in pretending they don't or shouldn't exist. The biggest risk is the ego blow if you're rejected. Many of us act as if the sky will fall down if anyone turns us down for anything, and the devastation will be especially great if it's clear someone doesn't want to be our friend. It may not even matter that it's someone we aren't much interested in, or even a person we actively dislike. If we learn she doesn't like us, we're wounded.

Women are particularly vulnerable in this respect because they usually have fewer experiences in sticking their necks out than men have. Because males have learned it's important to win and be successful, they start early — usually in sports — learning to risk failure and rejection and to handle it smoothly when it happens.

As a woman, you probably have little experience in risking the implied rejection of your offer of friendship being turned down. I say "implied" because even though it may be only your specific invitation that's rejected, you're likely to experience it as rejection of *you*. In order to determine which is true, you'll probably have to take further risks.

When you think about extending yourself to someone, remind yourself of these facts: it's okay to fear rejection; there are specific things you can do to reduce the fear; even if your worst fantasy comes true, you'll learn from the experience; your wounds will heal. But keep in mind the satisfactions that will come your way if your friendly gesture is welcomed.

Something else that may inhibit you from reaching out, especially if you're very critical, is the fear of unwelcome success. Suppose your invitation is accepted and the other person turns out to be a bore or worse? Then you're in the position of having first extended yourself and then of wanting to reject the other person.

This is really borrowing trouble. The person you invite for coffee, lunch or a movie may not turn out to be completely entertaining nor compatible enough to be your closest friend, but that's not what the invitation is about. When you ask someone to have coffee with you, it means just that, *not* that you'll have coffee every day, or that you're obligated in any way after that.

You may fear the other person will accept your invitation but find you boring or awkward or stupid. If, under pressure, your anxiety level tends to get so high that you become tongue-tied and really do appear stupid or awkward, now is the time to stop complaining about it and get help with that problem. Find an individual therapist or class where you can learn relaxation techniques or social skills. A class is best because it will probably be less expensive, and you'll also have a built-in opportunity to make friends who not only have a similar problem, but who understand some important things about you right away.

If you've lived in the same town all your life, if you have a close supportive family, if you have stimulating work and the time and money to indulge in hobbies, sports and entertainments, you might be able to enjoy the luxury of letting friendships develop slowly over a long period of time. In these circumstances there is almost no risk involved; by the time two potential friends go to lunch or the theater together they've been around each other enough to be sure of each person's responses. Often no one even has to invite the other, mutual plans just happen. But that slow, safe process of making friends isn't always available. Reaching out to new people may seem difficult or frightening, but it can be done and it's well worth the risk.

GETTING TO KNOW PEOPLE ON THE JOB

Coffee and lunch invitations are obvious places to begin making friends on the job, but they presume you've had some conversation and friendly exchanges already.

If you're new on the job and have had few exchanges of even the most casual sort, it may be tempting to decide it's everyone's fault but yours. "No one ever smiles or talks to me." "They've already formed into cliques and they consider me an outsider." Some of that may of course be true. But if you're the new person, you'll need to smile, say "hello" and generally initiate contact in order to let the others know you're interested in them.

If you've been waiting for others to speak first, they may have interpreted your shyness as unfriendliness, and you'll need to take some risks in the process of changing their impressions. For instance, if your co-worker, Mary, is not used to being greeted by you in the morning, she may be too surprised to respond the first time you smile and say "Good morning." That may tempt you to adopt an I-told-you-so attitude, which you can use as an excuse to give up. But if you persist, you may get a response the second time, and friendly conversation the third or fourth.

Shy people usually imagine that they're the only people who fear rejection, so when other people don't respond to their first offer of friendship they assume it's coldness or hostility, whereas it may be protection against rejection. This will be especially likely if you've established yourself as a "loner," or a strictly-business person. Give the other workers at least three chances to respond to clear offers of sociability before you give up. With some people it will take even more.

If your friendship is rejected by one person, resist the temptation to generalize. When you hear yourself saying, "Oh, they're a bunch of snobs," "No one in the office has time for me," or "They all have lots of friends already," *list* what evidence you have that your general comment applies to each one. You may be surprised that your judgment applies only to a few people, or maybe even to one. Our minds are endlessly imaginative when we want to avoid risks. *Make a list*, too, of each friendly gesture you've made to each person. Return to these two checklists whenever you make negative generalizations about co-workers or other groups of people.

Activity 22   Social Checklist

<u>"Why I think they don't like me"</u>   <u>"Friendly gestures I've made"</u>

1. _____   _____

2. _____   _____

3. _____   _____

4. _____   _____

5. _____   _____

6. _____   _____

7. _____   _____

Now that you have a record of your own efforts to initiate social gestures and you've modified your judgments about their attitudes toward you, you can begin a program of taking social risks.

Choose specific actions in particular situations that will be somewhat risky but that you're sure you can do. For instance, you might decide to say "Good morning" to two co-workers or to ask one question of your supervisor, or give one compliment to the person at the next desk. These are better self-assignments than "talk to group for thirty minutes at lunch" because you're more likely to do the lower-risk actions. You can build on your success until you're ready for that thirty-minute group conversation. And remember that "success" is accomplishing what you promise yourself to do each day. It has nothing to do with the response of other people which you have no control over.

Eventually you'll get some built-in rewards from the people you befriend as they respond to you in friendly ways. But for now, appreciate the fact that you're being brave enough to make those first gestures. You can also give yourself rewards for your efforts, as are suggested in other parts of this book.

GETTING TO KNOW PEOPLE IN CLASSES AND ORGANIZATIONS

These same principles apply to making friends through classes, church volunteer work or other occasional meetings. It may be difficult to cultivate friends in these situations, because you don't have a new opportunity each day. You may have to make a specific request ("Can you have lunch with me Tuesday?"), rather than seeming accidentally to sit with a fellow worker at lunch. This means you don't have the luxury of waiting for exactly the right moment or the ideal mood to approach them. If you postpone action six times, weekly class sessions might be over before you even get started. In a volunteer organization you may not work with the same person each time you volunteer. You may encounter an attractive person at a mailing party and then not run into her again for a month or more. So get in the habit of making some kind of friendly gesture at the very first opportunity.

How To Begin

When you're anxious about joining any new group, arrange to arrive ten or fifteen minutes early. The few minutes before a class or meeting provide a perfect opportunity for informal friendly exchanges. As new people arrive, you can introduce yourself and others so that everyone feels included. Early arrival will let you be among the first to meet people, and to get to know them a little better than is possible in large group exchanges. You'll feel more secure by the time the group begins. This will help you take the risk of being outgoing right from the start.

If there's an opportunity for each person to introduce herself to the group, use it to say you're open to new relationships. "I'm Jane; I'm new in town and would like to know more people." "My name is Sarah; I'm looking forward to getting to know other people who are interested in ecology." If there's no such opportunity, you might assert yourself by asking the instructor or leader to start off with introductions. Many instructors will be pleased with the suggestion and grateful to you for opening up a more friendly atmosphere.

Look around the room, listen, and decide who you're interested in getting to know. At the first opportunity, whether it's when you're asked to pair up for an exercise or at the coffee break, cross the room and say something friendly to her. I specifically state "cross the room" because that's hard for a shy person to do. In order to avoid being conspicuous, you may let yourself interact with the uninteresting person next to you, rather than walk over to someone you'd like to know. It may be only twelve feet, but it can feel like a stage ramp with 20,000 pairs of eyes glued accusatively at you. When you've exchanged a remark, relax and look at your "audience." You may be astonished that no one is glaring or pointing at you after all.

The content of your first remark is not too important. You might ask, "Have you taken classes here before?" or "How long have you been volunteering here?" Or be braver and say, "I wanted to talk to you because you said you had lived in San Francisco and I hope to go there for a vacation" or "I liked what you said about being nervous in groups; I am, too." A friendly tone will give the message, "I'm inclined to like you and that's all I'm trying to convey at the moment."

Following Up

If all goes well, you'll get into a pleasant conversation. You may have an opportunity to continue it at length (at a coffee break, for instance), but possibly you won't. In that case, be sure to say something when you leave, even if it means crossing the room again. "I enjoyed talking to you. I hope to see you next week." If you want to be very brave, you can offer her a ride next week, ask her for a ride, or suggest you come on the bus together (assuming you live somewhere near her). Or say "I'd like to talk to you some more about... Would it be all right to call you?"

This is moving fast, perhaps faster than you want to. But you're not sticking your neck out very far. Your invitation doesn't require a high degree of intimacy, nor much time, and it's closely tied to the activity you're both involved in. It's true that you won't have much time to feel out the situation, so you'll have some uncertainty about how interested the other woman is in getting to know you. If she says, "Thanks, but I'll be coming from another direction," you'll probably wonder whether she's telling the truth or doesn't want to become involved with you.

If you're easily hurt or given to feeling rejected, you might have trouble with this situation. You'll have to make a special effort to be open to the woman the next time you see her so she knows you're still interested. It may be that she took you literally, thinking you wanted transportation, rather than recognizing your gesture as one of offered friendship. At the next opportunity, you can make another overture that's more obviously friendly. If you get a second cool response (or if you're convinced the first was a negative message) you can look for someone else to befriend.

It might be that a person you approach is not interested in exploring friendship with you. Don't take that as a commentary on your personal worth. It may say more about her: she's extremely shy and can't quite believe you really want to know her; she's too involved in her career to have time for friends; she's wrapped up in her family or already has enough friends. Perhaps she's suspicious or critical of people and rarely sees good in anyone. If you want to play it safe, approach women who are new in town, newly separated from mates or who have indicated they're looking for new relationships.

Plan to use each opportunity that comes your way to do a "Courageous Act A Day" such as smiling and saying "Hi!" or asking about yesterday's lecture or inviting someone for coffee. If you make a friendly overture five times a day for five days to the same or different people you'll soon begin to get rewards.

MOVING FROM ACQUAINTANCES TO FRIENDS

Each time you increase the depth of a relationship, you'll be in a new risk situation, but you'll also have some successes to build on so remind yourself of them often. By "depth" I mean a combination of these factors: length of each contact, frequency of contact, amount of unstructured time spent together, and degree of trust for sharing intimate conversation.

If you're very lonely and have some initial success, it may be tempting to move quickly from a brief, casual acquaintanceship to daily or hourly intimate exchanges, especially if the other person is in a situation similar to yours. If you allow yourself to do that, it might be awkward to withdraw later, especially if you work closely together. It's better to build the relationship gradually. Don't leap from a casual conversation in the company cafeteria with an acquaintance to inviting her for dinner and a long evening of intimate talk. First try shorter, more structured and less personal contacts. Ask yourself whether you enjoy them and whether you feel you have more to say.

It takes time and some work to develop an intimate but nonsexual relationship — more work, perhaps, than one that quickly develops into sexual intimacy. Close friendships may also feel too risky in the short run, though ultimately a sexual relationship is much more likely to involve higher risk.

Working to develop a close nonsexual relationship requires continual alertness to the other person's boundaries, taking risks to judge the relationship toward each new step in the direction of openness, and calming one's fears after each new opening of a previously private personal space. ("Did I reveal so much that she'll think I'm a terrible or ridiculous person, or feel burdened by my problems?" "Did she reveal so much that she'll retreat to cover her embarrassment or fear of vulnerability?")

These risks present problems in a sexual relationship also, but they're made easier by the more readily available reassurance of a touch, a kiss, or a few words. Most of us need to work at developing comparable verbal skills to express caring and reassurance to friends. For instance, we can reassure ourselves when we're nervous about the growing openness in a friendship by saying, "I'm really glad we decided to get to know each other better," or "I feel good about finally talking to someone who feels the same as I do." We can learn to be more direct in checking out concerns: "We really talked about some intimate stuff today. Do you feel okay about it?" "I've got a personal problem I'd like some feedback on, but if this isn't a good time, let me know and we can talk about it another time."

It may seem alarming to say things like that out loud. Perhaps your fear stems from the idea that speaking directly about feelings will be looked upon as an unwanted escalation of intimacy. Occasionally that happens, but most of the time the other person will be pleased and flattered. If she does feel it's too much, it can hurt, but in the long run it's valuable information. If you want to form a close friendship, the person who readily feels intruded upon is probably not a candidate and it's helpful to know that early. (She can still be a welcomed casual friend.)

Even though it's new to you, you can learn to be open and direct about feelings and what you want and enjoy in a friendship, and you can incorporate this into your self-concept, just as you do any other skill you learn. The emotional risks of intimate friendships may seem difficult or frightening, but they are usually much less damaging than disappointments in sexual relationships. And, very often the rewards of friendship are more lasting and rewarding.

HOW MUCH DO YOU CONFIDE IN A NEW FRIEND?

Until recently, women have usually remained silent about the abuse they've suffered. Now that battering is out of the closet, attitudes are changing rapidly in some circles. But it's difficult to predict how people will react to hearing about your experience, whether they're new acquaintances or close friends or family.

When speaking to acquaintances, proceed with caution, protecting yourself from criticism. Many people still don't understand the reasons that women remain with abusive men, and you may be subjected to hints that you "must have asked for it," or that you were a fool not to have left much sooner.

You can protect yourself from these comments by starting a conversation about abuse in general to find out how the other person feels before you put yourself in a vulnerable position. If you don't think she'll understand your feelings or be sympathetic, wait until you know her better before exchanging intimacies.

This may be difficult if one reason you want the friendship is to tell your troubles to a caring person. But if you give it a little time you'll gain more. It may turn out several people you enjoy spending time with give no indication they'll understand. That's not necessarily a reason to drop the relationships, since they can still give you pleasure and help you keep loneliness at bay. Later, when they've gotten to know you and realize you're neither a fool nor a person who "deserves to be abused," they'll probably be able to listen with more understanding.

If you do find someone who's willing to hear about your past suffering and current problems, it will be tempting to spill your troubles out, once the emotional dam breaks. It may be such a relief to finally tell it all to someone who believes you and cares about you that you'll want to tell every horrifying detail. First check out whether your friend is up to hearing it all, and be sensitive to signs of boredom or impatience.

Having laid it all out once, don't go over it again and again. Even if you have the good fortune to meet someone who has had similar troubles so that you can trade stories, you may easily perpetuate each other's "poor me" attitudes by continually repeating the painful experiences of the past. Those "horror stories" will be a welcome relief at first, but if they continue, ask yourself, "Do I feel better or worse after telling them?" When you become aware of feeling worse, you'll need to explain the situation to your friend: "You know, I really get myself on a downer when I talk about being battered. I'm going to try not to talk about it anymore, and if I start, please stop me." That kind of declaration will usually be met with agreement and a similar request from the other person.

GETTING HELP FROM THE FAMILY

At a time when you most need their help, family members may not be supportive. If you've kept secret your man's abusive behavior, the family may have a great deal of trouble believing that he threw you against the wall or went after you with a knife. Their disbelief may indicate their confusion rather than their opinion of you. It may reflect their confidence that a woman as strong and wonderful as you would never put up with such abuse. They'll need to be educated about the problem of abuse, and they'll need time to absorb and understand what is happening.

You'll have to strike a fine balance between understanding *their* problem and protecting yourself from unsupportive attitudes and blame. Explain what happened if you want to, but give them some time to understand your revised marital history. ("Remember that time I said I was too sick to go to Thanksgiving dinner? I really had two black eyes." "That night we were at Mom's and everyone was congratulating each other on having such good marriages — How could I break in and say that Joe had raped me the night before?") If they react by saying, "Somebody's crazy, and I'm not sure if it's him, you, or me," don't be surprised. If they want to hear his side, try to be patient, but make your situation clear.

If you're still trying to protect the man's reputation by telling only about one or two of his lesser abuses, expect people to be skeptical of the necessity of your leaving. This doesn't mean you have an obligation to tell all or even to tell anything, but that information and the time to absorb it will make it easier for many people to support you. The best choice may be not to talk about it at all, depending upon your family relationships. In that case, you have a right to ask that family members trust you've made the best decision you could after long, careful and responsible thought. They don't have to agree with your decision, only to accept that you're doing your best.

Perhaps you've confided in the family all along and they've not only urged you to get out of the relationship but have insisted that as long as you stay, you deserve to be beaten. Now that you're leaving, they may be impatient if you express concern for the man's welfare or complain of loneliness. They might even seem contemptuous of you and your feelings. Even though you're feeling punished by them, try to place yourself in their shoes. They care about you, have worried about you, tried to help you and felt helpless when you decided to stay with or go back to the dangerous man. When you say something positive about him, or speak of your loneliness, they may be prone to instant panic, fearing it means you're going back.

Trying to understand their pain and frustration and confusion doesn't mean you should listen to their negative reactions. If you find you're subjected to negative reactions after two or more attempts to explain what has happened and what you're trying to do, protect yourself by not discussing the subject.

Sometimes the family's reaction will be subtle. You can't put your finger on any specific thing, but you find that after a visit to your sister or your father you feel vaguely depressed. When this happens remove yourself from the people who cause you to feel sad, to question your good sense, or otherwise start you on a downward emotional spiral. You don't need evidence or reasons; your feelings are your feelings. Simply tell your family you find you feel better if you spend more time alone. Suggest they do some reading about wife battering, and check every now and then to see if they've changed their outlook. Don't write them off forever. You may find you need them when you've all recovered from the crisis.

Dealing With Kindness

Families who do their best to be supportive can also be difficult. They may be so overprotective they reinforce helpless feelings you're trying to overcome. If you ran crying to them for help in the middle of the night and were rescued, you may now feel you have no right to reject further help. If you've taken refuge at your parents' house, they might encourage you to stay indefinitely. If you're afraid of the man, insecure about your ability to make wise choices or you're without other supports, it will be soothing to indulge your dependency feelings. Soon, though, you may find that while you don't feel ready to move out on your own, your family's protectiveness is stifling you. Your ambivalence may be masked by concern for your parents, who "need" you to be there.

If you find yourself in a situation something like this, accept the fact that sometimes you like being dependent, and that you're in the situation because you chose it. Become aware of what events increase your helpless feelings. Does your dad encourage you to talk about your fears and to enjoy his promise of protection? Notice whether that momentary increase in security is followed by a wish to curl up in bed, rather than to start organizing your life. When you talk of getting a job, do your parents or other relatives persuade you to "wait another week till you're feeling better?"

If you're faced with these seeming kindnesses which ultimately prolong your status as a dependent person, you'll have to tell your rescuers you appreciate their concern but must stand on your own two feet. You'll have to ask them to encourage your steps toward independence. Let them know that part of you wants to be helpless, and that's why it's hard to resist their indulgences. If they won't change, explain that you'll have to leave.

If you have a warm, supportive family who can extend support without overprotecting you, count yourself lucky and by all means accept what they have to offer. When you're in the process of leaving an abusive man it will help to be almost constantly in the company of friends, acquaintances or family.

The knowledge that there are people who care for you nearby will be important during the months after separating from an abusive partner as you adapt to a new style of life. In the next section I'll discuss some of the problems you'll encounter during the year or years after you separate and various ways of coping with them.

SECTION IV

After You Leave

Chapter 14

THE FIRST WEEK

The first week you're on your own will be stressful and possibly filled with fear and anxiety, but you can use those feelings to get your life reorganized. The scope and details of your immediate problems will vary depending on how badly you were hurt, whether your relationship was short or long and whether you have children. It will make a big difference whether you're unemployed or have marketable skills. Where you stay right after you leave the man will have an impact on how you feel, how you interpret your situation and how you start planning your future.

STAYING IN A SHELTER FOR BATTERED WOMEN

A stay in a shelter for battered women may be your best protection from the dangerous man, as well as from your own temptation to go back to him. You'll be surrounded by people who immediately understand why you had to leave. You'll get support for not contacting the man, and he may not be allowed to call or visit at all if the location of the shelter is kept secret from the public.

There will be someone in the shelter nearly all the time to help you sort out practical problems related to money, school or work, childcare and finding reliable professional help. Many shelters also have counselors available to talk to, and public assistance workers often make regular calls so you won't have to spend a day standing in the public assistance line alone. Talking with other women in similar situations will help reduce your loneliness and fears. Women who would ordinarily never meet because of differences, interests and lifestyles can be marvelously helpful to each other when they have the problem of a battering man in common. If you have children, it can be a great relief to get help in caring for them while you arrange to reorganize your life. Some shelters have full-time childcare, others have occasional volunteers. If it's not available on a regular basis, you can always trade childcare with other women in the shelter.

A shelter may have the disadvantages of lack of privacy, crowded conditions, too many children, and too much stress in small quarters. But you may not have time to ask, or care, about those conditions if you're escaping from an immediately dangerous situation. Even if you think you won't choose to stay in a shelter, it would be a good idea to get information now about the services they offer and how to arrange for housing in case you need it in an emergency.

There are also other kinds of shelters available, usually run by churches, the Salvation Army or YWCA's. These provide temporary housing to men, women and children who have no place else to go, and while they offer some of the same advantages of shelters specifically designed for battered women, they lack the special community feeling that often develops among people whose situations are similar. If you have to wait a few days to get into a shelter for battered women, this other kind of shelter is a good option.

Safe Homes

A *Safe Home* offers many of the advantages of a shelter but provides a calmer environment and the support of one or two people who may or may not have been in a situation similar to yours. This is someone's private house, which she offers to share for a limited period of time, often two or three days. Usually, you'll find yourself a cared-for guest, and you may be provided advocacy, information, referrals and sometimes even counseling on an informal basis. Safe Homes are often available in small communities where there are no shelters.

How To Find A Shelter Or Safe Home

There may be a toll free hot line in your state that will tell you where the nearest shelter or Safe Home is and whether it has room for you. If not, it may take a series of calls before you get the information you need. That's why it's a good idea to call when you're relatively calm and not in immediate danger.

Check your telephone book for all listings under "Battered Women" or "Abused Women." If the telephone company charges for each information call, see if your public library has an out of town telephone directory service. Take down all the numbers, not just one. Services for battered women change rapidly, so if one is no longer available, don't let yourself get discouraged from calling the next number. If you don't find what you need, try a crisis line information and referral service, a rape crisis line, the YWCA, the National Organization for Women, a community college or university women's center or any organization in the telephone book that begins with "Women." If your small town has none of the organizations suggested, try the same ones in the nearest large city or state capital. Remember that crisis lines are open between 11 pm and 8 am when long distance telephone rates are low.

STAYING WITH FRIENDS OR RELATIVES

Most of us are wary of being with strangers, so, given a choice, we would avoid a shelter in favor of friends or relatives, even if we don't have very good relationships with them. It's an advantage to be with someone you feel close to; however, that very closeness can seem to give the person permission to tell you how to run your life: "You should have left him long ago." "If you were more assertive (or less assertive) these things wouldn't happen." "If you go to work, you'll be in good shape." "Above all, you shouldn't try to go to work now." The bond between you and your friend or relative may mean there is no time limit on how long you can stay, but it may also set up feelings of dependency or guilt in you, and resentment in them, especially if you're staying with a parent or someone who has helped you in the past.

Once you've made your choice, accept all the help you can get as graciously as you can, without apologies. Let your mother babysit while you go to the doctor, lawyer or counselor. Borrow your friend's car to look for permanent housing or even to get away to a distracting movie. Just be sure you're both clear about the conditions for giving, lending or providing services, and when in doubt, ask. Don't keep talking about how grateful you are, but let your host know you appreciate the help and you plan to return it when you're settled. You might mention some specific pay-back such as offering childcare.

Your host probably won't mind some complaining and crying the first day or two, but soon it will become tedious. Avoid playing a "poor me" record, repeating your troubles, your fears and the awful things the man did to you. Friends and relatives are often glad to listen if they feel they're helping you improve your life, but if nothing changes they soon feel helpless and frustrated, and that's often followed by resentment. The resentment may yield to guilt and then more resentment over the guilt.

You can make it easier for them if you say what you want and encourage them to do the same. If you want advice, ask for it; if you want to be left alone, or just listened to, say so. Ask whether your host is willing to do what you want, and set a time limit, even if it's completely arbitrary: "I need to be alone tonight, is that okay?" "I might be ready to hear some advice in a couple of days, but until then could you just listen and support the way I feel? Or tell me you've had it if it gets to be a bore?" This will be particularly hard to do with parents or friends who may be eager to point out that you'd be all right now if you'd listened when they "told you so," but at least give it a try.

For your own sake, do as much as possible to help around the house, no matter how hard it is to get moving. This may be doubly difficult if your host insists you "just take it easy because you have enough to do to reorganize your life." "Reorganizing your life" may then take the form of lying on the couch brooding. You'll be much better off baking a cake, sweeping the floor, or painting the front porch. You can explain that to your host.

STAYING ALONE

You may decide to live alone, either in the home you shared with the man or in a new place. Even if you had to leave your home temporarily, for safety, don't assume you'll have to give it up permanently. If your children are in contact with your ex-partner, you may not be able to keep a new address secret and you might feel strongly that you refuse to be forced out of your home. If so, stay in the home and assess the risks carefully.

Even if you're pretty sure the man won't pursue you, it's a good idea to change locks, secure windows and perhaps to change your telephone number. If there's a chance the man will try to break in, add double bolt locks on all outside doors, including the basement and garage. You'll be safer if a friend or relative can stay with you until your situation is stabilized. Even having friends over frequently for part of an evening will let the batterer know — if he regularly drives by your house — that you're not often home alone. Stay away from the places he frequents and from his friends.

Even though it's embarrassing, let your neighbors know what has happened. If the battering has gone on for some time, they probably realize it anyway and will feel relieved to know you're doing whatever you can to ensure your safety.

If you've moved to a new place you might be reluctant to confide in neighbors you barely know, but a little embarrassment may mean the difference between life and death. Spend a few minutes talking to several neighbors, sounding them out on the subject of battering. Then tell them your situation and ask them to call you or the police if they hear anything that sounds like violence. Even though you may feel awkward in the telling, it can give you more sense of control, since you won't be worried about the man disturbing neighbors with his demands to be let into your house at two am. Instead, you'll be hoping they'll hear the commotion and call the police. Be more cautious in speaking to your apartment owner and manager. If they're determined to avoid trouble in the building at all costs, noise in the middle of the night may cause them to evict you. Get to know them a bit before you explain your situation.

As soon as possible, remove all of the man's personal property and store it out of view until you can get it to him. Where the signs of his absence are most noticeable, rearrange things so you don't have to look at empty spaces where his raincoat used to hang, his pipe, toothbrush or book used to be placed. Put something of your own in those places, and arrange things the way you want them, making it *really* your home.

Start projects that will take your mind off him and give you a sense of satisfaction. Paint a room or sand some furniture. Choose television programs that you really want to watch, but be very careful not to get hooked on one uninteresting program after another. TV can be just as much of an addiction as alcohol and drugs or love if you're susceptible, and right now you are. If there's always one more program to watch, you may never get out of your chair to make new friends and create a new life for yourself. The sooner you contact friends, relatives, a counselor or support group, the better. You need to know there is someone out there to call on if you're in need. If it isn't possible to arrange those connections quickly, post the number of one or more crisis lines by your telephone, and don't wait until you're desperate to use them. Review Chapter 12, "An End to Isolation" and Chapter 13, "Reaching Out."

GROUPS FOR ABUSED WOMEN

Unless you're in a shelter that provides regular group meetings, try to find a weekly battered women's group in the community. You may be a bit nervous at the thought of being with a group of strangers, but once you're there, you'll find they're not so strange after all. They'll be like you in many ways and are likely to understand your feelings better than most friends or family members because they've been in similar situations and felt some of the same feelings you have. Some will have started new lives away from their abusive partners and will be an inspiration to you. Most of these groups charge no fee, and you can attend as often or as irregularly as you like.

CONTACT WITH THE MAN WHO BATTERED YOU

Should you or shouldn't you call, write or meet this man? You can give yourself lots of reasons to make contact with him, each of which seems absolutely essential: you owe him an explanation or at least some information about your plans; you need to talk with him about seeing the children; you have to get some things out of the house. Your imagination may work overtime rationalizing your reasons for speaking to him. Don't do it. Wait.

Ordinary considerations don't apply when it's a matter of your physical or psychological survival.

It's probable your man will get along all right without you, but if you have doubts review Chapter 3. Later, when you're sure you'll be safe, you can arrange for visits with the children. As difficult as it is to risk having your property taken or destroyed, if you can't get it without encountering the man, you'll have to remind yourself that most of it is replaceable, but you're not.

Give yourself the same advice you'd have for an alcoholic who decided it's okay to have just one drink. It's not worth the risk. Whether or not you've decided that you have a classic case of addictive love, at this point you'll almost certainly behave like an addict. So make new rules for yourself appropriate to *this* situation, *this* week.

The first rule is not to see the abusive man under any circumstances. The second rule should be not to talk to him on the telephone under any circumstances. Give yourself at least seven days to think about your situation without his self-interested comments.

If you have a good friend who's looking out for your best interests and who's strong enough not to give in to your "reasons" for needing to contact the man, make an agreement with her that you won't call him unless she agrees it is both necessary and wise. If that kind of friend isn't available, you'll just have to promise yourself not to get in touch with the man for at least one week. If there's something that he *must* know, put it in a letter without a return address. The letter should be strictly business. No "I love you" or "I'm sorry" or "I hope you're all right." Just "the cat must have medicine three times a day. The prescription is on the kitchen table. Sue." Before you mail it, try to get a trusted friend to read it and to take out any hints that you want him back. In ordinary circumstance you can trust your own judgment, but this is an emergency situation and you're under a lot of pressure. You need to be protected from yourself, as difficult as that is to swallow.

If, in spite of this advice, you're determined to get some things from your house, be sure to go when the man is away from the house and take someone with you. A friend will help you take as few chances as possible and her or his presence may discourage the man's violence if you unexpectedly encounter him. In some communities, public service officers of the police department will stand by while you remove your things. If you decide to meet the man to discuss business, take a friend with you and meet in a public place such as a restaurant, where there are lots of people. Under no circumstances go anywhere in his car with him.

If you aren't willing to take these precautions, you're likely either to be coerced or seduced into going back; if you recognize that danger, rather than pretending you're beyond temptation, you can at least guard against it.

These may seem like easy precautions to follow the first few days after you've left. You may be able to both see and feel your injuries, and probably you'll swear this time you won't forgive or forget. But sometime during the first or second week, the memories of the good times will begin to surface and the evidence of damage he's done will begin to fade. This is a very crucial time, so be ready for it. Here are some simple but effective ways to keep your perspective on the relationship and on why you decided to end it.

Most Dangerous List

Make a list of the most humiliating and dangerous things your partner has done to you. Then put it in the form of a letter — not to mail but for you to keep. Writing in the first person ("I hate you for..." "I resent the times you...") can help you recapture your anger. Most important, don't leave things out because they're too awful to remember. Describe the pain and humiliation he caused you. Include the things he said to you afterwards, whether they were cruel or loving. It won't be long before you hear these "loving" promises again, and you'll need to refer to this sheet as a reminder of how empty the promises are and how little the loving words mean in the long run. This exercise will be painful, but it is extremely important. If you don't want to do it, or get too busy or forget, be suspicious of your motives. You probably don't want to remember the pain of the past. That's understandable, but if you let yourself forget, you'll be extremely vulnerable when the man tries to sweet-talk his way back into your life. You won't remember these are the same words you heard the other times he abused you. You won't remember they weren't followed by loving *action*, or that the honeymoon period lasted only a few days or a couple of hours.

At this point you may feel it's not a question of choosing to remember or not. You may believe you can never forget what the man did to you. But didn't you forget before, the last time you wanted to take him back? Write it all down whether you believe you can forget or not.

Activity
23

Activity 23   *Most Dangerous List*

_____

_____

_____

_____

_____

_____

_____

_____

_____

Best Memories List

But, what about the good times, you wonder. Make a list of them too. All the happy moments, the good conversation, the hopes, the dreams, and the qualities that you like or admire about your former partner.

Activity 24   *Best Memories List*

_____

_____

_____

_____

_____

_____

_____

_____

_____

Look at both lists and decide whether it's worth it to put up with one to gain the other. If the positive list is very short, it may be a little too soon to try to remember the good. If, after being separated for a week, you still can't remember many good times or things you like about your partner, you're probably hooked on a fantasy about the relationship rather than on the real thing. You may be mourning the lost dream; what you hoped the relationship would be. To check that out, compare your hopes and dreams at the beginning of the relationship with the way it really has been. How often and how recently did any of your dreams materialize? Let yourself mourn the loss of that dream, and then get on with your real life.

Change List

You may find yourself saying, "If only he would...we could be so happy." Put those "if only's" on paper and underline the ones that are essential to change. Turn that list into a letter to him that spells out what he would have to change in order for you to risk going back. Never mind, for the moment, whether it would be easy or hard for him, how long it might take, or what things you ought to or want to change in yourself. This, too, is a letter you won't necessarily mail, so don't worry about whether it's "nice" or fair. It's a list of things that would have to happen in order for you to be respected as a person who can make choices and who has a life she can call her own in addition to the relationship with the man.

Activity 25   Change List

_____

_____

_____

_____

_____

_____

_____

_____

_____

When you turn your Change List into a letter it may look something like this:

Dear Tom:

If I were ever to consider going back to you (which I wouldn't), this is what would have to happen. You would have to:

Never hit me, no matter what I do.

Not insult me or make fun of me, especially in front of other people.

Not put me down when we're alone.

See a counselor or go to a batterers' group for at least six months.

Go to A.A. for at least six months.

Not drink at all for at least six months.

Not interfere if I want to see my friends or go to school or get a job.

Give me a certain amount of money every month that I can spend with no questions asked (amount negotiable).

Joanne

The items that have a minimum time are the most useful. It's easy for him to say (and even to mean it, at least for the moment) that he'll quit drinking or start counseling, but the real test is whether he follows through. If you return to him as soon as the promise is made or the first appointment for counseling is kept, he'll have no incentive to continue. If he quits, you may entreat or threaten, but you probably won't leave until he's beaten you again.

This list, like the ones that preceded it, is for your own use right now. When you're tempted to call the man, look at the list of changes you said he must make, and note any he said he'd do but didn't, as well as those he flatly refuses to consider. Face the reality that he's unlikely to comply with any of them unless he's already made an impressive start. Realize that even if he did agree, it would be months before you could be sure he was following through. The point is that you won't return until he's proven his good intentions by action.

How to Use the Lists

Make a commitment to yourself that you won't even talk to him without reading the other lists first. Read the Most Dangerous List out loud and force yourself to live through the experience emotionally one more time. Remembering won't be as painful as living through it physically again. Keep the list near you so you can read it as often as you need to. Read the Best Memories List too, so that you can keep the two in balance and avoid an unexpected sentimental memory that eclipses everything on the Most Dangerous List. You'll then be in a position to keep a balanced perspective: "Sure, that vacation with Bill was the most romantic time of my life, and yes he's often been very nurturing. But those times don't come close to making up for the miscarriage he caused, the day he knocked me down the stairs and the daily hammering away at my self-esteem."

If you're tempted to go back to him even after you've reviewed your lists, if you're trying to persuade yourself he's changed, take a look at your Change List and mark the items he's actually changed and for how long a period. Compare what's actually happened with what you said he'd have to do for you to feel right about going back. The answer to what you should do will be right there.

COPING WITH FEAR

To feel afraid is a natural response, but it doesn't mean the things you're afraid of will happen. Statistically, there's small chance your husband or ex-boyfriend will hunt you down and kill you. But the possibility doesn't have to be very great to make you extremely frightened, and you might become a prisoner of that fear.

Even if your worst fear is improbable, you can't be sure, so you should take precautions to protect yourself. Spend as much time as possible with other people. If sometimes you have to go out alone, try to be on streets where there are lots of people. But once you've decided what reasonable safety measures you can take, start working on reducing your fears.

Pay close attention to what you say to yourself when you feel very afraid. The more you tell yourself terrible things will happen, the more frightened you'll feel. Statements like "He'll find me and kill me" and "He'll beat me even worse than before" are certain to increase your fear.

Start changing those fear-inducing statements to reassuring comments that reflect and reinforce your ability to cope. "He didn't come after me yesterday, and he probably won't today." "I protect myself by staying near populated areas when I'm in public and keeping my address a secret." "I can handle what happens, just as I handled frightening situations in the past." Remind yourself over and over that if you'd stayed with him you'd still be living in fear and it might continue for the rest of your life. But if you stay away, you'll endure heightened fear for a relatively short period and a time will come when you'll be free of it.

Check out your level of anxiety each day. Without your realizing it, it's probably diminishing as you make it through each day without your fears materializing. Many women who've left an abusive man find their fear steadily diminishes during the first few weeks after they leave. Then one day they realize with a start that it's gone. They can barely remember what it was like to be so afraid.

If the man does find you and attack you, double your efforts to find a safe place to stay and consider some big changes such as shared living quarters, leaving town temporarily or changing jobs. Don't hesitate to call the police. If you've been giving mixed messages for months or years, it will take time and require some firm and consistent action on your part to persuade the man you're serious about wanting him to leave you alone. This is a good time to start.

The odd thing is that when you're living with an abusive man you get used to a certain level of fear, and much of the time you believe it is only temporary. "It will all be different tomorrow or next time — or next week." Yet when you're out of the situation — even though your leaving has made it much less likely to continue — you tend to believe it will never change. Like any kind of pain, fear is endurable if you know it will last only a short time. Remind yourself that this fear really will pass, and probably soon.

LONELINESS

If you're at a shelter or with friends or relatives, you may not have too much trouble with loneliness at first. Keeping busy will help and that shouldn't be too difficult. You may have to see a doctor, lawyer or counselor and look for a place to live, in addition to working every day or applying for work or public assistance.

I'd like to tell you that loneliness will pass quickly, but probably it will get worse before it gets better. If you expect separation to be painless, you'll set yourself up to go running back to a dangerous situation. It's better to know that you can expect to suffer for quite awhile, and that you can endure it because in the long run you'll suffer less.

Coping with loneliness is still another area in which you can affect your feelings by what you say to yourself. Instead of "I'm so lonely, I can't stand it," try "I'm lonely and I can handle it" or "I was lonely with him, but now I have a chance to learn how to change my life so I won't be lonely." There's more about coping with loneliness in Chapter 20, "The Long Haul."

For some women, the first week is the easiest and they assume they've licked the problem of loneliness. It's important not to deny your feelings, so you'll know when you should make a point of being with people and when not to risk contact with the man.

Chapter 15

PROTECTING YOURSELF AND THE CHILDREN

It won't be so hard to end the relationship cold turkey if you don't have children in common. Children make separation more complicated, but you can overcome the difficulties by careful planning. Not all the problems will revolve around the children's relationships with the father. A long abusive relationship and the children's separation from their father or father figure can also create problems between you and the children. Children's methods of coping with a violent environment may be quite ineffective now that the violent man is no longer present. This chapter gives you some ideas about how to minimize contact when the father visits (or when you visit, if he has custody), how to deal with typical post-battering family battering problems, and when to get help from professional counselors.

VISITATION

Arranging for your children to visit their father will be difficult in the best of circumstances, and guilt about the separation can make it even harder. The father will know how to manipulate those guilt feelings and the children might also.

If you've been involved with several men who became important to your children and then lost contact with them when your relationship ended, you may be particularly vulnerable to guilt feelings. It's true that children suffer when they're separated from a father figure, but they suffer even more when they live with a role model who is violent to their mother.

Your involvement with an abusive man or with multiple "fathers" of your children has been a mistake and may have had destructive results for them. But that's not a reason to continue subjecting them to contact with a violent father figure. That would be a perpetuation of the same mistake and more likely permanent damage to the children.

If you're going to find it hard to stay away from the man, his visits with the children will create special risks for you unless you set them up very carefully. You can be pretty sure he'll use his visitation rights to try to lure you back by threats, by his charm, or by playing on your guilt feelings. During the first few months of your separation, arrange for him to pick the children up at someone else's house. Even if it's awkward or expensive or inconvenient, take them to a friend or relative's home, hire a babysitter or make arrangements through a child protection agency to leave and pick up the child there. Do whatever is necessary, so you won't be forced into contact with him.

He may object to that procedure, or may agree but then fail to come at the appointed time and try to persuade you to let him pick the children up at your house "just this time." At that point you're likely to feel angry at him, disappointed for the children, and frustrated over your own ruined plans. It may be impossible to redo your arrangements on the spot, or you may feel so defeated you don't want to take the time or trouble. It can then be very tempting to give in and concede that this time he can pick them up at home. That's an understandable reaction, but if you do that even one time you not only place yourself in a vulnerable position by meeting him in person, you also give him a message that he can manipulate you to get what he wants. He may interpret your conciliation to mean he can eventually persuade you to go back to him.

If you've left without the children or made the hard decision to give up custody your problems may be greater, but essentially of the same kind. If the father fails to show up with the children at the appointed time and place, you may be so eager to see them you'll give in to almost any plan of their father's. In the long run you'll be better off if you follow the same inflexible guidelines advised above. The father probably has looked forward to being free of the children and if you're absolutely consistent even when it's very hard he'll eventually believe you mean it when you say you'll pick up the children only at a certain time or place. Giving in to his demands even one time will give him hope and then you'll have to start all over again to make him understand you're serious.

You don't have to give him reasons for your tight regulations on visitation and you don't have to listen to his complaints. If you've followed the advice in Chapter 8 to have the specifics or visitation arrangements written into the separation or divorce decree, the situation will be much easier to handle.

CONTACT WITH THE BATTERER

A few weeks or months after separating, you may feel calm and friendly toward your ex-partner. Maybe you've relaxed your restrictions on visitation arrangements and have begun to talk to him for brief periods, either when he visits the children or to discuss other affairs you still share an interest in. If he's being reasonable and considerate and you're not afraid anymore, you might even have coffee or a drink with him now and then. You may begin to believe you can trust yourself, maybe even him.

You probably can't. To the extent that you've lost your fear and anger, you're vulnerable to his seductive promises and to your own wish to believe him. Perhaps you're feeling down, that you're not much good for anything, that no one loves, or could love you. Your ex-partner will tell you you're wonderful and lovable, and that he cares for you even if no one else seems to. Because you're emotionally isolated and dependent on him, you cling to him like a drowning person to a lifesaver. What you forget is that you wouldn't be in such desperate emotional need if he hadn't beaten you into believing you're worthless and hadn't insisted on isolating you from caring friends in the first place. His ability to nurture you takes on such importance because he's put you on an emotional yo-yo.

You'll find it difficult or impossible to stay away from him if you talk to him on the telephone or if you're around him and the children together. Once he sits down to chat about Susie's reaction to the animals at the zoo, or Johnnie's reading problem, it may begin to feel like the good old days (with the bad parts of those days forgotten). Before you know it, you may ask him to dinner and then encourage him — or be persuaded by him — to spend the night. It will be easy, then, to imagine he's a changed man, especially if he's considerate and romantic, or if he reads the children a bedtime story. It will be easy to persuade yourself they need each other and that you haven't the right to deprive him of his children.

If you don't have children in common to provide a reason to visit with the man you may invent others. Keep in mind that it's a short step from the dinner table to a few drinks together, and an even shorter step from these to the bedroom. The longest road on a destructive journey, as well as on a worthwhile one, begins with a single step.

You probably won't go back to your ex-partner if you don't go to bed with him. You won't go to bed with him if you don't cook dinner or go out drinking with him. You won't be tempted to cook for him or drink with him if you don't listen to his troubles or promises. And you can't listen to him if you're not in touch with him at all.

Don't Give In To Your Impulses

Refer to your Change List again (Activity 25 in Chapter 14). If you haven't kept it, question your motives. Losing it may be one way to avoid facing reality. *Make a new list*, being honest about your earlier demands. If you decided he needed six months of therapy or A.A. or one year of not drinking, or three months of treating you with respect, don't reduce those times now. He may have taken a small step in a constructive direction, but you'll have to wait at least several months to be sure of what it means. You'll also need verification of his changed patterns. You can insist on permission to talk to his counselor or other people who can tell you whether he's been living up to his promises. You may want to see his counselor once (which he should pay for) either together with him or alone, to be sure the counselor understands the degree of battering you were subjected to. More than one man has seen a counselor for months and months without mentioning battering, or related problems like drinking, as behavior he wants to change.

Activity 26   What Changes Has He Made?

Your former partner may try to make you feel guilty by accusing you of not trusting him. Your response should be, "Of course I don't trust you, after the abuse you put me through and the empty promises you made." He may play on your guilt feelings by insisting, now that he's taken steps in the right direction, that he needs your support to continue. Tell him he'll have to change because *he* wants to, and he'll have to do it by himself. If he won't do it by himself, he's even less likely to do it when he has what he wants — you. For your own safety and to be sure of how serious he is about changing, it's important to stay away from him. If you feel sorry for him or guilty, remind yourself that the best thing you can do for him is to stay away so he'll have the motivation to change. Providing him with an opportunity to be violent and destructive does neither of you any good.

You Can Control The Relationship

If you've gradually slipped into a friendly relationship, you may have to retrench; if you feel yourself getting more involved you'll have to retreat from once a week dinners to occasional coffees or from coffees to nothing but telephone arrangements about the children. This might be hard to do and perhaps he's been treating you reasonably well, but it's much too soon to tell whether it will last and you have a right to stay away. *You don't owe him an explanation.* Say something like, "I prefer not to go out with you anymore. I don't want to explain or answer questions about it. It's just the way I want it now." He'll probably act as if you're punishing him and try to make you feel guilty if you say you don't want to talk to him for awhile. If so, he hasn't changed because that pattern of inducing guilt and demanding explanations so he can talk you into going along with his plans, or batter you into it, is typical of abusive men.

If you do continue seeing him, for any reason at all, you're in for another period of turmoil. He'll most likely want more and more from you until he gets you "back home where you belong again." And you'll have to battle not only against his arguments, but also against your own vulnerability and guilt feelings. "He's trying," you'll tell yourself. "At least I could give him a chance." "He needs some motivation if he's going to change." "After all, I owe him something."

These are the ideas you have to get rid of, and you'll find it much easier to do if you don't hear them from him. You have to find out what life is like without him, and you won't be able to if you're sleeping with him once a week, or even involved in telephone conversations that keep you wondering when he'll call again. You have to get him not only out of your life, but out of your mind. Look away from him toward a new way of life. Start by convincing yourself you owe him nothing. This is a rigid attitude and may seem harsh, but it's necessary. You don't owe him another chance. You've probably given him too many already.

WHAT YOU CAN DO FOR THE CHILDREN

It's hard to tell the children you're afraid of their father, but they need to know the truth. With the possible exception of very young infants, all children will have been affected by the violence and fear in the household. If they haven't seen it, they've sensed that something threatening was happening. Vague apprehensions can be more frightening than the fact of violence itself. If they've seen it often, they've probably begun to accept it as a normal way for married people and parents to act toward those they love most. They may have begun to incorporate it into their own ideas of themselves as future spouses or lovers.

Children sometimes repeat the pattern of violence they learn at their parents' knees. You can reduce that likelihood by taking a strong position right now that violence is not acceptable, their father is not safe to be around and you're going to protect both yourself and them. You don't have to go into detail, nor need you talk about what a monster he is. You can explain that you do love him, which is why it's been too hard to leave before, but that now you're determined to stay away.

That determination is important for the children as well as for yourself. They can adapt to living separately from their father, but being separated and reunited and separated again is confusing to them. They may get a message that either it's not important to protect yourself or them or that you can't do it.

Tell the children that when you believe it's safe they can see their father if they want to. Whether or not he was violent to them as well as you, they may be too afraid or angry to want to see him, at least for awhile. Make it clear they don't have to see him until they feel safe. (If the court has ordered visitation you may have to seek a modification of it.) Sometimes children have a hard time saying that they don't want to see the father. If that's how your children feel, help them to know that their feelings are natural, that they may change and they have no reason to feel guilty about them.

Coping with children's problems can heighten your stress, but the responsibility can also distract you from your grief. Taking care to entertain and nurture your children will help them and you by keeping all of you busy. Let them know they can count on you to be there when they need you, and try to have meals, bedtime and school routine as "normalized" as possible.

If the children complain about the move you've made or their father's absence, try to be both sympathetic and firm. You might want to say you're not going to see him even though you miss him, or that because he hurt you, you're glad he's not there. Encourage your children to discuss their feelings and let them know they don't have to feel the same way you do.

One of the most difficult aspects of your situation may be that your children are frightened, depressed or angry and need more attention than usual at a time when you want to be mothered yourself. Try hard to get your emotional needs met by friends, family or shelter staff. Do it for yourself so you'll have something to give to your children. You may also want to arrange time for them to share with relatives or caring friends. Just be sure they know they have a place and a person in their lives that's stable. You may have to give the same reassurance over and over again, so try to be patient.

Old Coping Skills Need Revision

You may have developed a pattern of overprotectiveness toward your children in an effort to protect the children from the father's violence as well as to compensate for his harsh discipline or indifference. Perhaps the children received so much irrational and undeserved punishment from their father that you've been reluctant to discipline them. Another common pattern is to be overly punitive or even abusive to the children. You might have done that as a way of expressing the rage you didn't dare let out at the man, or in hopes of shaping the children's behavior to avoid the man's anger. You may have directed anger at your children because you were jealous of the father's devotion to them while you were ignored or abused. Still another way of coping is to become so depressed you don't notice or care about much of anything, including the children.

You may have to pay a price now for your previous ways of dealing with the children as you tried to survive an impossible situation. In addition, the children have developed their own ways of coping with a frightening, dangerous, unpredictable environment, which may have worked reasonably well for them in a chaotic household, but is counterproductive in the family now and in other relationships.

When you make a great effort, and rise above your lethargy or anger to provide good parenting for a week or so, you may hope to reap some rewards. If they're not forthcoming, you may slide back to your old patterns. It might be hard to realize that even the best of parenting won't necessarily get good results right away. Try to remember that your children have lived a significant portion of their lives in a state of tension (whether or not they actually saw the battering) and they'll take a long time to recognize and respond to consistent treatment. Some professionals who work with children of batterers say it take two years for their mothers to establish credibility as parental authority. You'll need lots of emotional support and the ability to reward yourself during this transition period.

CHILDREN'S REACTIONS TO VIOLENCE AND SEPARATION

Each situation in regard to children presents different problems and different advantages. If you or the batterer moved to a distant city and cut off contact, or if he isn't the children's father and doesn't choose to see them, you'll avoid the emotional turmoil that the absent parent's visits often cause. However difficult life may be for you and the children, it has the potential of at least being stable. Everyone can become used to being part of a one-parent family without the emotional upsets of the father's visits and eventually can learn to appreciate its advantages.

On the negative side, the children may long to be with their father. This will be especially hard for everyone if other children in the family have different absent fathers who come to see them and take them on excursions. If that's the situation, try to arrange your own special activities to coincide with those outings.

The children may also blame you for their father's absence. Even when they've seen him beat you, they may start rewriting family history, which will make it even harder for you to remember the past accurately. Try to help them keep a balanced picture and you'll help yourself. "Yes, it was sometimes more fun around here before Daddy left, but it was too dangerous." "Yes, I did tell him to leave, even though I still love him. He can't come back unless he can prove you and I will be safe, and he hasn't been willing to do that."

The children may blame themselves for the break-up of the relationship or even for the violence, particularly if they once called the police or tried to intervene. If they've frequently been disciplined by the father they may simply explain his absence as one more thing that's their fault. But often children don't need any reason at all to blame themselves. If you suspect that's how they feel, try to get them to talk about it. Ask, "What do you think you did that might have caused the violence or made him leave?" Listen carefully to the answer. Don't tell the child immediately that she or he is wrong, because that will probably shut off further talk. Encourage the child to express feelings about the father, whether they conform to your picture of reality or not. Then encourage careful reasoning by asking questions like, "Does hitting somebody — or leaving home — seem like something a person would do for an extremely important reason, or because another person didn't do the dishes?" You may have to say several times, "Daddy left because *I* told him he couldn't stay." After you've talked about feelings, you might want to say, "I used to blame myself when he beat me, but then I finally realized that he's responsible for what he does. I'm only responsible for what I do." Tell your child you don't think she or he is to blame, but that you understand the reasons for their feeling.

It won't hurt to limit the amount of violence your children watch on television, but when they do see it, you can use the opportunity to find out what they feel and think about rights and responsibilities in regard to violence and to tell them what you think about it. If a child is having a hard time adjusting to the new situation or persists in taking responsibility for the father's absence or his violence, consider professional counseling with a person experienced in working with children of batterers.

When A Child Becomes Violent

Your child may have learned by watching the batterer that the way to get what one wants is to bully: to take, to intimidate by loud shouts or threats, to hit, to break things. It may be especially hard to tolerate a bullying child when you've just broken away from the person the child mimics.

Consistent intervention is the key to changing this pattern. Ideally, each time the child bullies a person, you will step in and calmly state that she or he isn't allowed to do that and either physically remove the child or send him or her to another room until the child's self-control is clearly established. It's important to react the same way each time and not to hit the child to "teach him a lesson." The lesson the child needs demonstrated is that violence and coercion are no longer tolerable. If you want the child to take you seriously about this, don't strike her or him regardless of behavior. If you've had the habit of controlling the child's behavior by spanking, you'll need to learn other ways to discipline. This may be hard at first, so if you do slip up, be sure to explain that you're all learning new ways to treat each other, that you're working hard on it and when you fall back on old ways, it doesn't mean it's right. It just means you have to try harder. If this problem doesn't get much better soon, you'll need to get professional help, perhaps both to show you how to manage your feelings better and to teach you skills in coping with difficult children.

When you're upset about the way your child is acting and feeling sad or angry about your own life, it's hard to notice the positive. It's important that you try hard to appreciate a child's gentle and cooperative behavior, even when it seems nonexistent. Force yourself to acknowledge that the child is behaving well even if you're still angry about a recent outburst.

If your young child is persistently violent or subtly manipulative and controlling toward you or others, you may want to get a professional evaluation from a children's therapist. Consider having the child go to a special school or therapy program. If the violent child is a teenager, you may have difficult decisions ahead of you. You'll want to give her or him time to adjust to the new family life and learn new habits. But there may come a time when you'll have to consider your own or other children's safety and well-being, and take drastic action such as foster home placement. That will probably be a last resort, but keep it in mind as an option. It may be the best thing you can do for the child as well as yourself — the strongest way of putting across the message: "No more. You must not treat the people you love violently."

When A Child Withdraws Or Is "Too Good"

It's easy to overlook the good child who makes it her or his business to stay out of everyone's way and to be very obedient. This is the child who may be most helpful to you now, caring for younger children, comforting you when you're sad, easily forgiving your irritation. If you're nearly paralyzed with depression or fear, or drowning your sorrows in drink or tranquilizers, this child may start playing parent to you. Although it might be tempting to be comforted, keep in mind that the child needs to be a child and should know there's an adult in charge. You're probably the only anchor the child has now.

A child may also withdraw from everyone, escaping into books, television or drugs. You may vaguely wonder where the child is or how she or he feels, but as long as there are few demands on you, it will be easy to ignore the child. Though it takes a lot of energy, make a point of spending time with a withdrawn or "good" child. Talk about violence, fear and the new ways of living you're all learning. Encourage the child to express feelings, and be alert to hints about self-blame.

A withdrawn or overly good child may suddenly begin to act quite differently, expressing a lot of anger or destructiveness toward you or others or being generally disobedient. You may also find that one or more of your children uses the same psychological methods of control as the batterer, and you may react in the same way as you did to the batterer. Or the child who reminds you of him in other ways may trigger reactions that are not appropriate.

When to Get Professional Help

Many children outgrow problems and most probably don't need therapy, but children who have been exposed to violent and emotional abuse among the people who they must trust may develop lifelong scars. One way to avoid them is to get a third party to intervene. Don't worry about the child suffering from being labeled "sick." Rather than "sickness," it's a matter of learning or relearning skills in problem solving and relating in constructive ways. If you're not sure what to do, find a children's therapist who has worked with children of batterers and get an evaluation. The child may find it much easier to express feelings to a skilled professional than to you. Even if there are only a few sessions with the therapist, you'll be giving a clear message that it's okay to ask for help and that there are people outside the family who can provide it.

Chapter 16

THE PRACTICAL QUESTIONS OF WELFARE AND HOUSING

Soon after the first week you're on your own, you'll probably begin to plan where you're going to live and how you'll manage financially. If you've had a paid job, some of your immediate problems will be solved, but it's likely you'll still suffer a big drop in income and have to make decisions about whether the house or apartment you've been living in is affordable as well as safe.

If you have neither a good job nor other sources of income you may have to make some shifts in lifestyle and some compromises with your values. You might, for instance, have to rely temporarily on welfare or move from a comfortable house to an apartment or shared housing in someone else's home.

WELFARE

If you've never received welfare funds — and perhaps if you have — it may bring to mind pictures of unkempt children, harried or depressed mothers and snooping social workers. It's hard to dispel that image because like all stereotypes, there's some truth in it. The welfare grant is usually so small it's hard to dress children in clothes that haven't been patched over patches, and it's easy for parents to become depressed trying to make ends meet. Although social workers are no longer permitted to investigate the intimate lives of recipients, they do have to get some information from applicants that you might feel is personal. Nevertheless welfare can be a lifesaver in an emergency.

Categories of Aid

Old Age Assistance is available for anyone sixty-five years and older who lives outside a public institution. *Aid To The Blind* is for partially or totally blind people. *Aid To Permanently and Totally Disabled* is for people who cannot work because of permanent physical or mental disabilities. These payments are all made through Social Security and recipients are automatically entitled to Medicare. *Aid To Families With Dependent Children (AFDC)* supports families who have at least one child, at least one relative in the house with the child and at least one parent who can't or won't support and care for the child. When one parent is absent from the home, the child is considered deprived of support.

Applying For Welfare

What is commonly called the "Welfare Department" may be listed in various ways in your telephone book, and you can find out how by looking under "Welfare." The more you can learn ahead of time about what to expect, what your rights are, and what information you need, the easier the process of applying for welfare will be. You may be required to bring birth certificates for yourself and your children, receipts for rent, utilities, medical bills and other expenses and check stubs or other papers that prove your income or proof of residency. When you call for general information, ask what papers you need and be sure to take them with you. Arriving without the necessary papers will mean more delay and perhaps another frustrating morning standing in line.

Take a friend or welfare advocate with you and try to arrive fifteen minutes before the office opens. If you get there at ten or eleven o'clock, you'll wait a long time and soon be hungry for lunch but afraid to lose your place. If you get there in the afternoon, your name may not come up at all. In any case you're likely to have a wait so try to minimize it by arriving early. Having a friend to talk to will help to pass the time. If you're alone, take along a magazine, stationery or a crossword puzzle. If you can't leave your children with a friend, be sure to take along several small surprises for them to pull out at intervals when they've become bored.

As you wait in the welfare office, you may find yourself looking around skeptically, thinking all these people must be losers, somehow different from you, or worse yet, you must be a loser too. There will be a lot of people like you in that they have low incomes, they're women with children, people who have troubles. If you talk to some of them, it will help pass the time, and you can learn about the system from old hands.

Some welfare workers will act as if they're doing you a favor so it's important for you to keep in mind that you have a right to public assistance. Others will go out of their way to help you. Try not to let your frustration get the best of you, because you'll get better service if you stay calm.

Computation Of "Need"

Welfare funds are a combination of federal and state funds, and subject to regulations of both levels of government. State welfare guidelines indicate how much the department is willing to budget for various expenses such as rent, food, clothing and utilities. Don't be surprised if the amount they allow you is well under the "poverty line." What the welfare department calls your "regular recognized need" may be much less than what you recognize as your need, especially if you've left home with little but the clothes on your back.

Even after the state figures your "regular recognized need," it may not be willing to pay the full amount. Some states figure the need and then deduct a percentage from the actual grants given; others have a maximum payment per family or per person. Some have extremely complex systems that are difficult for most people to understand.

Once they've established an amount they think you can live on, the welfare department will subtract your regular income from child support, unemployment compensation, employment or other income sources, to determine the amount of the grant you'll receive. You'll be obliged to report any income while you're a recipient of a welfare grant, though in some instances you may be able to keep a small part of earned income.

If you have a fulltime job but are barely scraping by, it will be worth your while to call the welfare department to see if you qualify for welfare assistance for medical care or childcare while you work. Those extra costs might make the difference between a tolerable income level and financial disaster.

If you think you're being treated unfairly, it's unlikely you'll have the energy to fight the whole system, but you can work at getting what you're entitled to within the system. If you have questions or doubts about your grant, ask to see the rules that apply to your situation. Ask also whether there are special allotments for someone in your circumstances. There might be special allowances for transportation to doctors or for people who are old, blind, disabled or pregnant.

Know Your Rights
Don't be afraid to ask how each decision is made, what you're entitled to, whether there are exceptions, why you're being turned down, what you need to do to qualify for general or special aid, and what the department regulations are that apply to your case. They must let you know in writing within forty-five days if your application has been approved. Your first check will arrive within that period.

If you're applying for Aid to Families with Dependent Children (AFDC), the welfare worker will ask for the name and address of the children's father, so that the department can see that he pays child support. This is a requirement for receiving AFDC, but there are certain exceptions, such as for victims of rape or domestic assault. Explain to the social worker that you're in danger, if that's the case, and ask if there are special rules that apply to your situation. The caseworker may ask you for evidence of battering, such as court records. A letter from a counselor or shelter may be enough. At a later time the department may want to go after the man for child support, and you'll have to persuade them that he's still a danger to you, if that's the case.

If you're refused aid, you must be given a reason in writing. If you think you've been unjustly refused, or given too little money, call your local or state Welfare Rights Organization or the Urban League in the nearest large city. They can help you decide whether to appeal the decision.

If you have nothing to live on until the first check comes, explain to your interviewer that the grant will help next month, but you have nothing to live on for the next few weeks. You may get an emergency grant for rent or food stamps, or if you have a notice that utilities will be turned off, you may receive enough to pay them. If there are no emergency funds available, ask for referrals to agencies who will help with money, food, clothing or other necessary items.

It's Not Forever

It's demoralizing for anyone to be financially dependent on others. It's hard not to feel incompetent, helpless and that you have no rights. Sometimes a bureacracy seems like the most difficult of all dependency situations, because it's a giant machine that neither sees nor cares about individuals, whether they're workers or clients.

When you feel discouraged by it, remember the different kinds of hardships that accompanied your life with the man who battered you. The welfare department at least has regulations that you can see in writing, and will give you notice of them when they do change. Checks may sometimes be late, and welfare may take away some of your grant when the government decides it needs the money for something else. But there won't be changes and new unkept promises every day or week, and you won't be emotionally abused or beaten up.

Most important, it's not forever, unless you want it to be or you're elderly or permanently disabled. Even then there may be some hope of finding better solutions, once your life has calmed down. As hard as it is to have so little money, you can at least clear your head and begin to look at alternatives, which is almost impossible to do when you're involved with a violent man.

OTHER BENEFITS

If you received welfare payments you automatically receive Medicaid, which will pay for many medical expenses. You may qualify for Medicaid even if you're not getting welfare money if your income is quite low. To find out if you're eligible, call the welfare department of your state, a Welfare Rights Organization or your local Urban League.

If you're over sixty-five or disabled or blind you may qualify for *Supplemental Security Income (SSI)*, a government program to aid poor people. To qualify, you must have a very low income and few resources other than a home. Apply at your local Social Security Administration.

Social Security is designed to assist retired workers in their old age. A small monthly payment is even available for those who have never paid into the social security system through paid employment. You must be sixty-two years old to receive it and if you wait until you're sixty-five you'll receive more. If you were married for at least ten years, you're entitled to half of the amount your husband gets after he's sixty-five, or sixty-two if he retires then. Even if you worked for pay most of your adult life, you may be entitled to more from his account than your own, because you may have earned a great deal less than he did. Get information about your individual situation from the local office of the Social Security Administration. Take your husband's social security number and your marriage license, as well as your own social security number.

Food Stamps

Food stamps are available to people with low incomes, which nearly always includes welfare recipients. To find out how much you're entitled to, call your welfare department. Be sure to ask whether your age, the type of assistance you receive or particular expenses you have affect the amount of food stamps you're allotted.

Employment and Training

Special employment and training opportunities may be available through the welfare department, or even required by it. If you're willing and able to go to work, but have no marketable skills, ask about subsidies for training and assistance in finding on-the-job training. When you get the information about special welfare programs, compare them with those available through other community agencies.

If you need a lot of help getting started and you have a caseworker who will make it easier for you, a program like WIN

(Work Incentive Program) may get you started again in the paid work world. However most jobs available through WIN are poorly paid and dead-end. Their main advantage may be to get you out of the house and among people on a daily basis. In the long run you'll need to get training for a skilled job unless you already have it. There is more about searching for rewarding jobs, career planning and long term goals in the next chapter.

THE HOUSING SEARCH

Looking for housing takes a lot of energy. You have to get up early (when perhaps you'd rather not get up at all), and read the paper first thing. It's likely to be a discouraging process at best, but it will be even worse if you start answering ads at one o'clock in the afternoon. By then, the best apartments will be taken. If you don't have a telephone, ask a friend if you can use hers regularly at the same time every morning. Then you won't have to worry about feeling guilty for asking another favor every day. If you must use a telephone booth, be sure to get more than enough nickels and dimes the day before you call.

If there's an afternoon paper in your community, don't wait for it to be delivered. Find out where you can get it at the earliest possible time, and go there, even if it's the newspaper office itself. You'll be ahead of everyone who's waiting for the delivery at home or work.

Telephoning can be difficult. If you're feeling nervous or insecure, know that it's a normal reaction. When you need something very badly, it's easy to feel you're being personally rejected when you don't get it. Continually remind yourself it's okay to feel like putting off those calls, it's okay to feel rejected when an apartment owner says, "We don't take children," or "We need the first and last month's rent and a damage deposit." It's okay to feel that way, but you still have to make the calls. After being turned down several times, or rejecting the places yourself, you'll feel like giving up. But sooner or later, something will turn up if you keep working at it.

Review Chapter 11, "A Courageous Act a Day," and define this task, not as finding an apartment, but as "Now I'm going to make four phone calls." After each series of calls, reward yourself.

Don't neglect the possibility of walking or driving around desirable neighborhoods. In a tight rental market, many apartments and houses never get advertised, but are rented as soon as a sign goes up. You might be lucky enough to see the sign go up yourself.

Look into public housing. There are plenty of reasons it might not be your first choice, but it won't hurt to put your name on a list so if worse comes to worst you'll have some place to go. Public housing will give you some breathing space until you find something you really want. If there's a long waiting list, call every day, and politely but firmly explain that you're in physical danger and your situation is critical. You may be moved to the top of the list. I have known this to happen a number of times when abused women explained their situations.

SHARED HOUSING

Sometimes two women in a shelter hit it off right away and decide to find a place together. It seems wonderful to know someone who's in a similar situation and understands the problems. But the relief of gaining understanding about abuse and shared feelings of loneliness and fear may temporarily blind each woman to differences in values, lifestyles, attitudes toward children and other important matters. One woman may be afraid to tell the other about her doubts, and the other may have her own misgivings. If neither speaks up, it's impossible to find out whether their doubts are important enough to drop the plan or if they can be worked out through talk or compromise. Sometimes they go ahead with the plan because each is afraid to hurt the other's feelings, and eventually this leads to mutual hostility and the loss of a housemate as well as a potential friend. If you speak up about what you want and how you feel, you should at least be able to save the friendship.

Another thing to consider in sharing housing with an ex-abused woman who's just left her man is whether she's likely to go back to him in a week or a month, which will leave you with half an empty house, and may demoralize you and weaken your own determination to stay away. There's no reliable way to make that prediction, but you can at least think about your probable reactions if it does happen. You might prefer to share housing with someone who's in a more stable situation.

You might decide to move in with an old friend, or answer an ad for group living, or invite someone into your home in exchange for rent or childcare. Whatever the situation, talk frankly about your similarities, values and habits. Be sure you do this even if you feel you know all about the other person. Many old friends have been surprised at what they learned about each other when they began to live together.

QUESTIONS FOR A POTENTIAL HOUSEMATE

1. How much company do you like at meals, in the evenings, on weekends?
2. Will you be unhappy if I'm rarely home for dinner and the evening, or if I'm not always sociable when I'm home — or if I'm almost always home and almost always sociable?
3. How will you feel if I have guests several times a week, or if you do and I almost never do?
4. How will you react if I have a male or female friend spend the night, or if I object to your having a frequent overnight or dinner guests?
5. What can we agree to do if the man who battered one of us comes to the house or calls?
6. What will happen if one of us invites an ex-partner to come to the house?
7. What are the things that bother you about other people's housekeeping habits and what bothers them about your habits?
8. What are your attitudes about money, e.g., payment of bills, sharing expenses, impulse buying, etc?
9. How much common involvement do you want in the household, sharing expenses, childcare, cooking, etc?
10. If you have children, how do you want to divide space and expenses?
11. How similar are our lifestyles and values and how tolerant are you of differences?
12. What time do you like to go to bed and get up, and how do you feel about noise (conversation, music, etc.) at night and in the morning?
13. Will you or your friends smoke, drink or take drugs at our house?

Major differences, such as the type of work you do, people you associate with and how you entertain can be problems, but sometimes they're much easier to cope with than who left the frying pan dirty. Insofar as such things don't impinge directly on you, how tolerant are you? Will you express disapproval if your housemate spends all her spare money on records, or if she dates men who you believe aren't good for her? How will you react if she gives you a bad time about your habits or associates?

Working Out Differences

As you and your potential housemate answer and discuss these questions try to remember how potential problems were worked out with other people you lived with. Don't dismiss problems with the thought that it wouldn't come up with anyone other than your mother or your former partner. Instead, remember the things that bothered you and that bothered others about you. Be as honest as you can about whether you've changed in respect to those previously troublesome areas.

You won't see eye to eye on everything, nor can you predict how you'll feel about some of these things a month or a year from now, since life with a batterer tends to distort one's reactions to many situations. You'll go through many changes in the first year when you're physically and emotionally separating from the man and will make decisions about what's so important to you that it can't be compromised. If it's completely unacceptable to spank your child, you won't want to live with a woman who spanks. If it depresses you to be greeted by a sink full of dishes in the morning, you probably won't want to take a chance on someone who tends to put off washing dishes, even if she says she'll try to do better. You don't have to defend your likes and dislikes, or feel guilty for being too demanding. It's better to live alone than to start each day irritated by the habits of your housemate.

Once you each decide what items are not subject to compromise, you'll know whether you should continue talking. What are some of the compromises you each can make? If you're a night owl, you might agree not to play music after 10 p.m. during the week if you can play it as late as you like on weekends.

Most important is a plan for discussing disagreements and problems. If you've been with an abusive man for some time, you may have formed the habit of walking on eggs, trying to predict moods and behavior, and never asking for what you want. That can result in depression or smouldering resentment that periodically bursts out in angry shouting. You may have to do some hard work to learn to know how you feel, and then to tell your housemate about it and ask for what you want. If you at least agree about wanting to learn those skills and if you give each other permission to comment when one of you is sulking, irritable or otherwise indirectly expressing resentment, you can learn to clear the air before it gets too thick.

Sharing Your Home

If you decide to share your own house or apartment in which you've previously lived with the man, you'll have some special adjustments to make. Even if you feel you hate everything about him right now, there are certain habits of living together that you developed with him which may still seem the obvious or only way to do things. When your new housemate has different ideas, it may automatically seem wrong or ridiculous just because it's different. If you're alert to this possibility, you can prevent yourself from reacting until you've thought it over.

When setting a price for renting part of your home, include the cost of wear and tear on your things and put your agreement in writing. If all the furniture and household goods are yours, you'll start your relationship with more power in setting rules about how things are used and treated. You'll need to discuss this difference and sometimes you'll need to bite your tongue when you see mud on your light-colored rug. If you remember that the rental charge allows for that, it will be easier to take.

Shared housing presents the possibility of both expanded horizons and increased stress. If you haven't experienced group living outside the nuclear or extended family, you may be reluctant to try it. But shared housing may be your best choice for a while, because of the opportunity for low-cost rent and other household expenses and the availability of people to diminish your loneliness. Once you've determined where your immediate income will come from and where you'll live, you'll be able to look at some long range financial planning.

Chapter 17

THE ECONOMICS OF SINGLE LIFE

When you're separating or divorcing after a long relationship you might feel overwhelmed by the thought of starting over emotionally, socially or financially. If you're in a new city or neighborhood without your customary friends and relatives, or even familiar landmarks, you may feel especially bewildered. If, in addition to all that, you've lost a home and furniture, personal possessions or a job, you'll have some struggles ahead of you in establishing a new style of life.

On the other hand, starting over can have an exhilarating effect. Financial responsibilities that are frightening can also become a new adventure. Learning new things is stimulating, and can give you a sense of accomplishment and build your self-esteem.

Even if you were once confident about handling household finances, don't be surprised if they seem overwhelming now. Men who batter usually insist on controlling the money and persuade women they're not capable of making sound decisions or adding a column of figures. The longer you've been involved in such a situation, the more helpless you're likely to feel. This might be true, even if you're the one who handled the money or if you were the principle breadwinner.

PAID EMPLOYMENT
Costs And Benefits Of Working

If you have the luxury of choosing whether to be unemployed or to work outside the home, it may be difficult to decide what to do, especially if you have children. Once you're separated from the abusive man, rest may be the most appealing alternative. You'll certainly need to recover from your emotional turmoil and physical abuse but a vacation from work may not necessarily be the best way to get it. A lack of structured activity may add to loneliness, depression or fear. Paid work often creates a healthy tiredness at the end of a day that can distract you from a repetitive cycle of emotions.

If it's been quite a while since you did paid work, don't assume that you're too old, not qualified or that you can't work because of commitments to children. One or the other might be true, but you can't be sure until you've taken a fresh look at your situation and the current job market. You might not be sure until you've actually worked six months or more. Don't underestimate the emotional impact of paid work and its contribution to your self-confidence. Maybe you don't like the idea that our values are closely associated with paychecks. But that's the fact for most of us, and it's important to recognize it.

How Valid Are Your Fears?

Some jobs are better for self-esteem than others. Perhaps one of your fears is that you'll be stuck in a dead-end, tedious job forever — with some emotional abuse from your boss thrown in. Perhaps that's the only kind of job you've had, you didn't think about working toward something better because you thought you could depend on a man to save you from all that. Now that you're beginning to realize you can't count on a man's economic protection, what are the reasons you still believe a boring, low-paid, low-status job is your only choice? *Write* them down. They might look something like this:

Activity 27   *What Are Your Fears About Job-Hunting?*

1. I have no education or skills.
2. I don't know what I want to do.
3. Employers discriminate against women, minorities, single mothers...
4. I'm too young, old...

5. _____

6. _____

7. _____

8. _____

9. _____

10. _____

Look carefully at each reason you've listed. How many of your statements are specific and objective?

It's not objectively true you have no skills, training or education, though you may feel that way if your skills are not easily marketable, or if they won't get you a high-paying job. To say you're the wrong sex, age, or race is not precise enough to be useful, even though being non-white, under nineteen or over thirty-five and female may be a disadvantage on the job market.

You may be too old to be accepted as an apprentice in certain fields, you may not have the right kinds of skills or education to be a secretary or an engineer. These are different statements from the first very general ones. To make your statements precise, you need to ask: "Too old for what?" "Not enough education for what?"

Formulating Goals

To evaluate your strengths and weaknesses regarding employment, you need to have a specific goal in mind. What do you want to work at? What are your minimum financial requirements? Suppose you want to be an executive secretary at a minimum salary of $18,000 a year. Assess the situation:

Goal: *Executive Secretary*

Requirements	I have	I need
Typing: 80 wpm	*40 wpm*	*Speed practice*
Shorthand	*None*	*Introductory shorthand course*
High school graduate	*High school graduate*	*–*
Some college preferred	*–*	*Community college*
Usually under 32	*8 extra years of life experience*	*Courage and assertiveness*
Neat, attractive, etc.	*Not bad*	*One job-hunting outfit*
Ability to organize time and work	*20 years experience in family*	*–*

Activity 28   Evaluating Your Job Goals

Goal:

Requirements	I have	I need

_____

_____

_____

_____

_____

_____

_____

Instead of getting depressed over what you don't have to offer, concentrate for a moment on what you do have. Rather than
think you'll never be trained for the job, or that by the time you
are you'll have one foot in the grave, consider how you can start
getting what you need.

Traditional and Non-Traditional Jobs

I've chosen the traditional woman's job of secretary in the
example above to illustrate how to evaluate a career goal because
many women feel it's possible to do the job, the training period
can be fairly short, and jobs are plentiful. Moving into the responsible position of executive secretary offers special challenges
with appropriate rewards in some businesses.

Nevertheless, the financial rewards in a secretarial job will
rarely be as great as those in the traditionally male-defined jobs in
the skilled trades such as electrician, machinist, plumber. Just because you don't know anything about these trades doesn't mean
you can't learn. Until recent years, women have been barred from
almost all apprenticeship programs, and though it's still a struggle
to get into them, it can be done. So along with checking out the
secretarial and technical courses at the community college, why
not see an advisor at the counseling or career center or women's
programs office about training in the trades? Find out what each
job pays, how long the training is and other pertinent information, as well as making arrangements to visit the classrooms.
Don't overlook the possibilities in sales jobs either.

If you have several children to support or if you don't want to
depend on a man to provide a house, car or good life for you, it
may be necessary to challenge the traditional employment system. To live well, you'll either have to be assertive and imaginative about creating a responsible job for yourself, or move up
through the ranks, enter a traditional male trade or spend several
years getting professional training at a college or university.

In the example above, beginning shorthand and advanced typing at a community college might be a reasonable first step. Before you decide you can't afford it, gather information about costs and financial aid. Call the college to get information on courses and find out whether there's a women's center or a women's program office or career center. They often have special scholarships, information about financial aid and childcare. They may even act as your advocate with the financial aid office, and if you go there in person you'll probably meet other women who are in situations similar to yours. If you qualify as a "Displaced Homemaker" you may get help from one of the special programs designed for women who have been out of the job market while raising children. Perhaps the most important aspect of such centers is the warmth and understanding of both women staff and participants, many of whom have been where you are now.

GETTING AHEAD ON THE JOB

If you're already working at a job that seems dead-end, there are two major ways to change it without completely redirecting your career. First talk to your supervisor or personnel manager or the boss of the whole business about what you'd like to be doing, and how you can work toward it. Suppose you're working in a fast food restaurant at minimum wage. Tell the general manager you want to make more money and have more responsibility. If he or she replies to the effect that you would need managerial or technical skills, ask for specifics. Would you need classes, more experience, or to change the way you relate to co-workers now? Try to get specific answers and a commitment that if you did X, Y and Z, you'd be given an opportunity to step up to management.

Whatever your job, make it clear you want to advance, find out how to do it and arrange to have periodic evaluations on specific criteria. Even if you've mentioned to your boss that you'd like a promotion, you might not be taken seriously unless you follow through with a specific plan. Perhaps, like many people, the boss automatically assumes women aren't ambitious. He or she won't deliberately discriminate, but your ambition will have to be called to management's attention. Every time you read a book about your field or take a class, a workshop or hear a lecture related to your job or the one you want, tell your boss about it. Put all those things in writing and have them available when you're evaluated.

Perhaps your company doesn't often promote from within its ranks or your boss doesn't happen to like you or appreciate your abilities. In that case, apply at other similar businesses or agencies. When you're interviewed ask specific questions about what promotions you could expect within a specific time if you do the job well. Make it clear that you want to go as far as you can and don't be afraid to say how much you'd like to be earning a few years from now.

Even if you're sure you don't want to leave your company now, it's a good idea to know what opportunities are out there. If you get a good offer it can do a lot for you even if you don't take it. You might want to tell your current boss about it, stressing that you want to stay where you are but that it's costing you money. (Whether this is good strategy depends on your individual circumstances.) Even if you don't want to use it as a bargaining tool, the fact that you know you can do better can give you much more confidence.

Another strategy for upgrading your job skills is to look for a company that has its own training program, pays for the education of certain employees or gives you time off from work to go to school. Sometimes those opportunities go to men partly because women don't make it clear enough they're interested.

If you have evidence that management in your company discriminates against women, you can take your case to one of several government anti-discrimination offices or look elsewhere for a more promising job. The U.S. Equal Employment Opportunities Commission or your state or city office of Women's Rights, Human Rights or Human Relations Commission will tell you your rights, how to establish acceptable evidence and how to file a formal complaint. This takes a long time to gain satisfaction and can cause a good deal of emotional stress, so you'll need support from friends during that period.

There are many books available about how to succeed in business, how to decide on a career, and how to present yourself in the best possible way to a prospective employer.

HOW TO BUDGET YOUR INCOME AND EXPENSES

If you're not used to working from a household budget, it may seem too restrictive. But remember it will tell you what you can do with your money, as well as what you can't.

Activity 29   Making a Budget

First, *list* all income you can count on for the next twelve months. Include wages after taxes and other deductions, child and spousal support, gifts, welfare, interest and investment income and income tax returns from last year. If you're uncertain about the amounts, estimate low. If your husband has paid child support in the past, but only about one third of the amount that was court ordered, that's the figure you should project. Divide the total by twelve, so you'll know your average monthly income.

_____

_____

_____

_____

_____

_____

_____

_____

Next, *list* your fixed expenses for the next year, converted to monthly averages:

Housing: rent or mortgage, payments, upkeep . . . . ____

Utilities: heat, light, water, garbage, telephone . . . . ____

Medical and dental . . . . ____

Insurance: house, car, medical, life . . . . ____

Taxes: house, income . . . . ____

Now subtract the amount of your fixed expenses from your projected income, and decide how you'll distribute it for these day-to-day expenses:

Food: at home, school and in restaurants . . . . ____

Clothing: yours and children's; cleaning and repairs . . . . . . ____

Transportation: bus, gas, car upkeep, car payment . . . . ____

Entertainment: evenings out, liquor, cigarettes, childcare . . ____

Household supplies: replacements, cleaning, supplies . . . . ____

Education: self, children . . . . ____

Organizational dues and contributions . . . . ____

Newspapers, magazines, books, records . . . . ____

Vacations . . . . ____

Gifts . . . . ____

If your monthly day-to-day expenses total more than the amount you got from subtracting fixed expenses from income, you have a problem. Unless you were supporting the man you recently left, you'll probably have a smaller budget after separation than before. But don't lose sight of the fact that you'll have total access to whatever money is available and total control of how it's spent, which can feel very good.

Go over the day-to-day expenses again, cutting here, adding there. Consider a job if you don't have one or a second job for a short while during the transition. Borrowing may be an option if you're sure you can pay back the loan on time. The main thing is not to pretend to yourself you're going to spend less or earn more unless you have a very concrete plan. Don't, for instance, cut out cigarettes, if you've never been able to quit in the past. Don't cut out all entertainment, because you probably won't stick to the plan, and if you do, you'll pay a price in depression.

If your adjustments of day-to-day expenses still leave you short, review your fixed expenses for possible changes. Consider moving to a smaller apartment or sharing your house with someone. You might want to sell your car and buy a less expensive one that uses less gas or take a bus until you're in a better position. If you're tempted to let insurance policies lapse, consider very carefully. In addition to the risks that go with being uninsured for a period, you'll find it hard to get insurance after a period of being uninsured and you may pay a premium three times what you're paying now. However, you might want to get different kinds of coverage than you've had.

WORKING FROM A BUDGET

During the first couple of months after separation you might have to make adjustments in your budget, as you discover previously hidden costs and adjust to changes in some expenses. You won't always have to account to yourself for every penny, but during this period of transition it's important to keep a careful record of expenditures. In a month or two you'll know what you can handle on your current income, and you can plan what to change so you'll have more options.

If you are an impulsive buyer, or careless or impatient about keeping records, you may want to put a certain amount of money in an envelope labeled with each category of day-to-day expenses. If you're dipping into the wrong envelope to pay for something not budgeted, at least you'll be forced to acknowledge it on the spot. If you leave an I.O.U., saying what the money was used for, you'll be able to adjust your budget at the end of the month to reflect reality.

An alternative is to pay almost everything with a check or put it on a credit card. When your monthly statement arrives, go over each item to find out how much you've actually spent in each category and compare it with your budget. If you do this, take careful note of how much you're paying for bank charges or interest, and consider what you might buy with it at the end of the year if you shopped with cash.

The Importance of Saving

You may think you can't possibly save on your limited income, but the more difficult it is to do, the more necessary it is. Even five dollars a month will give you a cushion for unexpected expenses. You'll feel more secure if you have a small amount set aside for a car repair or doctor's bill. As you earn more money, raise your regular savings deposit and put part of extra income from bonuses, income tax refunds and so on in the account. Try to build it up to an amount twice your monthly salary, and keep it in an interest-bearing account you have immediate access to. Money Market Mutual Funds are available free. They pay much higher interest than banks or savings and loans and don't tie up your money for any length of time. (They give you free checks for checks over $250.) If you're like most people, you'll never put money in savings if you wait until you have enough extra. Take it right off the top, as soon as you're paid. In other words, "Pay yourself first."

Loans

If you're caught between the maxim "Neither a borrower nor a lender be" and the temptation to accept every offer to buy now, pay later, look for a middle ground. It makes sense to borrow, either for a special purpose or by regular use of a credit card, if you're sure you want or need the item, and if you can be sure you can make the payments when they're due and without increasing whatever stress you already have. Add the total interest you'll be paying to the price of the item, and decide whether the combined figures are what you're willing to pay.

At the time you separate you might have a number of unusual bills for medical care, moving costs or lawyer fees. Several bills may come in at once or be past due. If you're billed for insurance, medical care and house taxes, try first to negotiate terms.

Write to your creditors, suggesting a schedule of payments you're sure you can manage. If they agree, find out how much they will charge you for a longer payment period. If they don't accept your plan, consider borrowing. Gradually, you can get onto an evenly-spread payment plan for all creditors and major expenses, either putting cash aside each month for such annual expenses as insurance, or paying a fraction each month. It may take a year to get your new system working smoothly.

When you borrow, you're paying to use someone else's money, and in general the longer you use it the more you'll pay. But interest figures vary from place to place and sometimes change within a very short time. If you decide to borrow, either through a loan or by purchasing a major item on credit, shop around. Find out what fees will be charged in addition to interest, and get precise information on interest rates. If you don't understand the complexities, ask how many dollars you will be paying out by the end of the payment period. You may be shocked to learn how much it is. In some cases you might be still willing to pay it in order to have the use of the item much sooner, or because it's a necessity. Insist on a written statement of terms, read the installment contract carefully, including the small print, and when you've signed it keep your copy in a safe place. If you tend to get anxious over small print, take a copy to a friend you trust and go over it together. Don't be pressured into purchases (of money or things) by threats that this is the last time such a great offer will be made. You won't be able to tell if it's a great offer until you've compared it to some others.

If you borrow from a friend, relative or man you're involved with, you may pay in ways other than money: you may postpone payment beyond the time necessary and set up feelings of guilt and resentment in both parties. Consider the possible consequences carefully, and put your agreement in writing, so you'll each know when the repayment will be made. You might want to pay a small amount of interest, in order to emphasize the businesslike aspect of the relationship, and so that the lender gets something in return.

HOME MAINTENANCE

If you own property or investments you'll need to learn or relearn how to handle them. Before anything goes wrong with your property, ask friends, neighbors and co-workers to recommend carpenters, plumbers, electricians and other repair persons. Call each one, ask their hourly rate, terms of their guarantees for materials and labor and whether they charge for estimates. Find out if they'll come to your neighborhood on emergency calls and how long they usually take to respond to such calls. Unless you've been keeping close track of the cost and quality of work done on your house and have reason to trust the people who serve you, compare this new information with the costs and type of service you've had before. There's an advantage to continuous service, but you may also have paid top rates when it wasn't necessary.

If you have a major home maintenance problem, be sure to get several estimates before you contract for the job. By the time you've talked to the third person, you'll begin to understand the problem and you may want to talk to the first company to ask more questions. The lowest estimate isn't necessarily the best, but you won't even know what's low and what's high until you've talked to several companies. Ask them to put the estimate in writing and to itemize it. You may then be able to use the language of the estimate to get several more rough estimates by telephone, though you shouldn't accept a final one until the job site has been inspected.

If you can, watch the repair person at work, so you can understand the problem and, if it's a minor job, do it yourself next time. Your interest will also be an extra incentive for the person you hire to do good work.

You'll be surprised how much you can do on your own. Buy a few books on simple household repairs, invest in the tools the books suggest and take a risk or take a class in household maintenance. You'll find that once you stop being anxious and have the right tool in your hand, you can do many repairs yourself.

If you need major expensive repairs on your house, don't panic. The loan picture changes so rapidly it's hard to know what to do other than to keep inquiring. A bank that gives no loans when you call at the beginning of the month may give you a different answer at the end. One bank may say "No," and another — or even a branch of the same institution — say "Yes." If a credit union turns you down, a bank may accept you. Save yourself time and stress by calling a number of places and getting as much information as possible before you apply in person. Say whether you want a mortgage on your house, a home improvement loan (often available when others aren't) or a personal loan, and ask what, in general, is necessary to get such a loan or how they decide who will get it. They may give you a formula such as maximum mortgages are two and a half times your annual income or that your total debts, including the new loan, can't go over thirty percent of your income. To get that information, let them know you realize they have to look at your total financial picture before they can give you a loan, and be a little pushy about asking for their formulas. Ask what papers you should bring with you when you go for a personal interview.

When you consider where to invest money, or whether to refinance your house, or to buy for cash or credit, you'll need to understand the economy as it changes on a week to week basis. You may not know much about it now, but you can learn. Ask friends and colleagues to recommend a financial adviser. You may want to interview two or three before making a choice. Even if you're not sure which of them is giving the best advice — and like all professionals, they're likely to disagree — you'll have different feelings about how they do or don't explain things, or how closely they listen to what you want and whether they understand your values. Your financial future *is* your future — get expert guidance from someone you feel is really concerned with your best interests.

OVERCOMING FINANCIAL IGNORANCE

If you find yourself resisting the opportunity to learn more about money, give some thought to why that is. It may be that, like most women, you've bought the message from the time you were very young that girls don't understand math, that women are frivolous and extravagant about money and really can't be expected to understand it. You may believe high finance is men's business. You may be scared and quite uncomfortable with feelings of inadequacy. The way to overcome those feelings is to take one piece of the financial picture at a time and learn about it. There are many classes designed specifically for women to help them overcome their fears and ignorance. And it *is* ignorance, not stupidity, which means it can be overcome.

Another reason you may resist learning is that you still have the fantasy someone will take care of you all your life, and you'll be spared taking responsibility. Many men as well as women feel that way and aren't good at handling practical matters. Men are forced to pretend they're knowledgeable so they won't appear less than masculine, but women are let off the hook. It's also easier for men to cover their mistakes, because of higher salaries. Some women really have been taken care of by their men, but many find out too late that they weren't cared for at all. Just because your man made all the practical decisions doesn't mean he made the right ones. If you're willing to admit your ignorance and seek advice from various people, you may make much better decisions now that you have the chance.

At first you may only see the pitfalls of making decisions on your own and the burdensome aspect of responsibility for the consequences. You'll forget that you can find experts, as well as friends and family to consult with, and that your friends will help you pick up the pieces when things go badly. Later, you'll find yourself looking at some risks as the potential for success and an exciting challenge. You'll wonder why you ever let that man take away the good feeling that comes with standing solidly on your own feet.

Chapter 18

SEXUALITY

For many women, the decision to end an abusive relationship with a man means an end to sexuality as well. This is especially true if sexuality has been narrowly defined as orgasm through intercourse, and not a combination of needs and desires that include affection, sensuality and romance. Yet even orgasm, according to most recent research, hasn't been the reason most women engaged in intercourse, and it is not always what women miss most about the lack of sex.

Shere Hite, in a survey of over three thousand women, found that only about thirty percent of the respondents experienced orgasm as a result of intercourse (though some had orgasms during intercourse but as a result of manual stimulation). Yet most women (eighty-seven percent) said they did like intercourse and that sex was important to them.†

Hite says, "The most frequent reason for liking intercourse by far was that it was time of great affection and closeness."‡ Many of the women she quotes speak of being *one with a man, of warmth, love, closeness, wholeness, security, feeling loved, wanted, important and powerful.*

This chapter will give you some ideas on how to get your needs for intimacy and sensual stimulation met without intercourse. A first in that direction is to look closely at your own sexual desires and how they were satisfied — or not satisfied — in the relationship with the man you've left. As an aid in doing that, *write* the answers to these questions:

Activity 30   What Have You Enjoyed About Sex?

1. Do you enjoy affectionate touching? _____
What people do you especially enjoy touching, and which of

---

†Shere Hite, *The Hite Report* (New York: Dell, 1979), p. 612.

‡*The Hite Report*, p. 297.

them would you like to touch or be touched by more? (Think about friends, relatives, children, men, women and even pets.)

_____

2. Do you ever touch someone or want to be touched for sexual arousal, without wanting it to result in orgasm? How does it work out? _____

_____

3. Did you ever have sex with the man you just left or another one mainly for the intimacy, closeness, warmth, security or romance, rather than for orgasm? How often were you successful?

_____

4. How important is sex in your life? _____

_____

5. How often did you have orgasms with your ex-partner? Did they usually come about as a result of intercourse, clitoral stimulation by him or you, or other sexual activity? _____

_____

6. Were you unable at times to have orgasm with your ex-partner during intercourse? _____ What would have helped?

Did you ask for what you wanted? _____ If not, why not? _____

_____

7. How often were you left disappointed or frustrated after intercourse? _____
Did you ever fake orgasm? _____ How often? _____
Why? _____

_____

8. Were you ever sexually abused or humiliated by your ex-partner? _____

How often? _____

9. Are you ever left feeling frustrated or disappointed after masturbating? _____ How often? _____ Why? _____

_____

10. What other sexual activity do you enjoy? How important to

you are kissing, breast stimulation, caressing of hips and thighs, general body touching, caressing of vagina, oral vaginal contact, your caressing of your partner? _____

Which are important in reaching orgasm? _____

11. In the best of all possible worlds, what would sexuality be like? _____

_____

_____

LEARNING TO TRUST YOUR EXPERIENCE

If the questionnaire has been difficult for you to complete because of lack of knowledge about your own body and the nature of orgasm or nonorgasm, don't give up yet. Orgasm is a controversial topic when it comes to women. Through much of recorded history it hasn't been acknowledged that women could even derive pleasure from their sexual activities. Intercourse was seen (and still is by some) as a procreative function, entered into unwillingly by the female, forced by the male.

Whenever the subject of female sexuality and particularly orgasm has come up, the so-called experts have disagreed. Sigmund Freud promoted the idea that only immature women had clitoral orgasms whereas mature women had vaginal orgasms. Not until the 1966 Masters and Johnson study was there scientific evidence that women orgasmed through clitoral stimulation. Millions of women who had doubted the reality of their own experience were validated, yet the most recent findings indicate that women are capable of vaginal orgasms as well.†

Experts can both dispel myths and create new ones, which makes it hard for us to know how much to take on scientific "faith," when to doubt authorities and when to trust our own experiences. And that's complicated by the fact that some of our beliefs directly affect what experiences we have.

---

†These vaginal orgasms originate from an area on the upper wall of the vagina, called the Grafenberg spot. The size varies from about the size of a dime to that of a half dollar. It's extremely sensitive and when stroked it produces a strong desire to urinate at first, quickly followed by intense sexual excitement and orgasm. A woman may at the same time expel fluid which originates in the same spot. The existence of this fluid, expelled at orgasm by some women, has been denied and explained away as merely urine during most of our history, though it has also been recognized at various historical periods. Masters and Johnson reported that there is no such phenomena in women.

Many of us have been persuaded by experts that women aren't nearly as sexual as men and that men, due to their greater sexuality and vast experience, know and understand more about female as well as male sexuality. So we treat our male partners as experts and listen to them rather than to our own feelings. We do the things that seem sexiest to them, without saying what we want, for fear of seeming strange, wrong, sexually immature, too loose, or too prudish — or for fear of hurting or embarrassing them by casting doubt on their expertise.

There is clearly one area you're an expert about and that's what feels good to you and what doesn't. Regardless of whether it "should" feel good, or whether you've been told it's normal or the way women are supposed to feel, you're the authority. If you've been hesitant to tell a sexual partner what makes you uncomfortable or what you'd like him to do, this is a good time to get clear about what you do and don't like, and to resolve to ask for it the next time you're in a sexual relationship. On the other hand, you may be without a sexual partner for a while either by choice or through lack of an attractive enough opportunity. Such a condition can be tolerated, and even enjoyed, if you give yourself options to gain pleasure in a variety of ways.

SEXUALITY ISN'T JUST SEX

Sexuality is made up of affection, sensuality, eroticism, intimacy and romance and probably almost everyone would like to have a relationship that includes all of that. But if that's what you're longing for, there are some important questions to be asked: Was your partner affectionate? Sensual? Erotic? Intimate? Romantic?

Although it's true that there is a magical quality to life when these five components of sexuality come together in one relationship, it doesn't happen very often, so it will be useful to look at each separately to determine how to meet each need independently.

Affection

Affection can be expressed verbally, but more often is a physical expression of caring for a person by hugging, patting or stroking. Some people are quite free with their affectionate touching, others reserve such expression for intimate family members or long-term friends. If such an expression of friendship or concern is important to you, look at your patterns of getting those needs met and consider changing them if necessary.

For instance, if you've reserved affectionate contact for the family or friends you're close to, let yourself open up to touching new acquaintances and potential friends. Women in many groups — for instance, at some YWCA's or NOW chapters — interact in an affectionate style. You may want to explore several groups before becoming involved with the one that best suits your needs.

If you do have friends you'd like to touch more, don't assume that they don't want it too. Let yourself stroke a friend's arm, or put your arm around her shoulders, or give her a hug when you're feeling good — or sad or lonely, or especially close to her. Pay attention to whether she feels uncomfortable. Ask her how she feels about expressing friendship by touching, or say, "I'd really like to hug you now, okay?" And unless you get a negative response, do it. You might want to review Chapter 13, "Reaching Out."

If, like many women who've been in abusive relationships, you have no friends or family available, there are still some things you can do to meet some of your affectional needs. Get a cat or dog or another pet that has almost unlimited pleasure in being stroked, and makes virtually no demands. Of course, it's not the same as what you can get from a person, but it will help. And after what you've been through you can stand some affection from a creature who expects very little from you and doesn't criticise you at all.

Sensuality

Sensuality is an important part of sexuality for many people and on a continuum of stimulation or excitement it falls somewhere between affection and eroticism, having some of the characteristics of both.

Sensuality refers to the gratification of the senses or appetites. The more intensely you become emotionally involved with the pleasures of your five senses, the more sensual you are. For instance, hearing music, smelling or tasting food or drink, looking at paintings, sculpture or snow-covered mountains, or touching or being touched may give you great sensual pleasure. Though the context is different, the feelings may be similar to those you have in a sexual relationship.

What are the greatest sensual pleasures of sex for you? The touching of an entire body by another whole body, exploring crevices, curves and angles that otherwise you hardly know exist? The sounds of juices flowing, of your partner's panting, satisfied moans or your own gasps or cries? The smell of your partner's body? The salty taste?

Think about other activities in which you gain similar satisfactions. If there are few, consider which ones you might develop. You might indulge in a weekly full body massage. If a professional is too expensive, trade massages with a friend. Or massage yourself slowly and lovingly with an aromatic body cream. Contact sports, running and swimming can also provide satisfying physical stimulation.

Develop your appreciation of visual and auditory experiences by really looking and really listening. Put aside some time for visiting art galleries, looking at lakes, or mountains or sand or trees — just looking without any purpose other than the visual experience, without analysis or judgment. Do the same with music, experimenting with symphony, jazz, rock. Let yourself feel sad or lighthearted or excited. Dance to it if the spirit moves you. When everyone else has gone to bed, read poetry aloud.

It may take some time to develop your sensual nature fully especially if you've previously relied on sex with a partner to satisfy you completely. Part of this development is remembering to notice. *Notice* when you enjoy running your hand over a velvet pillow. *Notice* when a singer's high note or a trumpet's call sends "chills up and down your spine."

The next thing to do is *enjoy*. Often, when you unexpectedly experience a sensual reaction, you'll immediately sense that a surge of longing threatens to follow it, a longing for that particular man and sexual intimacy with him. When you feel that threat, you're tempted to stamp out the sensual urges in order to deny the longing. Maybe for a while that's what you'll choose to do, but you don't have to. You can learn to enjoy sensual experiences for their own value, not just as a prelude to, or reminder of, sexual intimacy. And if you want to, you can let them build in an explicitly sexual way until you're ready to treat yourself to an orgasm.

Eroticism

By eroticism I mean orgasm and the explicitly sexual arousal and tension that is most often associated with it. For some women this may be the aspect of sexuality that is longed for most, yet it's the easiest need to meet without a partner.

If you've been telling yourself that the "right" or "normal" or "mature" way to have orgasm is during intercourse with a man, start telling yourself now that the "right" way is the way that satisfies you without hurting anyone else. And if you haven't learned the pleasures of masturbation you might want to begin now. If masturbation is something you "give in to" and try to get over with quickly, consider looking at it a different way. If you think of it as something shameful, either because of moral or religious training or because it's something only sexual "losers" do, you might want to reevaluate. Almost everyone has masturbated at some time, religious and nonreligious people, those who are in good relationships and unsatisfying ones, and those who have no sexually intimate relationships.

If you're going to masturbate, you might as well get the maximum pleasure from it. You probably don't appreciate a "Wham bam! Thank you ma'am!" approach from a man, so why treat yourself that way? Use your sexual urges as an opportunity to appreciate your physical and sexual being. Take it slow and be loving and affectionate to yourself. Once you become used to your own caring and satisfying touch, you'll be less likely to settle for less.

Intimacy

Intimacy implies first of all closeness; it also means warmth, depth of relationship, familiarity and affection. Shere Hite's research indicates that women enjoy sexual intercourse because of the intimacy they experience. Here are some of the things women wrote about the reasons they like intercourse:

"The touching and tenderness then makes me feel warm and secure, safe and close."

"I love intercourse. It feels really close, like he is really mine and cares for me."

"...it is a time when I get his individual attention, and feel very loved and secure."†

These and the other answers quoted from *The Hite Report* indicate that reassurance of a special man's love, and being close, are important aspects of sex for many women. We can assume that for many of Hite's respondents, intercourse caps a relationship that is warm, close, and reassuring in other respects. But it's also clear that a certain number of women only feel close to their lovers during intercourse.

Take a second look at your responses to the questions at the beginning of this chapter and consider them in relation to the satisfactions, care, communication, security and intimacy you experienced in other aspects of your relationship. If it was rare for you to experience those feelings except during sex, perhaps that indicates a serious flaw in the relationship. If you didn't get those satisfactions even during sexual intimacy, then you're not missing so much after all. When you're tempted to believe you're missing an intimacy you actually had, read the list of pleasures you did and didn't get, read the list and consider whether you're longing

†*The Hite Report*, pp. 423-25.

for a lost dream rather than a reality or even a potential reality, with that particular man.

All of this doesn't mean there isn't a special wonderful quality to sexual intimacy, but there are other close relationships which, if not quite as exciting, are sometimes more reliable and ultimately satisfying. Review the section on "Moving From Acquaintances to Friends" in Chapter 13.

Romance

Regardless of how well you organize your life, neither your successful career, your delightful children, good friends, sports or art activities, nor the joys of masturbation provide quite the same excitement as does romance. It's this special quality of romance and the search for it that gets many of us into trouble.

In defining romance the dictionary uses these words: "heroic," "colorful," "chivalrous devotion," "supernatural appeal to the imagination." Another definition is: "A baseless story usually full of exaggeration or fanciful invention." Synonyms for romance are "story," "fiction," "falsehood," "fable."

Our longing for romance is often a longing for the unreal. Real life is hard for many of us. It can be tragic, boring, lonely, frightening or oppressive. Sometimes there's nothing we can name that's wrong with life, so we tell ourselves we shouldn't feel depressed or restless, yet there's something missing. What we crave, often, is that unreal something called romance.

As discussed more thoroughly in Chapter 5, romantic love is often a kind of addiction that lifts us out of our everyday doldrums. Falling in love is a very special experience, one that ought to be treasured, but not expected to continue indefinitely. A continuous fall will eventually end in a crash. At this time of your life, if you feel you're too vulnerable to risk falling in love, you need to look for other ways to rise above the tedium of everyday life.

There's an overlap between sensual and romantic pleasures, and you can experience both through drama, music and art, which lift you out of the daily rounds of chores and nuts and bolts reality. They put beauty into your life and help you make imaginative leaps. If you have a little money that you normally spend on beer or the hairdresser or lessons for the children, set aside enough instead to go to a movie, concert, play, art exhibit or dance program. Choose whatever is likely to grip you, whether it's country music, ballet, a sculpture exhibit or science fiction film. Let yourself be transported without indulging in a fruitless longing for the other kind of romance. Enjoy the experience for itself.

If you really have no money to spare, plan your television

watching carefully so that you're not using it to kill time, but watching something that truly captures your interest. Avoid the "soaps" which focus on the tragic aspects of love and problems like your own.

An important part of romance is the suspense. Will he call tonight? Does he love me? What if he finds out I'm not as wonderful as he thinks? The very things that often make a new romance tortuous are the same tensions that make it deliciously enticing. And to the degree we allow ourselves to be transported, we risk serious damage to our egos, careers, life goals and the ability to be in control of our lives if the object of the romantic feelings doesn't feel the same way. Yet this is one of the few risks in life that most women don't hesitate to take.

There are ways to compensate for the lack of that romantic excitement in our lives. Any activity that carries with it the risk of loss, rejection or failure and of winning, acceptance or success can provide a similar titillation.

Sports provide the best arena, since they allow for the sensual pleasures of the body as well as the opportunity to win or lose either publicly or privately, alone or with teammates.

Art also provides suspense. Art doesn't necessarily mean the creation of a great painting. Writing a poem, experimenting with watercolors or modeling clay will stimulate you to develop skills you may think you're "not good at," but may never have tried. Art includes many media: crocheting, cabinet-making, playing the recorder, creating macrame, ceramics, photography, woodwork, upholstery and many, many other activities you can do at home alone or with friends.

Business or other career involvements also may include excitement and risk. Any career, including parenting, can involve you in learning, creating, risk-taking and the stimulation of peak experiences. Short-range, one-time adventures can give you a thrill that's similar to romance. Anything you've been afraid of trying, whether it's climbing a ladder or a mountain, can provide a feeling of suspense and anxiety, success or failure. The "small" pleasures you can find daily or even hourly are at least as important as those occasional dramatic happenings. A sunny fall day can be experienced as a sensual marvel rather than as wasted because you can't share it with a lover. Remember that romance is sometimes low key and don't compare each small pleasure with the fireworks at the height of romantic excitement.

An important part of romance that often makes the risk worthwhile is the ego-enhancement of knowing someone really believes we're the most wonderful person on earth. Even though our minds tell us the absurdity of such a view, it feels mighty good. To be adored, to be thought brilliant and clever and good and beautiful is intoxicating, so what can substitute for that?

Nothing, really, except some drug, perhaps, that allows for an equal amount of fantasy. But part of the joy of competing in sports or of developing other talents is in basking in the praise and appreciation of others. You don't have to be the best to get it, either. If you knit a sweater or create a beautiful garden that gives you pleasure, your friends will tell you it's terrific and you're clever to have done it. Not that you're perfect, no. Still it feels good. That, and developing the ability to admire yourself will help you to get along better without a lover's romantic illusion that you're perfect.

If each week you hug your good friends several times, masturbate, focus on the sensuality of music, nature, food or art once or twice for several hours, play on a team or run or swim once or twice, and create something of your own, whether decorating a cake, running a small business from your home or designing a stained glass window, you're certain to get some excitement from taking risks, and to enjoy being appreciated by other people. You won't have much time to pine for that man and the sexuality you associate with him.

LESBIANISM

Much of the discussion in this chapter on sexuality and in the next on romance focuses on women with or without male partners. Yet a significant percentage of women are additionally or only attracted to women. For some, lesbianism is an early choice, others come to the realization only after years of relating to men sexually and often after having been wives or mothers. While there still exist laws and taboos against lesbianism, the last ten years have in general brought about greater public acceptance of the reality of women loving women.

Lesbians teach school, win custody battles, are congresspeople, tennis stars, actors. There are lesbians in every field, just as there are gay men. Being openly lesbian is not a decision to be taken lightly, yet many women find they're comfortable for the first time in their lives when they accept their same-sex orientation and adopt a lesbian lifestyle.

A number of women find it easier to form egalitarian relationships and to meet their needs for affection and sexuality with other women. Certainly all the problems of intimacy aren't solved. Battering even occurs among some lesbian couples. But many women find that a common style of emotionality, nurturance, talk and sexuality make it easier to solve problems and bring out the best in each other.

If you think you might be at least as attracted to women as to men, don't deny it. Think back to your sexual impulses as an adolescent and young woman. If you were attracted to other women at that time it might have been "just a phase" or it might have been the truest expression of your sexuality. You're the only one who can know that, and it may take you awhile to think it through.

Wanting to touch or hug another woman doesn't mean you're a lesbian. If you're afraid of being misunderstood you can avoid it by being sensitive to the other's feelings. If your affectionate gestures are met with a cool or ambivalent response, you have only to back off to reassure the other person. You don't have to act on your affectionate or sexual impulses toward a woman any more than you do if you're attracted to your friend's husband or a strange man on the street. You might feel sexually aroused and want to follow those feelings or you might want to pass right on by them in favor of building a good, solid nonsexual friendship.

What if you do want to follow through on those feelings, not only towards a particular woman but women in general? These days there are many books published, by and for lesbians, that explain what lesbians do and how they feel. Most cities have at least one gay or lesbian organization now, and colleges and universities with women's resource centers have referral and drop-in services. There are networks for lesbians living in rural areas and many newspapers and periodicals to connect you to others.

It is important not to be threatened by your feelings and to realize that even if you do decide to act on them you may not be a lesbian. Throughout history, societies have recognized that people can be bisexual. That is, they're capable of being attracted to both sexes, even though most people deny or repress attractions to people of the same sex.

This book is about, among other things, making real choices. You can't make choices until you investigate your feelings and learn to accept them. Fortunately we live in a time when choosing a woman lover can be seen as a healthy and positive option. Whether you choose to exercise that option is up to you.

Chapter 19

THE NEW ROMANCE

They say there's nothing like a new romance to heal the wounds of the old one. If you're lucky and careful enough to find a man who treats you well, your lonely hours may be reduced to a tolerable level. You'll have concrete evidence that men can be loving and affectionate without threatening or abusing you. If you don't let it become addictive, such a relationship can be helpful in getting you through the rough times after your separation from the batterer. Whether or not it turns out to be forever, you'll want to be careful who you choose this time.

WHAT ARE YOU LOOKING FOR IN A PARTNER?

The first step in developing a healthy, nurturing relationship is knowing what kind of man you want. And the best time to think seriously about the question is when you have no special man, so you won't pretend to yourself that your new man perfectly fits the description of what you want.

List the characteristics you'd want in a man, including those you think you have no right to. For instance, if you don't consider yourself smart or good-looking, you probably won't think you deserve a smart or good-looking man.

Activity 31   *"What I Want In A Man"*

1. _____

2. _____

3. _____

4. _____

5. _____

6. _____

7. _____

8. _____

9. _____

10. _____

11. _____

12. _____

Now *add to the list* whichever of these characteristics you find attractive in men: dominant, worldly, confident, aggressive, unemotional, independent, funny, affectionate, smart, sexy, dependable, personable, expressive, dependent, submissive, insecure, modest, artistic, interesting, family-oriented.

Put parentheses around each characteristic you'd be willing to do without if there were other important ones. *Underline* the ones that are absolutely essential.

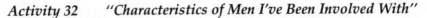

List the characteristics of the men you've been involved with, including the man who abused you. How many of them had the traits you now say are essential? If few of them did, what are the other characteristics they had in common, if any? In other words, what was it about those men that "hooked" you even though they didn't have the qualities you say are most important?

Activity 32   *"Characteristics of Men I've Been Involved With"*

1. _____

2. _____

3. _____

4. _____

5. _____

6. _____

7. _____

8. _____

9. _____

10. _____

If there's a pattern, you can use it to be wary of certain kinds of men, and suspicious of your reactions to them. For instance, if essential characteristics are "kind," "considerate," and "good-natured," yet you were involved with three men who lacked those qualities but who were either "sexy," "good looking," or "good dancers," recognize the contraction between what you want and who you actually choose. Then you can be especially careful when you're attracted to that kind of man. The man you choose to go dancing with may be very different from the one you want to live with. If you're attracted to a good dancer who's bad-tempered, then dance with him, but don't invest yourself emotionally and if he begins to mistreat you, walk quickly to the nearest exit. If you're romantically or sexually attracted to a man, it doesn't follow that you should love or marry him.

Consider the possibility also that you're not attracted to kind, considerate, good-natured men. Maybe you just think you ought to be, but usually you find such men dull. Perhaps you've bought society's message that a "real man" must be adventurous, tough, and keep you guessing. If you added to your list quite a few of the first six characteristics listed after Activity 31, you're looking for the stereotype of what a male is supposed to be. The trouble is that a man who's developed most of those characteristics is likely to be a controlling kind of supermale, and to expect you to be a superfemale — that is, to have the opposite of his characteristics. He might be the kind of man who abuses a woman who doesn't conform to his expectations.

WHAT IF YOU KEEP FINDING
THE SAME KIND OF MAN?

If you've frequently become involved with abusive men, it's either because you tend to find them in more or less the same places, something about them attracts you, or something about you attracts them.

Abusive men are found in all classes, races, ages; at all educational levels and in all employment categories. However, there are families, neighborhoods, taverns and social groups in which it's looked upon as okay for men to beat their women and battering may be more common there than in groups where at least lip service is given to the idea that battering is unacceptable. Men who drink or use drugs excessively probably batter more than those who don't, even though their drug use doesn't necessarily cause the battering. Women who abuse drugs or alcohol are more likely to be beaten, simply because they may lose control of their environment. If you're in a high risk environment, you'll have to look hard and be extremely careful to find a gentle, considerate man. It will be safer to move to a different neighborhood, stay away from certain crowds and make an entirely new set of friends. If that doesn't change things, then you should look into yourself.

Family Patterns

Although a few women who've attached themselves to several abusive men may believe they deserve punishment, it's not a typical pattern. There are other reasons for a woman's involvement in more than one battering relationship. Many people find mates with whom they repeat the kind of relationships they formed with a parent. This sometimes happens even when they didn't like that earlier relationship and consciously looked for something different.

If you were emotionally or physically abused by a parent, you may unintentionally continue to find abusive partners because that's the intimate pattern most familiar to you. You meet a new man and feel some sense of excitement or comfort or both. It's warm and familiar to you, a little bit like coming home. Only later is it clear that the comforting familiarity is similar to what you experienced as a child. Whatever else it may be, the feeling is known to you and therefore seems safe. It may even be that a non-punitive intimate relationship is so alien you feel insecure and uneasy with it and don't know how to react.

List the characteristics that best describe you, your mother, father (or parent figure) and compare them with those of your intimate partners (Activity 32). Pick out the ones that most of the men in your life have in common and see whether they are much like those of a parent. That will tell you whether you have a tendency to find partners like your father or your mother — or whether you seek the opposite traits of one of them.

Activity 33   *Your Family Characteristics*

1. _____
2. _____
3. _____
4. _____
5. _____
6. _____
7. _____
8. _____
9. _____
10. _____

If you regularly become involved with a person who's similar to an admired parent and yet who abuses you, consider whether there's a previously unrecognized streak of abusiveness in the parent. Perhaps you've called it independence, humor, protectiveness or strength and when you've found it in your romantic relationships, it's more like selfishness, sarcasm, control or stubbornness. In that case, think about the precise meaning of each of those traits and when you meet a new man, consider whether there's evidence of that trait. You may not be able to tell for sure until you've seen the man in a number of situations, including stressful or embarrassing ones.

In your search for the opposite of a parent who was abusive and who was also alcoholic and lazy, you might make the mistake of assuming an energetic nondrinker can't possibly be abusive. That might cause you to overlook some early signs of a potentially destructive relationship.

Repetition of Patterns

If you were in love with a man who seemed quite different from your abusive parent and discovered the similarity too late, think back to an early point in the relationship when you felt uncomfortable about how he treated you but let it go without complaint. Ask yourself what it was you wanted that caused you to overlook the discomfort. Keep pushing your memory back to the earliest point. Do the same thing with each relationship in which you didn't realize what kind of man you had until you were already deeply involved.

Define as precisely as you can what you wanted or were trying to avoid. Perhaps you were afraid to risk hurting the man's feelings, so you didn't say you disliked his plan for your evening. If you're often compliant because you're afraid of hurting someone's feelings, start being considerate of your own feelings and heighten your awareness of what you want and enjoy. Review the Rights List (Activity 6) and the *Be Good To Yourself* section in Chapter 11. Maybe you didn't want to pay your way, so you felt you had no right to object to the restaurant he wanted to take you to. Maybe you were afraid that if you told him you were hurt or insulted he'd become angry and leave, or if you asked a question he'd think you weren't very bright. Is it a pattern you learned trying to prevent abuse from a parent? The man might have interpreted your passivity to mean you cared so little for yourself that he could easily abuse you.

If there's a clear pattern, you'll find it easier to know where to begin making changes. If you habitually let people's unacceptable statements go unchallenged because you're afraid of appearing stupid, you can begin changing now. Enroll in an assertion training class or force yourself to begin speaking up in a variety of situations and with different people.

When you have some practice, you'll be willing to tell a new man your opinion whether you expect him to like it or not. You'll find out at the beginning of the relationship whether he's going to use the opportunity to insult your intelligence. If he is, you can leave before he becomes seriously abusive and before you're so involved it's hard to do.

Avoid The Appearance of a "Soft Touch"

Many women are drawn to men who call forth their nurturance and protectiveness, which makes them vulnerable to the very men who may be especially likely to mistreat them. Men who had difficult childhoods, were mistreated emotionally or physically by parents, served time in jail or have drinking problems often seduce certain women into feeling sorry for them. The women believe they can compensate for the men's troubles by loving them. Many abused women have said, "I thought if I just loved him enough for long enough, finally he'd believe in me and trust me and learn to love himself — and he wouldn't want to hit me any more." If you have the urge to rescue, steer clear of men who call forth that response in you. If you're prone to guilt feelings, you're doubly vulnerable, because when you want to separate he'll trigger the guilt by saying he can't get along without you and you're cruel to abandon him.

If you're the woman on the block to whom children bring stray cats or wounded birds, if your heart — and money and time — goes out to anyone who has suffered, abusive men will spot you very quickly. When you're with someone new, there's nothing wrong with being warm, but try not to let him know your weakness for troubled and inadequate people. Part of the problem here is that you let men choose you, rather than deciding who you want to be with.

None of this means there is something wrong with you or that you want to be punished. It does mean you have to take special precautions to avoid abusive relationships. It means you should go slowly in becoming involved with new men and continually question yourself about their behavior and motivation, your feelings and responses and the character of your interactions. When you find yourself "falling" for a new man or being sought by one, use the list of traits for your ideal man from Activity 31 to evaluate whether he's really the one for you. If he isn't, don't stay with him while waiting for someone better to come along. Stay uninvolved and begin an active search in the places you're likely to find a man who will be good for you.

You can't always predict whether a man will be a batterer, because some are gentle and considerate during the dating phase but change radically soon after marriage or when the woman becomes pregnant. But if you let the relationship develop slowly, in most cases you can save yourself heartache and injury. Here are some other things to look for.

Activity 34   Questions to Ask Yourself About A New Man

1. Can you state particular characteristics of his that you love? ...._____

2. Can you give examples of them? ...._____

3. How many essential characteristics of your "ideal man" does he have? ...._____

4. Does he accept your right to decide if you'll use birth control? ...._____

5. Does he think it's a wife and mother's right to decide whether to work at a paid job? ...._____

6. Is he willing to have you spend time alone, even if he'd like to be with you? ...._____

7. Is he glad you have other friends? ...._____

8. Is he pleased at your accomplishments and ambitions? _____

9. Does he think women can and should be as wise, worldly, confident, strong, decisive, and independent as men? ._____

10. Does he sometimes ask your opinion? ...._____

11. Does he both talk and listen?......................_____

12. Does he tell you when his feelings are hurt? ...._____

13. Does he think it's okay for men to show they're weak or vulnerable and to cry sometimes — aside from right after he's abused you? ...._____

14. Is he able to express affection aside from the times he's sorry for abusing you and when he wants, or you're having sex? ...._____

15. Are there some special traits about women (ability to express emotions, willingness to be vulnerable) that he admires? ...._____

16. Does he like and admire his mother or sister? ...._____

17. Does he have good friends? ...._____

18. Does he have interests besides you? ...._____

19. When angry does he break or throw things? ...._____

20. Does he lose his temper suddenly over small things, especially when he doesn't perform as well as he'd like? ..._____

21. Does he ask you about other men in your past life? ...._____

22. Does he want to know where you've been when you've been

out? ....—

23. If you stay out late, does he insist on an explanation? .—

24. Does he believe husbands should make the important decisions? ....—

25. Does he think there are any circumstances in which it's okay for a man to hit a woman (for instance, if he finds "his woman" with another man)? ....—

26. Is he jealous of your friends or relatives? ....—

27. Does he think you're with another man if you're not home when he calls? ....—

28. Does he think you're going to "cheat" on him when you talk to a man or dance with an old friend? ....—

29. Does he think men should earn more than women? ...—

30. Does he especiallly want boy babies and associate fathering boys with masculinity? ....—

31. Does he think you have enough education, even though you want to go to school? ....—

32. Does he get angry if meals are late, or the food isn't just right? ....—

33. Does he have the traits that often "hook" you into involvements with abusive men? ....—

34. Does he take over when you're having trouble doing something, whether you want him to or not? ....—

35. When he's hurt, does he act angry instead? ....—

36. Does he silently sulk when angry? ....—

37. Does he drink or take drugs almost every day or go on periodic binges? ....—

38. Does he ridicule you for being stupid or for characteristics that are "typical of women"? ....—

39. Do you like yourself less than usual when you've been with him? ....—

40. Has he spent time in jail? ....—

42. Was he abused as a child? ....—

42. Does he sometimes put you on a pedestal, saying he doesn't deserve you? ....—

43. Are there some qualities you especially like about yourself that he disapproves of or ridicules? ....—

44. When you've acted independently, has he sometimes called you a "women's libber" or "dyke?" ....—

45. Has he been in fist fights or hit other women he's been involved with? ....—

If you have many "no" answers for the first 18 questions, if you haven't many answers to question 3 or you have many "yes" answers to questions 19 through 45, the man in question is likely to be abusive. Look especially at the answers indicating anger that comes easily and is expressed destructively, that is, he breaks things or sulks, rather than stating directly what has made him angry and asking that something be done about it. Be wary of a man who's jealous, doesn't want you to be well educated or to have many friends. Look out for a man who shows contempt for women or feels it's unmanly to express affection or admit vulnerability or hurt feelings. If you can't name the characteristics you love in him and you don't feel good about yourself when you're with him, be suspicious of yourself. Be especially suspicious if he has some of the traits that attracted you to other abusive men.

GIVING UP CONTROL

In the beginning of a relationship it may be difficult to spot the ways you give up control. It feels good to be with a new man and you think nothing could possibly go wrong. But listen carefully to the things you're careful not to say, comments that might break through illusions he has about you, point up a difference in opinion or risk having him think you're wrong or stupid. Count the times you're silent about your legitimate grievances because you're afraid of hurting his male ego. Notice the times you shrug and say, "Oh well," to yourself. For instance, "I disagree, but... oh, well, I guess it doesn't matter, so why say anything?" In the long run all those little things will become big things that do matter.

The first thing to go might be your opinions about politics or other subjects you think he knows more about than you. Next you become silent when he criticizes friends or family members. You don't tell him much about how you spend your time or money because you're afraid of his criticisms. Then you begin to "walk on eggs," waiting for him to be in a good mood before bringing up certain topics. He makes more and more of the decisions about the things that concern you both (whether to go out to dinner or stay "home" at your house) and becomes more decisive about the things that should concern only you ("You don't need to go to school, I like you just the way you are").

Perhaps each time he makes a decision about an aspect of your life, you interpret his action as wisdom, leadership, superior intellect, or an ability to rise above mere emotions. Like many women you've looked for a man who's smarter and more experienced than you to fulfill your romantic ideal. You then have an investment in maintaining that image of the man, and it becomes important for him. You confuse superiority — real or imagined — with control and being controlled with being taken care of.

From Control to Abuse

Control and abuse are closely intertwined, though physical violence is not always a part of the picture. Control, in itself, seems to be almost addictive for some men. The more they get, the more they need. Their self-concept is severely threatened when their women seem to be slipping out of their control. These men begin by making decisions about how to spend the couple's money; soon they decide what the woman should wear or how she should act. Since the scope of approved activities becomes very narrow, the occasions for doing the "wrong" thing and being punished by psychological or physical abuse become frequent. And that increases a feeling of helplessness and dependency, which in turn causes resignation to even more control.

PROTECTING YOURSELF

In order to avoid becoming involved with a man whose "protection" becomes control, develop your own ability to protect yourself and to control your own life. That means a whole range of activities — from moving furniture or understanding something about how your car works, to carrying out plans for a better-paying job and managing on however little money you have.

We all want to be taken care of to some extent, in some ways, at some times. If you're occasionally depressed, a good man will fix you some tea, rub your back and do the laundry (and you'll do the same for him). He'll take care of you *when you want it*, without taking advantage of those low times to increase your dependency on him. He won't try to make your decisions or take over your jobs when you've made it clear you want to stand on your own feet even when it's hard. If you have mixed feelings about maintaining your independence because you feel weak but want to practice being strong, your new man may be confused about how to act. Talk to him about your feelings (and about his probable ambivalence toward rescuing you). Either he'll have to be very sensitive to your attempts to be independent or you'll have to negotiate an agreement that he'll resist the impulse to take care of you unless you directly ask. You'll have to agree not to give him mixed messages by frequent hints for help or helpless sighs when you don't know what to do next.

When you do need help, it needn't always be from a man. You can find women who teach mechanics, repair plumbing, and who are willing to share their knowledge and skills. Each time you successfully struggle with something alone, or accomplish a "masculine" job together with other women, it strengthens your belief that you don't *have* to have a man but can choose one when you want to. That's part of your self-protection.

Establish Limits

Remembering that you can choose when you want to be with a man will help you to involve yourself slowly. Even if you want to spend every night with him, don't do it. Several evenings a week tell him you have other things to do. Practice enjoying a good book, doing some work around your home or sharing the company of women friends. If he insists on knowing what you do when you're not with him, or if he tells you he can't be parted from you even for a day or two, he's probably becoming addicted. If you give in early in the relationship you'll find it hard to exercise independence later. When you try, he'll probably feel threatened and in turn threaten you. You'll be right back where you started, but with a new man.

The beginning of the relationship is the best time to establish limits, although it's hard because you may want to please the man and be with him constantly. It's important to separate what you want from what he wants, even if at this point nothing seems to matter much but being with him. If one evening you feel like going to a movie and he wants to stay at your house to watch TV, you may be tempted not to mention the movie or immediately list the reasons why you'd rather stay home after all. *Don't do it.* Establish right now that you're a separate person with desires of your own, apart from his. That doesn't mean you shouldn't compromise. Just be sure you state your preference, and that you get what you want some of the time. This is even more important if he's paying for the date. If you think that gives him the right to make all the important decisions, you're setting the scene for a relationship in which you'll never have equal power.

If you feel you're losing control of decision-making, it's far better to go out less but pay your own way more. However, if he earns three times your salary, there's no reason you can't agree that he'll pay three quarters and you'll pay one, and each have an equal part in the decision making.

Don't take on wifely or motherly duties right away, either. It's fine to invite the man to dinner occasionally, but don't let him assume he can join you for a meal any time he drops in. When he does come for dinner, ask him to do the dishes or part of the cooking. The important thing is to keep some time and space and decision-making to yourself. Once you let him make certain assumptions about your availability and compliance, it will be difficult to establish your independence.

One of the ways women are sometimes seduced into destructive relationships is through the comforts a man with money can provide. When you're tired, discouraged and struggling to make ends meet on a welfare budget, late child support payment or meager paycheck, a generous man can be hard to resist. And when he pays, it's tempting to let him have his way, take you to the places he chooses, buy you clothes he likes to see you wear and pay for vacations that would never be your first choice. Or it's easy to go along with other things he wants of you, because he buys you gifts, helps with the rent or takes you to places you could never afford on your salary.

If you tolerate activities or statements you would normally challenge because you're afraid of losing the man and all those nice gifts and the outings you can't afford, you'll be putting yourself in a position for potential abuse. To change that situation renew efforts to earn more money by taking classes or making other long range plans. Work double shifts for a while, ask for a raise or find pleasures that aren't expensive. Women are nearly always underpaid, and this advice isn't easy to follow, but in the long run it pays off in better feelings and more control.

If you tend to let men do as they please as long as they pay your way, ask yourself what the money means to you. Is it important only for what it can buy, or is it tempting because you enjoy the feeling of being taken care of, of not being responsible? If the value is mainly in being taken care of, remind yourself that sooner or later the bill comes in and with an abusive man it's very high. You'll need to protect yourself by making friends who are interested in mutual caring and who don't exact a price.

What Do You Tell a New Man?

Another way to protect yourself from a controlling or abusive man is to keep your previous relationship with the abusive man to yourself. When you're with a new man, you may have the urge to pour out your life story, especially the terrible experience you had with the man who battered you. Resist the temptation. No matter what he says about it, no matter how hard he tries to convince himself otherwise, you take the chance that such an admission will reduce his respect for you, especially if you continued a relationship with a batterer for a long time. Even though you both agree it shouldn't have that effect, in the back of his mind the idea may lurk that you were abused once and you could be controlled and abused again. It may rise to the surface at a later time when he wants you to do something you don't want to do.

Even if you're in love, even if you're going to marry eventually, there's no rule that says you have to tell a man everything about other relationships. If he asks, you needn't make up a story, but can simply say, "It's past, and I'd rather not talk about it." If he persists in questioning you about past relationships, it may be a warning that he's unreasonably jealous and possessive. Later, when it's clear you've become an independent strong person who cares for herself, telling him will have a different effect.

Proceed Slowly

Perhaps you're beginning to see why I advise not being closely involved with a man during the first year of separation. It's much easier to struggle with the hundred pound sand bag if there's no one ready to toss it easily into the sandbox. It's easier not to cry too often if there's no handy shoulder to lean on. It's easier to make mistakes and learn from them when there's no one to relieve you of that responsibility. And it's much easier to learn to get along on a very slim paycheck if there's no one near to slip you a five dollar bill, buy you a television, take you out to dinner, pay the babysitter, buy your cigarettes. You can pay your own way if you have to, but if you don't have to, it's tempting to say, "Well, why *not* be dependent? Why *not* let him take care of me?"

Pay special attention to the difference between wanting a rest and wanting to retire. Even if it's satisfying to take care of yourself most of the time, there will be times when you're sick, feel tired, burdened, overwhelmed with responsibilities. These are the times when you should be especially careful. Along comes Mr. Right, he helps you make some important decisions, pays off one of your debts, and oh, it feels so good to lean on someone. You *like* being taken care of.

Don't confuse this momentary restful lull in your exhausting routine with a lifetime of being financially and emotionally dependent. If the man says he'll marry you and you can quit work and devote yourself to the children, does that mean he will want more children? Do you agree about that? Does it mean that when you're ready, you can go back to work without the least objection from him? Does it mean that when you want more independence he'll feel as good about you taking care of yourself as he does now about taking care of you? Don't just think about those questions, and don't just ask him. See how he reacts when you spend time with other people, when you do things for yourself, when you refuse financial help.

Give the relationship at least a year before you make a decision to move in together, or marry or have a child together. Not only does love blind people to the loved one's faults, those faults often temporarily disappear. When they're newly in love, stingy people suddenly feel generous; gloomy people become cheerful; rigid people flexible. A big part of the intoxication of love is the changes in one's self. One tends to believe the changes are permanent. The best way to tell whether they are is simply to wait a year.

If you live alone for a year, without complete involvement with another man, you'll begin to know yourself. If you don't like all that you come to know, you'll begin to change some things and as you become better company for yourself, you'll become better company for other women and men. You'll get pleasures out of being by yourself sometimes, as well as from being with friends and co-workers.

When you meet an attractive man, you'll say, "I'd like to be with him," rather than, "If he doesn't want me, I'll die." If the attractive man begins to take advantage of you, control or threaten you, you'll tell him immediately that you don't like it and won't put up with it. If he persists, you'll say good-bye and mean it. You'll be going ahead with your life, even if you'd like to be involved with a man, but if you can't find a man who's good for you, you'll make it just fine on your own.

Chapter 20

THE LONG HAUL

You're finally free. You've gotten safely through the crisis stage of leaving and reorganizing your life. You keep telling yourself you should feel great...and you wonder why you're depressed instead, and if the emptiness you feel will ever go away.

Believe it or not, there are some benefits to being in a continual state of crisis. There's always something that must be done immediately, and feelings of fear or rage can sometimes mobilize you into action. If you've had to make several moves, job-hunt, cope with the children, deal with your ex-partner and learn quickly how to survive on your own, you may not have had much time to feel depressed or lonely. But sometime after you've finally settled into a more stable routine — a week, a month or three months after you leave the man — you may begin to experience the hardest period of all.

LEARNING TO COPE WITH LONELINESS

Perhaps when you're lonely you become irritable, or keep to yourself, or are especially self-critical or find it difficult to sleep. Maybe you get a perverse pleasure from looking sloppy or having a cluttered house. Each person has a different way of coping with loneliness. If your individual ways are destructive and increase the problem, try behaving as if you're not lonely. Make a point of talking to one person a day in person or on the phone and make at least two plans for the weekend with other people.

If your lonely moods aren't immediately obvious to you, learn to recognize their early signs in order to control them before they get out of hand. Notice changes in your sleep, TV-watching, eating and drinking patterns. Increased consumption of food or alcohol or lack of appetite are likely signs of depression, which in turn may be a sign of loneliness. When you notice one of these patterns developing, substitute an opposite activity, or something that will give you the same satisfaction without the guilt. When you feel like an afternoon nap, go for a walk. When you want an extra piece of chocolate cake, treat yourself to a bubble bath.

Make a coping plan during a time when you're feeling on top of things. Write the plan out, so that when you first notice you're slipping into a lonely state you can put it into action.

Activity 35   Coping Plan for Loneliness

<u>"What I Do When I'm Lonely"</u>   <u>"What I Can Do"</u>

Snack all evening alone

Brew some special tea, start that long historical novel I've always wanted to read

_____

_____

_____

_____

_____

_____

_____

_____

_____

Loneliness may never completely leave you. It haunts nearly everyone occasionally, whether we're actually alone or not. So don't assume a love affair will necessarily banish the empty feeling. Remember, too, that even an excellent relationship can end with sickness, death or unexpected divorce, so your ability to create your own satisfactions and excitement is the best insurance against loneliness in the future. That same capacity for enriching your life as a single person can add to the quality of a new love relationship when the opportunity arises.

The satisfaction of having responsibility for your own life is also the anxiety of having to take care of yourself. It's a new experience, almost a new job, and it will feel frightening for a while, so allow yourself time to become used to it. The fears and loneliness won't go on forever, and in the meantime, you're learning how to cope with them. Here are some more ideas for getting through the hard times:

Find out what makes you feel up and down. Anything that makes you feel useless, lazy, helpless or out of control will contribute to your feeling low. Be especially alert to self-critical statements that accompany your low periods (see Activity 15).

Pay attention to how you feel after you talk on the phone or in person to your friends or family. If you feel sad when you hang up or leave them, ask yourself if that's the way you usually feel after talking to that person. If so, stop calling or seeing them. If it's someone you really must speak to regularly, keep the conversation short, and refuse to discuss things that make you feel sad, angry, guilty or lonely. Do something that lifts your spirits as soon as you hang up or are alone.

Notice if there are special times of the day or the week when you miss your man more than usual. Do something different at that time from what you did when you were with him. If he sat across the breakfast table from you every day for twenty-five years, have breakfast in a different room, or go out for coffee. Try to change the habits that are associated with being with him, so it isn't as noticeable that there's someone missing.

Be equally aware of what makes you feel good. If it's been a long time, you may have to experiment with new activities. Go to places where you feel comfortable or pleasantly excited. Get a radio, tape recorder or record player. Play music that cheers you and makes you feel energetic, not music that reflects your low mood. Never play love songs.

YOU MAKE YOUR OWN LIFE

You may go through a period in which you're not acutely miserable, but life has lost its savor. You ask what happened to the ecstacy that comes from intimacy, the trust and security that come from long-standing friendships and the stimulation of new experiences.

The short answer is, "It's where you make it happen." You have to make those friends, then risk letting the relationship deepen to a more intimate level; you have to work at overcoming difficulties, developing trust and allowing yourself to be vulnerable, until new friends become old friends. You have to look for new experiences, take the risks and find new rewards. You also have to know what you want from a lover, and see that you go where you're likely to find the right kind of person.

It's up to you, but you don't have to do it all by yourself. The right person, or better yet, the right group, can give you both support and courage.

Group for what? Courage for what? Possibly you don't know yet. The longer you've been involved with an abusive man or married or a mother, and the longer you've been out of the job market, the less certain you probably are about who you are and what you might enjoy. So this is a good time to find out. You're free to do what you want without the constraints of a man who easily feels threatened or who says everything you want to do is too independent, expensive, or silly. (I'm not forgetting the constraints of children and poverty for a single woman. They're important but can be worked around.)

Reactivate Your Dreams

Now is the time to rise above the sameness of your days and explore the risk of testing your abilities, the expansive feeling that comes from intellectual, physical, social, career, or psychological growth. Perhaps you've been taught that while everyone, of course, wants all that, it's just adolescent nonsense to expect it. Maybe you believe mature people settle down to a dull life and make do with what they have.

It may, indeed, be impractical to recapture and act upon your girlhood dreams. This may not be the time to go (with or without the children) off to Hollywood to become a star. But don't count it, or anything, out until you've come up with some good reasons why you can't or don't want to do it. If you really "always wanted to act," don't go to your grave saying that regretfully. Get out and join a little theatre group, or take acting lessons at a community college.

Acting is just one example. It could be mountainclimbing, skiing, learning archeology, dress designing, studying medicine, sailing, painting, coin collecting, car racing, horse grooming, landscape gardening, hair dressing, hiking, nursing, joining an encounter group, camping, "swinging," singing, teaching, being a mathematician, taking up ballet, upholstering furniture, sky diving, gourmet cooking, car repairing, interior decorating, skating, biking, whitewater canoeing, visiting different churches, getting into politics, joining a rap group or joining the neighborhood campaign for good government.

The list can be endless when you let your imagination play. But you may have trouble getting started, so think back to the things you wanted to be, do or have when you were young. Turn back to Chapter 2 and look at your answers to Activity 1. *Make a new list*, using ideas from your previous answers and your own memory. *Underline* all the items you might like to try if there were no obstacles in the way. *Put* a $ sign after each one that requires money, a T after each that takes more time than you seem to have, a C for each that's difficult because of childcare responsibilities. *Put* an A after each that requires more ability than you think you have (brains, beauty, personality, strength, etc.), O for any you think you're too old to begin and P for those you might do if you lived in a different place.

Activity 36   *Recapturing Your Dreams*

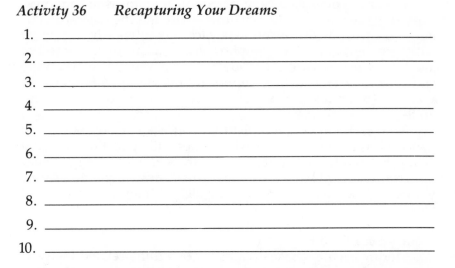

1. _____
2. _____
3. _____
4. _____
5. _____
6. _____
7. _____
8. _____
9. _____
10. _____

If age or ability or place are major factors holding you back, chances are you can overcome those barriers with enough determination. Lack of time and money are likely to be more difficult to contend with. But before you give up, estimate how much time, money or other items you lack. How much of it do you need? Be as specific as possible. Decide what you're willing to sacrifice in the short run for long-run satisfactions. How much money would you need to go to school, how many years would it take to develop a particular ability? If you don't know the answers, call an employment or educational counselor, community college Women's Center, travel agent or whoever might give you specific information. You may want to review Chapter 17, for ideas about how to solve money problems.

Abilities Can Be Acquired

If a specific ability is the big thing you think you lack, it's probably a skill that you can acquire with practice and some instruction. Some people do have what seems like a natural gift for certain achievements, but often we don't know what our "natural" talents are until we try them out for awhile. Have you ever admired a craft done by an amateur, read a story that was not great literature but that pleased you? Have you watched the thrill of a child when a blob of clay resembles — even slightly — an animal? If you'll let yourself, you can recapture that childlike pleasure. It's not the great product or prize at the end of the rainbow that's the thrill, it's the process of getting there. You can feel yourself growing as you learn new skills, whether your small steps are visible to anyone else or not.

If you're going to escape boredom, loneliness and depression, you have to take some chances — though the risks won't be nearly as great as those you took each day of your involvement with a violent man. More importantly, you can be in control of just how much risk you're ready to take at any particular time, and you can arrange to have supportive people and other rewards available to comfort you when you feel scared or don't measure up to your own standards.

Take each item on your list that you wish you'd done when you were younger, and note which ones still appeal to you. That is, if you could have it happen magically — if, with a snap of your fingers, you could have the brains, talent, beauty, youth, or time to make those dreams come true, which of them would you still want?

Modify Your Dreams

Modify each of those dreams to something related that you can easily do now. If you always wanted to be an opera star, you can still take singing lessons, or sing alone with a record. If you wanted to build houses or cabinets, you can scrounge some scrap lumber and make a doll house for the kids or put together a bookcase for yourself. If you wish you'd studied architecture, you might enroll in a community college drafting course or start reading books about architecture from the public library. If you'd like to be a world traveler, but lack time and money, find out where you can see travel films, send for maps of places you'd like to go, and start planning and saving. Meanwhile explore the parks, museums, and neighborhoods in your own city. If you "would have been an artist except that you lack talent," take some drawing courses, or try pottery, jewelry-making, or macrame. Don't assume you lack talent until you've worked hard to develop a skill.

WHAT CAN YOU DO NOW?

List all the things you'd like to do that take only a little energy, time, money or skill. *Add* activities that will develop skills related to the "talents" you wish you had. *Mark* two of them to begin this week. If there are others that appeal to you, but would take elaborate planning or a good deal of money, don't discard the ideas. Later you can make a long-range plan to encompass them.

Activity 37   Start Now List

1. _____

2. _____

3. _____

4. _____

5. _____

6. _____

7. _____

8. _____

9. _____

10. _____

Never mind, for now, which you're most interested in. Choose the one you can start tomorrow. The sooner, the better. If you find you're stalling, saying you don't want it enough, do it anyway. Act as if you're eager to devote the time or money to it. Get started. Make the telephone call, gather the materials, check out a book from the library — but get going. Right now it's not so important what you do, as that you do something.

Whatever you've chosen will probably be hard work at first, but as you see yourself developing you'll discover new activities and interests can be very exciting and rewarding. You'll then be on your way to creating your own life's excitement.

From time to time it may be difficult to find energy for new activities. Read Chapter 11, "A Courageous Act A Day" as often as necessary. As soon as possible get involved with other people — through classes, clubs or special interest groups — who have similar interests. There's an excitement that comes from talking with others about shared work, paid or unpaid, that can be as stimulating and intimate as a love affair.

I speak of "work" where others speak of recreation or hobbies, because to gain the most satisfaction you should treat the activities you do like a job. Devote yourself to them regularly, take them seriously and try to improve your skill. This doesn't mean you can't do many things lightly as well. But if you haven't been able to find paid employment that valuable and absorbing, you need to develop another activity that's important to you.

Most of us live narrow lives, without taking advantage of opportunities to learn or to be stimulated. Check your newspapers from coming events. Note how many you're not interested in and ask yourself how many of them you've never actually tried and know almost nothing about. List those you might experiment with and try one new thing at least once a month.

When you do take up a new sport, hobby or "work," don't

stop until you've given yourself a chance to practice it quite a bit. Then if you're satisfied you're not going to like it, try something new. Even if you take up something different every couple of months, it will be valuable to find out what you don't like. It's one way of getting to know yourself better and learning to appreciate your own individual tastes. When you meet lots of people and have new experiences, you'll be too busy growing, learning and changing to be bored or depressed.

Remind yourself it will take time to build a new life and that whether you're feeling good or not, you can tough it out. Even with ups and downs, in the long run you'll have a much better life than the one you left. In the next and final chapter you'll get some ideas about how other women adapted to their new lives.

SECTION V

The Ones Who Got Away

Chapter 21

THE ONES WHO GOT AWAY

Why do they leave and why do they stay away?

Very little is known about what enables women to develop the strength to leave an abusive man and to create a life that is satisfying. Theoretically, women who leave and stay away should have the opposite characteristics of those who continue the relationship. We ought to be able to say about a woman who left a man after years of battering, "She reduced her economic dependency by getting a job," or, "She stopped feeling emotionally dependent on him..." "She stopped loving him... felt better about herself... changed her ideas about traditional values and the role of the father as head of the household..." But it isn't necessarily so. Many women leave *in spite of* continuing feelings of emotional dependency and love, and in spite of poverty, isolation and traditional values.

In order to get first-hand descriptions of what it's like to break away from a violent man, to stay away, and to discover a new way of life as a single person, I asked nine women to tell me their stories. They answered my questions about their feelings and relationships before, during and after their involvements with the men.

Most of this chapter is about their lives as single women, but in order that you may know something of what they endured in the abusive relationships, I'm including very abbreviated versions of their life stories. In some cases I have used initials, in some fictional names and slightly altered facts, and in some real names, according to each woman's preference.

LIFE WITH THE BATTERER

Jan

Jan was married at seventeen, right after high school graduation, and has worked and attended school for most of her married life. Her husband, Ron, was often unemployed and floundering in his career as a salesperson. Jan, at twenty-four, is an exceptionally assertive person, and has been as long as she can remember. No one would have called her dependent at the time of her marriage, yet now she has questions about that. "I would say I was not dependent. Yet I felt the only way I could get out of that situation (living with her mother and a violent stepfather) was to marry someone. I didn't think I could get out by myself. I was feeling real scared, even though everyone said, 'Oh, Jan, she's such a strong person'."

Jan, in fact, was the dominant person in the relationship with her husband. She was the worker, the planner, the organizer. Unlike many abused women, she was neither socially isolated nor economically dependent. She was convinced that she could overcome the marital difficulties by "persistently loving Ron and talking to Ron." "He didn't hit me all that often, at most, six times a year. Sometimes, he might go five or six months, so that gave me hope. I was very much afraid of his outbursts, his uncontrollable anger."

Jan left him several times, once for nine months, after which he didn't hit her for two years. But when it happened again, she left him for good. She has made a very satisfying single life for herself.

Sandi

Sandi says of herself, "I was so introverted in junior and senior high school that no one ever talked to me, only Ernie." He fathered her twin sons who appeared on the scene shortly after her eighteenth birthday. But that relationship didn't last long. Bringing up mixed race children alone was not easy and when Merle came into her life, she was glad to have some help, to be "rescued," in fact. She had been dating him only a short time the first time he hit her. "I opened the door and his arm came at me, he just smashed my whole body to the floor and broke my nose." After a couple of other hits, Sandi retreated to her parents, who sent her to Tucson to stay with an aunt. She was so lonely there that she called Merle, who brought her back to Seattle. Periodically, she called on him to rescue her, but she always paid a price in physical or emotional abuse.

Merle never hit her during the times she lived with him, but he found other ways of abusing her. Sandi, who was on welfare, was expected to pay all the household bills, even though Merle had well-paying jobs with the city. He refused to admit that the twins needed food or clothing so that she had to sneak these basic necessities to her children.

The second time Sandi went to a shelter was final. She has now been away from Merle for over two years and is discovering exciting things about herself in community college classes.

Patricia

Patricia met Tim when she was in a foster home at the age of fourteen. "Tim came in saying, 'I'll be your mama, I'll be your daddy, I'll be your world'." And I never had one, and I took it. I felt like I knew him and we were of the same cut or something. In the beginning we had fun together and we were two wild ones, let me tell you, he could keep my pace. He's still the same. I grew up.

"I was with him for six years, from the time I was fifteen and he was seventeen." During these years Patricia attended high school and worked as a prostitute. "The worst I was beaten was when I was first out on the street. He broke my nose, broke out a couple of teeth, broke my tail bone. After a while people at school knew what was going on, but they didn't say anything."

After several miscarriages, Patricia gave birth to a baby girl. "As the kid got a little older it got to be mind abuse as well as physical abuse, but Tim's physical abuse would be only every three or four days instead of every day, the way it had been."

Finally, Patricia left for the last time three years ago, putting several hundred miles between them. She now lives with a man who is "the opposite of Tim," and she's planning to learn drafting at a community college.

E.S.

E.S. was a twenty-three-year old radio technician student in her native Philipine Islands when she began a correspondence with the man she was to marry. He was an acquaintance of her cousin, and had been living in the United States for some years.

After a year of exchanging letters and pictures, Pete went to the Philipines to ask E.S. to marry him. She was almost twenty-five, and having turned down four marriage offers, was becoming concerned about whether she would ever marry. In addition, she had fallen in love with Pete's picture. Almost before she knew it, she was married to this fifty-three-year old farmer and was embarked on a new life in the United States.

Their life in the States was one of constant hard work in the fields, and E.S. supplemented their farm income by working as a hotel maid. She also cared for their daughter who was born two years later and a son three years after that.

From the beginning, Pete lied to her, denying, for instance, the existence of his ex-wife and five children, pretending his oldest daughter was his sister, even after E.S. had met them. Insisting that E.S. sit in the cold in the car waiting for hours while he visited that other family was one of the first of many humiliations she suffered. The humiliation was worse than the physical abuse.

Four months ago, after thirteen years of marriage, she left

Pete. She was no longer able to persuade herself it was God's will. E.S. has already passed her G.E.D. test and is starting electronics school through a CETA program.

Virginia

Virginia had an adventurous life before she became involved with Bob. In the sixties she left Seattle to work in the Civil Rights struggle in the South. Later, her company transferred her from Seattle to Anchorage. In those days, before the pipe line boom, there were few black people there, which perhaps exacerbated the loneliness she had felt. Nevertheless, she did have some friends, and it was through them that she met Bob, who was gentle, kind and romantic.

After they were married he continued to display those traits at times, while at others he was morose and uncommunicative. His was a "Jekyll-and-Hyde" pattern common to many abusive men.

Virginia was twenty-five when she married this thirty-five-year old father of four boys. Immediately after the marriage, she became an instant mother to three of his children and maid to the household of males. Although she felt used and demeaned by Bob from the start, the physical violence didn't begin until they had been married several years and the boys had returned to their mother.

It took Virginia three years to regain the confidence she had lost during the first five years of her relationship with Bob, and to gather the courage once again to strike out on her own. She has now been divorced for three years and is a student, with plans to be a counselor or teacher.

Marilyn

Marilyn, now in her early thirties, loves a good time. Married at nineteen, she was "true blue" for the duration of that six-year marriage. But once out of it, she devoted a good deal of her non-work and nonparenting time to partying. Monty, whom she met during the first year after the divorce, became a part of that life. He was "sneaky" from the start, and the relationship was volatile, but not violent.

Only when Marilyn said she wanted to break off the relationship did Monty become physically abusive. He had said, "Once you tell me that you're going to be mine, I'm never lettin' you go," and to her sorrow, she later realized that he had been serious. He followed her, harassed her, and threatened both her and each new man she began an involvement with. The reign of terror culminated in his forcing her car off the street with his car, and threatening her with a gun. Neighbors intervened.

Marilyn took him to court and now feels relatively safe as a result of the "no contact" order she obtained. She has begun a new relationship with a man she enjoys being with, but she worries that he too is destructive to her. For the first time in her life she is beginning to think about making real choices about her life.

Corrine

Corrine says she cried at her wedding. "I felt I'd betrayed myself and realized I didn't like Marty enough. I was wretched, but my mother and sister encouraged me to go through with it anyway."

During the first year of marriage she became pregnant, she and Marty "fought and fought" and there was "emotional upheaval all the time." Although Marty hit her "in fun" during the first few months of their involvement, it wasn't until the fourth year of their marriage that he struck out in anger. Her injuries during the next seven years included small cuts from broken glass, a black eye, bruises and a broken nose. Perhaps even harder to take, he was involved with four women in a period of four years.

Although Corrine acquired a bachelors degree and a teaching credential, she "couldn't imagine taking care of the kids" — two girls, now nine and ten — "without a partner, having to do everything myself."

Corrine, at thirty-five, is divorced, has lost custody of one of her children, and has not spoken to Marty for well over a year except on essential business. She has an unsatisfying relationship with another man, has not been able to find a teaching job and is still undecided about whether she wants to be an artist or a social service worker. Nevertheless she has no questions about her decision to break up the marriage.

Shirley

Shirley grew up in the south and is still very much a traditional Southern woman in some ways. At forty-five, she has been a suburban housewife and mother of two for twenty-five years.

Shirley speaks of emotional abuse and sexual humiliation as the intolerable aspects of life with Clarence, her engineer husband. Only when questioned specifically about it does she say off-handedly that yes, he was physically abusive too. One of the things he did to her was to push her down the stairs when she was pregnant.

He criticized her cooking, her housekeeping and everything about her. He was so rude to everyone that they had no friends.

Over the years, Shirley became convinced that she was incompetent to do anything, so that now, six months after leaving him, she worries about whether she'll even be able to rake the leaves adequately.

Shirley had several strokes, which she attributed to the stress of living with Clarence's abuse, yet even long hospitalizations didn't worry her enough to propel her out of the marriage. But when Clarence put their thirteen-year-old daughter out of the house, Shirley finally gained the strength to separate from him. After six months she is slowly learning to regain her ability to handle everyday tasks, her health has vastly improved and she's considering taking up the nursing school classes that she dropped twenty-five years ago.

Valerie

Valerie, at sixty-four, has also had a struggle learning to take care of herself, after forty-two years of being alternately protected and slapped around by an alcoholic man whom she fell in love with at twenty.

Valerie still admires Jim's mind, his ability to understand international politics and remember the information he absorbs from his reading. For forty-two years he was her window to world affairs. But almost every weekend he was drunk, and periodically she would become the victim of his violence.

Two years ago she left him for good, and she now enjoys handling her own money, meeting new people and learning new things. Although she is partially disabled from a youthful bout with polio and a later stroke and heart attack, she is managing a fairly independent life in a senior citizens' apartment building. She would take Jim back in a split second if he would stop drinking, but she doesn't believe he will.

THE UNEXPECTED

In earlier chapters I noted what you might expect to experience right after leaving your man and at various periods during the first year or so. Those experiences are common to many women.

You'll find, though, that you can't predict quite how you'll feel or what you'll do. Each woman's experience is both the same and different from others'. Below are some of the surprises that these particular women have experienced after leaving violent men.

Although Shirley often feels sad and lonely since leaving her twenty-five-year marriage six months ago, that's not the whole story. She says, "My health is surprisingly good since Clarence left. And I sleep so well. I thought at first something must be wrong with me, because I can go to sleep at night. And my daughter said to me that I ought to be sorry. My whole family has broken up, so why am I so happy?"

Now, after eight months of total distance from Monty, Marilyn says, "I never thought I'd feel so good about being on my own and sometimes I really feel great about it. It surprises me that there are times when I can't even imagine being involved in a relationship with a man."

Patricia was surprised to find that leaving Tim didn't solve all of her problems. "There were things I blamed totally on him 'cause he was messin' with me so much. I think a lot of women will do that. They think the grand person who they are, inside, will just bloom once they get out. Everything will be just fine. But no, I still have a lot to change. Like, I drag ass. I have to be inspired to do something. I always thought it was him holding me back from doing the things I wanted to. It's just me. I don't push myself when I should. For a while I was in a stage where I thought, 'He did it to me!' Now I realize it's up to me to change it."

Virginia had a similar rude awakening when she finally got away, after six years. "I thought I would be happy and I wasn't. I thought I would be independent and self-confident and have high self-esteem and really enjoy life. But I didn't. I thought it was the marriage that made me depressed. I thought the anxiety was around the boys and Bob, but I'm still (three years later) quite anxious. I thought marriage would just solve everything and it didn't. And then I thought divorce would solve everything and it didn't. It was sort of a low blow to my ego that I had a couple of problems too. I'm working on them, but I still have them."

Corrine also found a number of unexpected difficulties. The most profound disappointment was that one of her daughters chose to remain with Corrine's ex-husband. "I never considered that either girl would leave me. It was a great shock." In addition, Corrine at first felt "anger and shame about public assistance, social workers' investigations, the legal system and the divorce trial," and there were continuing problems in finding or choosing stimulating relevant work and being always poor or broke and worried about money and the kids.

Nevertheless, when Corrine was asked what things have been easier than expected about being a single woman her emphatic answer was, "I've had no regrets about leaving." She was also surprised that some very immediate fears of retaliation from her ex-husband didn't happen after all. "He hasn't hunted me down yet. Apparently, he's respected the authority of the restraining order, and after coming to my house three times, has taken seriously my threat to call the police."

Jan thought she'd never be able to manage rugged backpacking trips again, since she and Ron had always done them together. "A few weeks later I met Mary (who also was used to taking such trips with a battering man whom she'd just left) and I realized I could do it without him. I realized I did have the skills and those I didn't have I could learn. And I could make up for muscles with the right kind of equipment."

Jan had other pleasant surprises during the first few weeks after leaving Ron. "At first I thought I'd be lonely. That lasted just a couple of weeks, though. I started taking all those classes. I took six different class, a different one every night: "What to do when your husband or wife walks out," "Intimacy," "Wilderness camping," ...then after I was away for about a month I started liking living by myself. I didn't expect that to happen. I think I thought I'd just keep myself busy until I went back to Ron."

Jan had been pessimistic about her future. "I was damned sure last fall (one year ago) that I was never going to be happy again — not until I got back to Ron. I did not expect to do all this growing this year."

THE GOOD OUTWEIGHS THE BAD

As you can see, it's not all unreasonable for you to fear being lonely, poor, depressed or otherwise unhappy after you leave that violent man. Almost no one says it's a bed of roses, and nearly all admit to having bad times at first, with some continuing for quite a long time. But, on balance, all say the bad times are worth it, because the rewards of the new life are more lasting or more important than the painful times.

Shirley: "I'm about as lonely (after six months) as I was when Clarence was here. But I think it's worse when there's somebody in the house with you and you're still lonely, and you know it shouldn't be this way, but it is."

Virginia: "I like myself better, with all my flaws. I used to hate myself. I hated myself for being there. For believing all that crap. At least now I'm not worrying about, 'Oh, why am I doing this.'"

Patricia: "I had a lot of fear (before I went into court over custody). I guess what you'd say is my soul is washed of him. I don't carry around that fear anymore."

GETTING THROUGH THE STRESSFUL DAYS

One of the things that all these women have learned is that even though some bad times must simply be endured, there are ways to cope with the stressful and dreary days so they're less painful or don't last so long. The methods of coping exhibit some striking similarities, as well as a high degree of individual imagination.

Loneliness, especially on weekends, nights and holidays, is a pervasive problem for many women during the first year that they're not part of a couple.

Patricia: "Weekend nights would be the hardest. I'd see couples going out and stuff. I'd just grab up my kid and go to a girl friend's house who had kids and me and my girl friend would let the kids play and sleep while we had a good time. If I was at home I'd try to find little things to distract me. I'd try to be real good with the kid, so I wouldn't feel guilty when I put her to bed. And then I'd write big plans about what I wanted to do."

Shirley: "I cannot go into Fred Meyers on weekends when it is such a husband-and-wife store. We used to go there on weekends and buy tulip bulbs and grass seed or whatever. I don't want to go there on weekends 'cause it will make me feel bad. All those couples... and they probably go home and fight like cats and dogs!"

Virginia: "Holidays and weekends were hard. I didn't stay home, but spent them with friends. I lived with a friend who was divorced and we helped each other. She was really supportive to me."

Sandi: "I can con myself into being in a good mood. I can recite what things are good about me and what I really want to be and I like that. I don't depend on somebody else."

Valerie: "I was a little bit depressed but I found Barry, a good friend. He took me under his wing and we became fast friends. I think he's filled in the gap of being lonely."

"I've got to have somebody and I'm still fighting that, but I'm getting better. Now I can stay home two nights a week — maybe three — by myself, instead of running to Barry. I'm also going to the library and reading books which I never did before."

Marilyn: "At first just being alone was real hard to accept. I can't really remember when it stopped being hard."

Jan: "I had a real hard time last Christmas. I didn't send out any Christmas cards last year. I didn't know how to sign my name — Jan? Ron? Thanksgiving I volunteered to work and in the evening I went to Donna's house for a nonfamily Thanksgiving. It was fun but it just wasn't Thanksgiving. I had always spent it with Ron's folks."

Corrine: "I've done volunteer work, made new friends, I write letters to old friends, write in my journal, swim, walk, read, paint, take courses, job hunt."

HELP COMES FROM UNEXPECTED SOURCES

In the relative isolation of an abusive relationship, it's hard to imagine that you won't be alone if you separate from the man. Yet, help comes through agencies, shelters, and friends and relatives, sometimes unexpectedly.

Patricia: "My girl friend from Utah moved here. Hot mama, one and two! That's just somebody who knows everything about me! We're like teenagers sometimes. Somebody said we're like primates picking out fleas, and we are. We give each other that kind of attention. She's the only one I'll do without for. She sat in court with me every day for eight hours."

The group leader at the shelter was helpful to Patricia too. "I asked myself how flowery was she going to be. I was suspicious of social workers in general. And then here she was, cussing and confronting people and I thought *this* woman's for *real.* She's not going to feed me a line. So when she told me something I trusted it."

"The shelter was real helpful. They would come up with things I never dreamed of, and when somebody is that willing to help, you get real enthused about helping yourself. For a long time I only socialized with people at the shelter. I didn't want to go 'out there' yet."

Shirley (separated for six months) doesn't yet socialize much and found it hard to tell the few neighbors she talks to that she was getting a divorce, but it finally came out. And after twenty-five years of being told she couldn't even rake the leaves right, she gains solace and encouragement from seeing how these other women manage. "Marion is very nice.. She comes over and helps prune away a dead bush. She's very capable because her husband doesn't do a darned thing so she's had to learn all these things. Sandra raised four kids by herself and I guess she had to learn absolutely from scratch. Her husband was one who had done everything before. It can be done, I guess."

Particular women at a shelter had a positive impact on Sandi. "Every time I left, I intended to stay away forever. I think the only reason I did the last time was because of the people at the shelter. I was saying to these people 'How could you go back? And they were saying, How could *you* go back?' I was saying to Vera, 'God, someone did that to you and you still care about him?' She got mad; she said, 'Look at *you*. Who do you think you are to tell me that when you do exactly the same thing?' And she was right. But not just anybody who hadn't been hit could say that to me and get away with it."

"Joan never talked much, but she had a real impact, being around someone who's been in that situation for twelve years and got battered for twelve years. It's easy to do it little by little but when you see somebody who's done it for that long it's easier to say, 'I'm not going to do it for twelve years. One more is going to make three'."

Valerie finds solace in the friendship and help of a man. "Barry's eighty-six years old; he's a big-hearted fellow willing to do anything. We all need a man to fix this or fix that and he does it for every woman in this building. We have a nice friendship going and that fills the void of talking to a man. I've got to have... no, 'got to' is the wrong word, but it's *nice* to have a man to talk to."

E.S.: "I got lots of friends. If I need help they can help me. They're giving me more support. All the old friends we had, they didn't change."

"I call the telephone counselors at the Abused Women's Network and I just talk and talk; it makes me feel good, not hurt anymore."

The Second Phase group (for women who have determined to stay away from abusive men) at the Abused Women's Network was helpful to Marilyn. "It's all a learning process about myself and if I screw up at all, I can't go in there and lie, can't cover up. I feel that when I do, I'm not fooling anyone."

ADVICE TO WOMEN IN
ABUSIVE RELATIONSHIPS

For the most part, these women admit to bouts of depression and loneliness ranging from moderate to great. Some are beset with illnesses that have limited their activities, have chronically incapacitated them or are life-threatening. Nearly all are continually beleaguered by money problems. Yet, none regret the decision to leave, and when asked for their advice to women who are involved with abusive men, their responses are almost identical.

Shirley: "Can this marriage be saved? I have one word: 'no.' It's not going to get better. It will only get worse and you'll get older."

Virginia: "Get out quickly. The longer you stay in it's just more defense for the opposition to say, 'You can't make it.' And you begin to believe that, and it *is* tough. But you only get out by doing something for yourself. That's the hard part, getting out by yourself. Going to a shelter is a big step — that phone call."

Sandi: "Go to the shelter. Be around people who are in the same situation. It helps to be around people who are also debating or in the process of leaving and saying 'Yep, we did have good times. When things were good they were *great*, but when they were bad they were *awful*'."

Valerie: "I say to a young girl or even one twenty years married, 'Get out of it while you're still young enough to start again, even to finding another man and starting another marriage. Get out before you're too old and sick.' I'm not that old, but I'm too old to start again in a marriage."

E.S.: "Think it over. Think of your future. If he's doing that all the time you can do something, say something, get a divorce."

Marilyn: "Get out. I feel very strongly after what I've been through, that the situation is not going to change. It might be all right for a while. It's the exception that battering stops."

Corrine: "You might as well leave now as later. My situation did not improve. But then I left when I was psychologically ready and I have had no regrets and no temptation to return."

HINDSIGHT

Corrine's philosophical aceptance of her need to leave when the time was right typifies many women. It may even help some women to leave if they can accept their past decisions as inevitable and to accept or forgive themselves for staying with the man. Those who can't forgive themselves may feel they must stay and stay until they can turn the frog into a prince.

I asked, "What would you change if you could live your life over again?"

Patricia: "I would have stayed with the foster family and gone to school. I wouldn't have gotten involved with Tim if I'd stayed there. And even if I had, I would have left the first time he ever laid a hand on me."

Shirley: "I think I would have left in 1956 instead of now. I would not have left nursing school, but I suppose better late than never is the only thing I can say now."

Virginia: "I would have had counseling before we got married. I would have had him bring his boys up *before* we got married, instead of becoming instant wife, mother and maid. I think I should have left in the first week."

Sandi: "It all formed me, who I am now and I really like myself more than I did. So whatever it took, it was good. I don't think if I hadn't of went through that relationship, I would have had the strength to be who I am now. I wouldn't have had the drive."

Valerie: "If I had my life to live over again, I'd be a more educated person. I used to read any kind of cheap novels. Now my mind is changing to the point that what I'm trying to do is increase my knowledge, which I never felt like before."

Marilyn: "I guess if I had never even fraternized or gone back at all, it would have been easier. But I think every time I did, I learned something. And because I did, I have no regrets. I mean I know how terrible it can be. I don't have any question marks in my mind as to maybe if I'd stayed, it might have been wonderful and maybe he'd of really straightened out. All those questions are answered for me. I *know* what it would be like."

Patricia: "I wish there was some way I could have known how to get from point A to point B without going through all the shit I've gone through. But there's no way I could have known, and I had to go through all that. I would have filed for divorce the day after I left Tim for the last time if I had known what I know now. But there was no way I could have known that and if someone had told me that, I would have told them they were downright wrong."

ADVICE TO YOU IF YOU'RE
THINKING OF GOING BACK

In spite of the seeming complacency of some of those answers, these women want you, who are separated from abusive men, to consider carefully the temptation to go back.

Virginia: "Think about the worst thing that has happened to you. It will probably happen again. Think about how you didn't like yourself when you were there. Think that it's a hell of an environment for kids to stay in, watching their mom being kicked around."

Shirley: "Think about how you're going to pay for what you've done while you were gone: the money you've spent, the embarrassment you caused your husband. And no magic is going to occur, unfortunately."

Patricia: "Do whatever you can to keep yourself busy, and hang in until you can build yourself a new life. Socialize a lot with women who are trying to get out of it too. If you haven't got that, the best thing to do is to pack up and move many miles away, so it takes a couple of days to get back, 'cause he may call. And your heart will go flutter, flutter and you might want to dash right over there, but wait a couple of days before you go back. After the emotion passes, your head will take over."

Some other things that might help you endure staying away and the feelings that sometimes overwhelm you:

Patricia: "When I first got away from him I enjoyed it every day 'cause I'd get up in the morning and I'd say, 'Today I can change my life and there's nothing he can do about it'.

"I make a list every week, still, and some of the things hang over from week to week, so then I ask myself, 'Why is it so hard to do?' And then when I think about it, I see what was hard and it's not so hard after all. And I just go do it. And if it *still* looks hard, I make sure I get up in the morning and go do it, just get it over with."

Shirley: "I'm not sure I'm ready for church yet. I think I would cry when I heard the songs. But if I keep hiding behind this, 'I'm not ready for it,' I will never get out from behind the kitchen table. That is something I'm going to have to do. Take a chance and do it."

Sandi: "Every time I felt like I needed him I would think about a certain situation and getting hit and how I felt, and then I got into those feelings and then I didn't want to go back.

"I knew that even if he went into counseling and changed I would still feel the same. I would always be afraid.

"It was really hard for me to start being less introverted. School helped a lot. The immediate reinforcement of school helped. That 'A', that '85' on a paper that kept telling me I was okay, the accomplishment of being in a man's field, finding out it's nothing."

Valerie: "I've made a lot of my own friends, I'm going to church every Sunday which I didn't do before, and going to pot-lucks and meeting people. I go swimming and to Bible study and when I wake up and get out of bed I look forward to my exercise class, and I am glad to get up."

E.S.: "Before, I don't know what to do. I don't know whether I can make it or not, if I and my children have a future or not. Now as long as I can get my training and get a job that makes me secure."

Jan: "At first I thought I was deserting Ron when he needed my help, really not believing that leaving him was the best thing I could do for him. It took probably about six months for me to believe that. I realized I had to work things out for myself and then I realized, 'Oh, yeah! It's the same thing for Ron'.

"Now I have other people who are closer to me than my family, and because of that, this holiday season is not going to be as difficult. I've redefined family, I guess.

"During the first four months after I left Ron I used the drop-in group at the Abused Women's Network. I also used my mother as an example. I told myself, 'I'm not going to live with a jerk for twenty years like my mother's been doing'."

Corrine: "I wish I'd told all his relatives exactly what had happened instead of being discreet. I think they believed his stories that I was emotionally feeble and unstable, a lousy mother and having an affair. I think you should tell *everyone* about him. Visit with friends, go to groups, get counseling for yourself and your kids, do enjoyable things with your kids. Get the best lawyer you can find, don't listen to the man, don't visit him, don't call him and don't let your kids talk to him."

LIFE IS BETTER NOW

In spite of loneliness, poverty and depression, these women who have stayed away from violent former partners — whether for several years or a few months — are unanimous in their assessments that life is far better now.

Corrine: "I *love* my independence. I'm relieved and *glad* to be away from him. I consider it an accomplishment that *finally* after so many years I *did* leave. No more arguing, scapegoating and blaming in front of the kids. I don't have to listen any more and I don't. Life, even including the routines (which I don't have too many of), is more of an adventure, a challenge, and more rewarding."

Jan: I miss the intimacy of just being held — and yet... I just realized... I can get those needs met right now with my friends Betty, Nan and Doris.

"Another thing I like is getting off work and getting a yen to go to the park to feed the ducks, not having to make a phone call to say, 'I'm going to be a couple of hours later tonight,' not to get permission, but just to let him know. And being able to do with my money what I want.

"Now I know what's important to me, and I do what's important to me. A trip is more important than a house, reading a book is a higher priority than washing dishes, going canoeing is more important than vacuuming."

Marilyn: "The best part of being away is being free, not having anybody criticizing me or telling me what to do. When I'm out and it's late I don't have to call anybody to make up an excuse about where I am.

"At work I can concentrate, because I'm not in crisis all the time.

"I think I'm in the process of probably making major decisions which I've never done. I never made decisions about what I'm going to do with my life. I'm wondering about that now and I'm very slowly looking into possibilities. I'm asking for what I want. I never felt like I could do that before."

E.S.: "When you come home you're not scared. I have lots of things I can accomplish. Before if I'm talking on the phone, I'm laughing and if he's here he says, 'What!? Are you laughing like a kid?!' Before I could not even say what I want, express what I want. I'm always in fear before.

"Now I like to go to school. I'm free. Even if I'm poor, I'm happy. I can feel happiness inside now."

Valerie: "I'm getting away from that loneliness. I can talk to anyone. When he took care of the money, I didn't have that responsibility; I didn't think I wanted it. But now that I've got it, I know a little bit about how good it can feel to have your own and do as you please. I use my money for a little entertainment and trips. I'm going to get along on what money I have and not depend on a man to take care of me."

Sandi: "I wake up in the morning and maybe I'm depressed for about a half an hour and then I say, 'Wow, you know you got to get up and do things or *of course* you're going to be depressed and it's going to be a boring day.' So, I get up and have a good day, usually."

"I'm twenty-four but I never had a chance to be a kid. Now I go to school and I think a lot. This creative writing class is making me get into my head and making me express things I never could express before. I really want to be able to do that, tell people how I feel. I've never taken a class before that I was really wanting to put everything into. I want people to understand me. Before it's always been, 'I'll understand you, I'll listen to you,' and now I want to take turns and I really want to know what to say when it's my turn.

"Being mostly without a man for almost two years is really lonely sometimes and it's real depressing sometimes, but I don't think I could have developed who I am with somebody around, or it might have taken real long and I'm in a space where I really appreciate me. I can believe that I can make decisions on my own, I can raise my kids on my own. And you know? Everything I have is more than anybody else I know has, and they all have men!

"And they all look to me for advice. They think I know it all. I don't know *anything*, to me. That's really good for people to respect me, and I like that a lot. It's independence in a way. I can deal with my kids without sayin, 'Wait till your father comes home'."

Virginia: "The best thing is my privacy. Before, the boys were always there, or he was always there, I couldn't say, 'Hey! I want to have Sunday to myself'. I would say it but I never got it. And I really treasured my privacy. I like not worrying about so many people — four boys and a man and their games and their schedules — and I don't know, somehow there wasn't time for my schedule, my problems. I had so many mother-type shoulds, ball game shoulds, PTA shoulds, and wives' club shoulds, the things you're supposed to do if you're married or a wife or a mother.

"I'm planning to get a four-year degree and to be a counselor or teach teenagers to work with victimized women. On the good days I like myself."

Shirley: "I watch TV, I go to see my counselor twice a week, I go to Safeway a lot, you know, maybe to just buy one thing, and I go to the post office box twice a day. I'm going to be in the phone book in my own name next year, isn't that nice?

"I don't think much past Christmas right now. That's better than it was before, when I didn't think past next week. Things are better for me now because at least there's hope. Before I left Clarence, it was a hopeless situation. It could only get worse."

Patricia: "I'm living with a man who is totally the opposite of what I had before. It's give and take now. I've learned that. I live a normal life now. I have a normal relationship. I guess that's what I was always looking for, that was the void. I never had those normal things through childhood. I kept on feeling that loneliness. I put all that dependency on him, instead of learning how to give and take with another person. That's one of the best things.

"I feel like I fit in the world. I'm not being kept in the basement."

None of these women found it easy to get away, or stay away or to make a new life. Many of them still don't find it easy. But none of them regret leaving. Several refrains stand out:

I'm learning...

I like myself...

I feel free...

Their message is that you can learn new ways, you can like yourself, and you can get free.

SECTION VI

NEW DIRECTIONS

Chapter 22

TEEN ABUSE

If you're a teenaged woman or her parent, this chapter is written for you, though women beyond the teen years who are abused in dating relationships may find it of use as well. It focuses primarily on sexual, physical and emotional abuse of single, childless teenagers by their boyfriends. It doesn't assume that if you're a teenager you aren't married or don't have a child, but if that's your situation, you'll probably find most of the other chapters of *Getting Free* just as pertinent to your life as they are to those of older women's. This chapter gives information about battering in teenage dating relationships and points out the other parts of *Getting Free* that may be most helpful to read. If you're the parent of a teenaged woman who's abused, you can use this book to understand your daughter's situation. (You may also want to give her a copy.) The last part of this chapter is addressed specifically to you.

If you're a teenager you may experience all of the fears and hardships of older women in abusive relationships, but there are additional problems as well. In your struggle to free yourself from your parents' control, you may find yourself confused by feelings related to your relationship with a controlling man. It's difficult for most women to talk about being abused, and as a teenager you may have even more reasons to hesitate. For instance, you might worry that if you confide in your doctor, minister or teacher, they will tell your parents, and then you'll have to face their hurt, anger or punishment. Your parents may refuse to let you continue seeing the man you're involved with before you come to that decision on your own.

If you're the parent of a teenager, you may experience all the fear you would have for an older friend or relative in a dangerous relationship, as well as special concerns because of the relative lack of experience and vulnerablity of your daughter. This may be combined with rage that you can't control her as you "should" be able to and jealousy of the man who does control her. In addition you may be asking yourself what is wrong with the way you raised your daughter and why she pays no attention to your entreaties to leave the dangerous man. If you're the mother of an abused teenager and have been abused yourself, you may feel special responsibility, even if you left the abusive man in your life some time ago. This chapter offers suggestions on how to help a teenager identify abuse, how to support her and how to cope with your own feelings.

HOW COMMON IS TEENAGE BATTERING?

The information that battering is widespread among all kinds of married and co-habiting couples began to come out in the mid-1970s, but almost nothing was known about teenage or date battering until the early 1980s. Even now, about all we know for sure is that many teenagers, like adults, are subjected to physical abuse in their intimate relationships. Maria Roy found, in interviews with 4,000 adult women who had been battered, that many began the relationships as adolescents.† Surveys of high school students' couple violence are few and the responses give us a wide range of figures. One study of fifteen- to nineteen-year-olds found that seventeen percent of the women and eight percent of the men admitted to experiencing some type of physical violence with a dating partner. In over three quarters of the cases the violence began after the couple became seriously involved, but most of the couples were only fifteen the first time it happened. For about a quarter of the students violence began in casual dating relationships, and almost sixty percent of them had the courage to end the relationships.‡ Another study found that thirty-five percent of high school students reported various levels of violence in their relationships. Although some students admitted to extremely dangerous acts, most of them spoke of pushing, shoving, slapping and threatening. There were no reported differences among races or social classes.*

It should not surprise us that violence between high school students is common. Violence between brothers and sisters, more than other kinds of family violence, has often been viewed as inevitable, normal and acceptable. One study found that sixteen percent of children aged three to seventeen beat up their sisters and brothers.** If you've been fighting for years with your brother,

---

† Maria Roy, ed., *The Battered Woman* (New York: Van Nostrand Reinhold Co, 1977).
‡ Mildred Pagelow, *Family Violence,* (New York: Praeger, 1984), p. 292, citing a study by Henton et al.
* Karen Susan Brockopp, et al, *A Descriptive Study Surveying the Frequency and Severity of Intra-Couple Dating Violence at the High School Level,* unpublished Ph.D. thesis.
** Pagelow, op. cit., p. 68, citing Murray Straus, Richard Gelles and Suzanne Steinmetz, *Behind Closed Doors.*

it might not seem too different to fight with your boyfriend. If an older brother has beaten you up periodically, it might not be shocking to be beaten by a boyfriend. If you're in that situation, think carefully about whether you want to go on living with fear and violence or whether you'd rather start a new pattern.

Among college students surveyed, some of whom were teenagers, about half had been victims of sex aggression during a single academic year. That is, the man attempted to make the woman become sexual in a way that was unacceptable to her, and she resisted. Of those attempts, forty percent succeeded.† Legally, many of these acts would be defined as rape, although the women might not realize it. Only two percent of them reported these offenses to police or parents or other authorities.‡

Other surveys indicate that between twenty-one and sixty-eight percent of college students have been violent to intimate partners or dates.* Some women who were hit before marriage say the main cause was their boyfriends' unfounded jealousy and refusal to allow the women to be independent.** Many of them hoped that once they were married or living together, the man would feel secure and stop the violence. Unfortunately, marriage is often viewed as a license to increase the violence.

HOW TO TELL IF YOU'RE ABUSED

Sometimes it's harder for a teenager than an adult to tell whether she's being abused. Teens are more likely, for instance, to engage in horseplay and teasing that sometimes can turn into physical or emotional abuse. You might be playfully wrestling with your boyfriend when he gets the upper hand, twists your arm behind your back and refuses to let you go until you are hurt or feel humiliated or until you grant him a favor. Later he says it was "just play" and that you shouldn't make an issue of it. He might tease you by throwing you into a swimming pool or taking your purse and showing people the private things in it. You feel scared or furious at being forced into an embarrassing or powerless position, but you laugh to show you're a good sport. Your boyfriend insists it's just fun, and you try to persuade yourself you agree.

Cars offer some young men important ways to display power. Some of them speed or drive recklessly in order to scare and intimidate their girlfriends or to impress them with their courage

† Pagelow op. cit., p. 292, citing Parcell and Kanin.
‡ Pagelow, ibid.
* Pagelow, op. cit., p. 293, citing works by Laner and by Makepeace.
** Pagelow, op. cit., p. 286, citing Dobash and Dobash and a study by Bowker.

or driving skills. If you feel frightened or intimidated or helpless when your boyfriend is showing off, you have a right to insist he stop the car and to get out whenever you want to. There is a wide range of abuse, from "joking" remarks about women, to tickling, to forced sex, to threatening with weapons and using them to maim or kill. (See pp. xxv to xxx in "Who The Book Is For," for examples.)

Emotional abuse can be particularly confusing (see Chapter 24), especially when it is in the guise of friendly playing around. Teasing is one example. You may be expected to be a good sport when your boyfriend makes "jokes" about things you've done or said that you're embarrassed about, or when he makes demeaning remarks about your body, your feelings, your friends or women in general. He might brag about other women he's interested in or who are chasing him. If you feel embarrassed, hurt, humiliated or inadequate as a result of his comments, you're being emotionally abused.

If you think he can't help being that way because he doesn't understand how it affects you, it's your job to explain it to him. Find a time when you can be alone with him, and explain what bothers you without laughing, apologizing or flirting, so that he knows you're serious. If he still doesn't understand or tries to tell you you're wrong, too sensitive or have no sense of humor, you have a right to tell him you don't want him to do that regardless of whether he understands or agrees with you. If he persists, it's a message that he doesn't care enough about how you feel or that he deliberately teases you to make you feel bad about yourself. In either case he is exercising power and control over you, and your self-esteem is in grave danger of being gradually chipped away so that it will get harder and harder to state how you feel or what you want.

WHO'S RESPONSIBLE FOR THE VIOLENCE?

Hitting is always potentially dangerous, because it tends to bring on more violence, and then more, until finally someone may do serious injury to the person he or she cares most about. Even if it's not immediately dangerous, violence is an indication that one person is either out of control or is using a display of anger to control the other person. Either of those situations will turn a potentially good relationship into a battle zone filled with fear and hostility.

Having said that, let's look at what kind of hitting we're talking about. Setting aside the probability of escalation, some hits are worse than others. When men hit women it usually has much more force and is a greater threat than when a woman hits her boyfriend. For instance, if you hit your boyfriend, it may be a punch on the arm or pummeling him on the chest. If he is three to ten inches taller, thirty to a hundred pounds heavier and in good physical shape, it may feel to him like playfulness, and not at all threatening. He might not even bother protecting himself. Yet, eventually, if he gets angry, he may hit you with his fist, which is likely to hurt and scare you, and begin a process of his controlling you. Then he might blame you, because after all you started it.

It's true that you started it, and you should take responsibility for what you did, but that doesn't mean you're responsible for what he did. Only he can start or stop his violence, just as only you can start or stop yours. It might be that you've hurt him with a weapon or your fist, in which case you should take your problem seriously and get professional help to work on it. If it happens when you're taking drugs or drinking alcohol, you should consider that a problem, too, and get help to stop.

There is some indication that teenaged women tend to think violence has a bad effect on their relationships, whether they are hit or the ones who do the hitting. Teenaged men, whether they're the abusers or the abused, tend to believe violent acts have a positive effect on the relationship or no impact at all.†

If you agree with other young women that violence has a bad effect, you'll probably be able to control your anger as you mature. But your boyfriend may not even try, since he may feel it's not important or even a good thing to do. This might be a reason women become less violent and men more violent to their partners as they grow older.

The pattern may also change because of marriage or childbirth. There is a tendency for more violence to take place in marriages that occur when the couple is very young. Women who are pregnant are also at high risk of being beaten by their husbands or boyfriends. Few teenaged men or women are skilled enough to acquire well-paying jobs, and the lack of money, sudden responsibility and insecurity about living up to adult roles can all add stress to a teenaged couple's lives. The stress is not the cause of the violence, but it can provide an excuse for the man who is willing to control by violence, and can mislead the woman who's being abused into believing her partner can't help what he does.

WHAT TO DO IF YOU'RE HIT

If your boyfriend has slapped, pushed or threatened you, it's important to take it seriously, whether you've been injured or not. It means he's willing to use physical force to control you, and there's a good chance it will get worse unless you make it

† Brockopp, op. cit.

absolutely clear you won't allow it. You have to do more than just complain. If you're not ready to break up, which would be the safest thing, you can still say you won't see him until he comes up with a plan to control his anger. A plan is different from a promise, and even good intentions are not enough. If his anger is so close to the surface that he has hit you even once, he will need help in learning to control it.

If your boyfriend wants to continue seeing you, insist that he go to an anger management class or a counselor or make particular changes that will enable him to stop the violence. If he has hit you only when he's drinking, you might tell him you'll agree to continue seeing him only if he stops drinking entirely and attends a program like Alcoholics Anonymous. You may think you don't have the right to decide he has a drinking (or drug) problem, but if he hits when he drinks, the drinking and the hitting are both causing you to suffer and you have a right to protect yourself. He will probably be angry at you for "telling him what to do." You can agree with him that it's up to him what he does, and add that it's up to you to decide whether you're going to continue seeing him. That is, you will or won't see him depending on whether you'll be safe with the decision he makes. If he says he only drinks or is violent when he's terribly unhappy or when his father beats him or because he lost his job, you can let him know that not everyone reacts to those troubles by hitting the person they love. Let him know that regardless of his reasons, which are really excuses, you're going to take responsibility for staying safe.

Right after your boyfriend has mistreated you, you might be tempted to tell him he has to do certain things or you'll never see him again. That's a good idea if you're absolutely sure you mean it. But if there's any possibility you'll change your mind when he brings you flowers, turns his irresistible "little boy" look on you or when you get lonely, don't do it. You could tell him you're getting to the end of your rope and that if he does it again, there's a chance you'll walk out on him. An advantage to saying what you *might* do is that when the time comes to act you won't feel guilty about not warning him. Every time you make a threat and then don't carry it out, he gets the message that you don't mean what you say and he doesn't have to take anything you say seriously. Wait until you are sure you can carry out what you say. Then it isn't a threat, but the announcement of a plan.

ENDING THE RELATIONSHIP

Sometimes it's hard to leave a boyfriend who takes you to exciting or expensive places and buys you gifts, especially if you have very little money yourself. If that's one of your problems, try to keep two things in mind. First, there are lots of other men out there who would probably do the same for you and would treat you in a loving way. You may not notice them, however, until you stop focusing on the man who's abusing you. Secondly, if it's important to you to own good things and to go exciting places this is a good time to plan the job training or education that will enable you to buy yourself luxuries. Then you'll be secure knowing that if you're involved with a man it's because of who he is, not what he can buy you.

Some teenaged women (and older ones too) are reluctant to end a sexual relationship, because they're afraid they can never have another without being considered "loose" or a "slut." If you do separate, perhaps you'll want to take some time before you get involved with a second man, so you're sure you know your feelings and that they're directed to someone who deserves them. You might decide not to become sexually involved again unless you're married. On the other hand you might decide you have the right to express your sexual feelings in whatever way seems right to you and your partner. The main thing is that you can take this opportunity to think through your own values and decide whether you're going to make yourself stay in this relationship as a life sentence for a mistake, or whether you're willing to give yourself a second chance at finding a loving sexual partner.

There are many other aspects of teenaged life that make it especially hard to cope with an abusive boyfriend, and it may take some time to find a counselor or to persuade your parents to understand your situation. But keep trying. Most importantly, try to find some trusted friends, whether teenaged or adult, whom you can talk to about your situation. If you keep talking and keep analyzing the relationship, you'll soon be able to decide what's the best decision for you.

HOW TO USE *GETTING FREE*

A relationship with a violent boyfriend is physically dangerous, yet when you're intimately involved with a steady boyfriend, the thought of breaking up with him can seem like an even bigger risk emotionally. *Getting Free* is designed to help you weigh the pros and cons of the relationship, to decide what's best for you and make the most of the consequences. If you leafed through the rest of the book you might have seen references to parenting and long-term marriages and thought they didn't apply to you. But *Getting Free* is designed to fit the needs of all abused women, regardless of age or circumstances. For instance, most of Chapter 1 and Chapters 4 through 7 are just as pertinent to you as to an older women who's more established in family life. They will help you understand the social aspects of battering, your rights and your feelings of love, and give you suggestions on how to decide whether to leave the man or continue the relationship.

You may think that because an example in an activity doesn't precisely apply to you, the exercise itself won't help you. For instance, on page 56 I suggest that the worst fear a woman has about leaving her man might be losing the house and garden she's tended for twenty-two years. If you're seventeen years old you may think that has nothing to do with you. But instead of skipping the activity think of what your biggest fear is. Maybe it's being without a date for the senior prom, or being treated like a "loser" by your friends, or having to admit that your parents were right, or just being lonely all the time. All of those, and any other fears you have, are important. The thing is, you can overcome them by using the activities in the book to help you recognize them, analyze whether they're likely to happen, and think through the ways you can make things go well. At the same time, if the worst can't be avoided, you can plan how to cope with it.

Some of the activities emphasize long term relationships and decisions about children, because those are often the most complex situations and therefore the hardest to change. But it's also true that some young people's situations are especially hard to handle. If you're still in school and financially dependent on your parents, you have fewer choices than many adults. In addition, you have fewer recognized rights. The social pressure may be more intense than in adult communities and there's a tremendous emphasis on love and romance. Perhaps, like many teenagers you're socially isolated or have lots of acquaintances but few people you can tell about your fears and dreams. So don't underestimate the difficulties you face in making changes.

Many women take on family feelings and values as soon as they become seriously involved with a man. You might feel loyalty and concern for your boyfriend, place his needs before your own, and sometimes even feel about him that he needs to be nurtured like a child. If those feelings seem like signs of being grown up and having adult responsibilities, you might be paralyzed by feelings of guilt and failure when you think of leaving him. It might feel as if you're abandoning a family member; many men who batter, even very young men, know how to play on those feelings. So even if you're unmarried and have no children, Chapters 2 and 3, which focus on family issues, can help you get a balanced perspective.

Section 2, *Getting Professional Help,* applies to you as a single teenager or young woman, with the possible exception of the chapter on "Making Legal Decisions." Each state has different laws for adults and juveniles, so you'll have to get local information about how the law applies to you. You might also need information on how your local courts are likely to deal with your boyfriend, especially if he's a teenager. A justice system that is harsh on adult men who batter may not take the violence of a teenager seriously.

All professionals are obliged by federal law to report abuse of children under eighteen to police or child protection agencies, though this is sometimes interpreted broadly in various communities. Medical personnel, counselors, shelters and safehomes may refuse to help you without your parents' permission. It doesn't mean they don't care, but that they would be breaking the law if they did. To avoid these situations some teenagers who can't get help from their families feel forced to make up a name or lie about their age. Try to get information about what to expect in your community before you are in a crisis by calling a battered women's shelter, a teen runaway center or a crisis line. It's easy to be anonymous over the phone; when you feel that you can trust the people, you can arrange to see them in person.

Parts of Chapters 14 through 17 are more relevant to adult couples who have established households together or who share children than to single, childless teenagers. In addition to the restrictions on shelters and safe homes already mentioned in most states, you won't be eligible for public assistance unless you have a child, so the sections about shelters and welfare grants may not be of immediate use to you. But other parts of those chapters can be important for you to read and act upon. Activities 23 through 26, which include lists of dangerous things your boyfriend has done to you and a "Best Memories" list, can be extremely helpful in keeping you safe, no matter what your age or situation. Check the table of contents to see which sections you want to read.

The rest of the book, which includes the chapters on "Helping Yourself To Survival," "After You Leave," and "The Ones Who Got Away," will apply as much to you as to adults. You may also want to read the parts of the book that are about long term marriages and child custody problems, so that you can see what might be in store for you if you decide to break up this relationship in ten or twenty years after you've had several children. I hope the book will enable you to get free now, while you have many options for the future.

WHAT CAN A PARENT DO?

Few things are more painful than to watch one's children make dangerous choices. If your daughter is involved with a violent man you certainly will be right to consider it a serious situation. There is usually no way to predict whether a man will confine himself to moderate or infrequent violence or whether he is going to do permanent damage or even kill. In addition to physical injury, the emotional damage is often severe. So what can a parent do that will at least not make matters worse?

As with all teenage-parent conflicts, it makes a crucial difference what kind of relationship exists. The age of the teenager is also important. Some advocates of "tough-love" might advise telling your daughter not to come home until she has severed her relationship with the man. Although in certain cases this might work, there isn't any guarantee; by the time you know the results it may be too late to change your mind. Abandoning or rejecting your child is the most dangerous thing you can do. The man she is involved with is likely to perceive you as a threat already and to try to cut off contact between you and your daughter. If you send her away, you will play right into his hands and take away the very support your daughter needs to eventually break away.

You may be under a great deal more stress than you can easily handle if you patiently stand by or intermittently rescue your daughter when she has been beaten up, and there comes a time when you must take care of yourself. You may need, from time to time, to limit your involvement with your daughter. If you find yourself too angry or too depressed or too critical to be of support to her, try to enlist another family member or friend to stand by and explain to your child in the most loving way you can that you need a temporary separation. Make it clear that you care about her and want her to be safe because you love her, but that your feeling of helplessness, fear or anger make it impossible for you to be with her and help. Let her know you will be back with her as soon as possible, and be sure she has the names of others she can call on.

If you can, listen to your daughter, let her talk about the man and swallow your outrage when she tells you how handsome or loving or needy he is. Think of all the ridiculous things you did as an adolescent and an adult, even if many of them weren't life threatening. Try to understand that she can love her boyfriend at the same time as she hates him, and that you may only see her when she is in pain or feeling enraged because of what her man has done to her. If you won't listen to the positive aspects of the relationship, she will be even more embarrassed than she already is to talk honestly to you. Nor will there be any likelihood she will listen to your advice. The more she is silent, the more it plays into the isolation which will help the man abuse her.

When you do have an opportunity to spend time with her, try to arrange some of it alone together and some of it joining valued friends or relatives. The more time she spends with people who have been important to her, the better the opportunity to remember she can be liked and loved without being abused. Give her an opportunity to do things that help her feel adequate, whether it's making cookies or playing tennis. The man is, no doubt, regularly assaulting her self-esteem, so it's important for you to take the opportunity not to criticize, but to compliment.

You will be fortunate if you can do those things. Some of you may have lost contact with your daughter because her man has taken her away, and demanded she not be in touch with you. If she's a juvenile, calling the police is an option, and it's a better one if her boyfriend is an adult who can be charged with kidnapping or statutory rape. The law in each state varies, so get reliable information about what the likely results will be before you act. Your decision will require weighing legal possibilities as well as how your daughter is likely to react. If the police find her, don't be surprised if she refuses to go with them. There may be nothing you can do if she continually runs away to the man. If that seems likely, you may want to quietly find out where she is, and then carefully arrange brief contacts. As long as you are in touch with her you can remind her someone besides her boyfriend cares about her and will nurture her if she decides to leave. As ludicrous as it may seem, she probably feels that he is the only one who loves her, so that message must be countered at every opportunity.

There will be a time when it's appropriate to put all your energy into rescuing your child, and you may feel you have to go on doing that, even if it's to no avail or counterproductive. Resist the temptation to continue when it seems to be harmful to her or you. Go about your usual activities and also be sure to be in touch with people you can rely on for support. If you and your partner disagree about what should be done, don't let it put a wedge in your relationship; it's a time when you most need each other and when your daughter needs you to be in the best possible condition. Talk to a third party and try to come to a compromise or at least understanding and respect for each other's positions.

If your son is the violent person, do everything possible to get him into an anger management class or at least to a counselor, and be sure to let the young woman know you understand he is in the wrong and that she should not stay with a dangerous man, even if he is your son.

Above all, don't let anger overwhelm you. You may feel like doing violence to the man or even to your daughter, but that is the path that I hope we are all trying to change. To paraphrase the prayer, work at developing the courage to change what you can, the patience to accept what you can't, and the wisdom to know the difference.

Chapter 23

LESBIAN ABUSE

In the years since *Getting Free* was first published it has become all too clear that violence is a serious and widespread problem among lesbians. If you are a lesbian who's been battered you may have been one of the many who were reluctant to have that disturbing news come out of the closet. You might now be among those who feel strongly that open discussion is essential, so that you and other lesbians who are battered can gain the support and practical aid you need. It is a sad irony that so many lesbians worked alongside heterosexuals to establish shelters and safe homes and a national movement against battering, but virtually no services are available for lesbians who are battered and only a handful of articles have been published about the subject. The National Coalition Against Domestic Violence has recognized that disparity and doubled its commitment to work against homophobia within the battered women's movement and to promote services for lesbians.†

On local levels both the movement against battering and lesbian communities need to take the problem seriously, working together where they can for mutual education and cooperative services, so that lesbian victims can be assured of safe havens and supportive assistance. The women who need help will be reached as a result of lesbian communities conducting widespread educational campaigns to the effect that the community is concerned, the community wants to help, and that the victim is not to blame. Services also need to be made available for lesbians who batter and who are determined to change the way they relate to partners.

THE QUESTION OF WHO IS BATTERING

You might find yourself confused over whether you or your partner is "the batterer." Perhaps you have struck back at your partner in self-defense a few times, or maybe you're being battered

† A step in that direction is the lesbian battering anthology initiated by the coalition: Kerry Lobel, *Naming the Violence: Speaking Out About Lesbian Battering,* (Seattle: Seal Press, forthcoming 1986).

now, but in your last relationship you were the violent one. Possibly you're still carrying that guilt and the identity of "the batterer," which is not accurate in this relationship. It may even be that you and your partner hit each other with about the same amount of force and frequency. In addition, if you are both emotionally abusive, the picture can become bewildering, especially if your lives and feelings have become so merged that you're sometimes not sure where your personal boundaries are.

There is controversy in the movement over whether "mutual battering" exists. Some workers insist that only one person is the "batterer" and that she is always in control of her partner, even though sometimes it may look like "mutual battering" at first. I am among those who believe that pattern is just one among several, that some women who are fairly evenly matched fight each other with about equal force and regularity, as well as that couples go through a period in which one abuses and batters the other, and then the second one gets the upper hand and abuses and batters the first one. Or a woman may batter and control a partner who never even strikes back and may rarely resist, yet in her next relationship she is the one who is abused, and who doesn't retaliate. I make these judgments on the basis of what women have told me, whereas others have said they distrust the reports of women who are in the midst of these relationships, especially those who have battered.

How To Identify Abuse

Until we have more knowledge about these issues, there are several things that can be kept in mind to help you clarify what's happening to you. Ask yourself if you've been physically threatened or hit by your partner. If the answer is yes, you're physically abused. Are you free to be with friends, dress, cook and speak as you please, or take courses or do work that you like, without fearing punishment from your partner? If not, then you're being controlled by her, which is the core of abuse. Using the brainwashing and "crazy-making" criteria in chapter 24 as a checklist, ask yourself if you've been emotionally abused by your partner. If you're being physically, sexually or emotionally abused, you need some time away from your partner, primarily to be safe. Secondarily, you need time alone and with good friends to regain a clear perspective on what has happened to you.

Here is another set of questions for you: Have I hit, emotionally abused or tried to control and punish my partner? Have I, for instance, insisted she dress, cook, speak, keep house, make love, drive and otherwise behave in just the way I think is right? If the answers are yes, you are the only one who can stop it, and you will need to get away from her in order not to hurt her, while you learn the skills of anger management and relating intimately without the need to control.

If either one of you hit the other in self-defense, but it was severe enough to injure one of you or cause either of you to be afraid, that behavior is harmful enough to warrant methods of preventing it in the future. If it was with more force than necessary or even if it was just the amount necessary for defense, there is a serious problem to be dealt with.

THE NATURE OF LESBIAN BATTERING

Some people believe battering between lesbians tends to be "mild." It's possible this attitude exemplifies a need to deny or minimize the existence of violence among lesbians. Perhaps it reflects the fact that many counselors and group leaders have heard about lesbians throwing things, pushing and shoving, with no evidence of serious injuries. Or that politically sophisticated lesbians, feminists and workers in the movement against battering tend to be appalled and frightened at even a small amount of violence in their lives. They realize it is likely to escalate and, like other women, tend to seek help from counselors at an early point in their relationship problems. Even if these speculations are correct, it is also true that there are many dangerously violent lesbians. We know that at least some lesbians who batter defend their actions as necessary and are unwilling to change. Possibly the most dangerous women won't admit to their battering practices until they're confronted by the justice system. We will know more about them when large numbers of lesbians take the risk of calling the police, when police and prosecutors take lesbian battering seriously, and when lesbians who batter are court-ordered to groups.

There has been little research in the lesbian community about battering, but we can expect more in the next few years, some of which will be designed to determine its extent and severity. If we discover that the level of lesbian violence is as great as violence by heterosexual men, what will that mean to our theories that a major reason men batter is that simply by virtue of being men they have implied or explicit permission to be violent? That they can get away with it because they have superior resources and weaker ties to children? The short answer is that we simply don't know.

One study attempted to find out if lesbians who battered had resources that were superior to their partners', but there was no significant correlation. There may be an imbalance of resources that weren't considered. Perhaps one important resource that gives power is simply the willingness to use physical force. Since most women are not trained to react physically, if a woman chooses that method of combat, her partner may become quickly intimidated and start a pattern of giving in, not to superior power, but to the violent woman's willingness to use it.

When lesbian battering began to be publicly acknowledged, there was speculation that it was the "butches" who battered the "femmes," but it now seems quite evident from informal observation by counselors and others that this is not a widespread or typical pattern. In many couples where there is battering, "butch-femme" roles aren't played at all. When they are present, it's sometimes the "femme" who does the battering.

Responsibility For Battering

Some things we do know. Whether the battering is alternately done by you and your partner, whether you fight with equal strength at the same time or whether you or your partner is in physical and psychological control, the person who abuses another is the person responsible for it. Only she can stop it. The abused woman is not to blame for what happens to her. If you are abused, you probably will have to leave your partner to break the pattern, and she will have to do some very hard work over a long period of time to change her pattern of violence and control. Meanwhile you will have to get some help in rebuilding your sense of self-worth and your social network. You probably will not be able to continue the relationship in a way that is safe and in which each of you has equal power. Where there is a chance of that, you will need some help from a third party after you've done your individual work, to negotiate and keep a new style of relationship.

HOW TO USE *GETTING FREE*

When *Getting Free* was first published I discussed with the editors whether we should include information about lesbian battering. After careful thought we agreed that anything I could have said about it would have been based on little knowledge and a great deal of guesswork, so we made the choice not to try to speak specifically to the needs of lesbians. I did hope, as I mentioned in the original introduction, that much of the book would be useful to lesbians and gay men who were beaten by lovers. Many readers have told us it was true. They used their well-practiced skills in "translating" heterosexual reading matter into language appropriate to their sexual orientation, discarding what didn't fit.

Except for the first chapter of *Getting Free*, which is about traditional male and female roles and marriages, most of the material applies with language modifications to lesbians as well as heterosexuals, though there are certain sections that will have special ramifications for you, as a lesbian. To know what you can expect of police and prosecutors, for instance, you will have to make inquiries about the current practices and attitudes toward lesbians in your own community, and they may be changing rapidly. The same is true for child custody problems, though in general we know that a nonbirth-giving lesbian partner is likely to have few, if any, custodial rights to children. However, the law differs from state to state and is subject to wide variations in interpretation from one location to another, dependent upon the prevailing or most vocal community values and the biases of individual judges.

Because issues of confidentiality affect all aspects of lesbian life, you will have to use your imagination in applying some sections of the book, especially if you're in the closet. This may be especially true of the chapters on "Ending Isolation" and "Reaching Out." In addition, the sections about self-esteem, such as the chapter on "How To Be Your Own Counselor," should be read in the context of how your life and self-esteem has been affected by homophobic societal abuse of you as a lesbian by representatives of many institutions. Careful attention should be paid, as well, to self-criticisms that stem from internalized homophobia reflected from that hostile "real world." Because much of the world is homophobic and ready to verbally abuse you just because your sexual orientation is not the same as theirs, it is doubly important that you not collude with them by abusing yourself.

EMERGENCY SERVICES

If you need emergency housing your choices in almost all cities will be limited. In rural communities individual families may provide "safe homes," for a few days, but there is no guarantee they will have any understanding of lesbian issues. If you are fleeing for your life, you may not care about their attitudes for the first twenty-four hours, but when you're in crisis it will not improve your state of mind to be the guest of homophobic individuals. So try to develop an emergency plan before you need it, that enables you to be with accepting, nurturing people.

If you decide to go to a shelter, you'll need to find out whether the staff are conservative about things like sexual orientation or are open to housing a lesbian. You might find an empathic lesbian working there, or other staff and administrators who are committed to serving all women and who provide an atmosphere of acceptance. In some shelters there are open-minded staff members, but they may be prohibited by an administrator or board of directors from even discussing lesbian issues, nor will staff attitudes tell you much about how you'll be accepted by the other women. Some lesbians who are battered have pretended they were involved with a man, and found welcome sanctuary in shelters, but the deception has certainly taken a toll.

You're probably hoping you ever won't need emergency housing, but if you have ever had reason even momentarily to consider it, that's an indication you might need it in the future. So if you're not in crisis now, this is the time to gather information. You'll have more time to collect it and you'll be in a better emotional state to absorb and evaluate it.

ENDING ISOLATION

In many communities it is difficult for lesbians who are battered to break through the isolation that was typical of all battered women ten years ago. But it can be done. If you're out of the closet and a part of the lesbian community you will know what agencies are available to assist lesbians with various issues, and you might know which are going to be appropriately concerned about your safety. If you're not sure, and you want to preserve your privacy, make a few discreet inquiries, of the "I have this friend..." variety, or by telephone. The response will give you an idea of the agency stance regarding battered lesbians. If it seems positive, ask whether there's a group, housing or individual counseling available, and whether the women providing it are experienced in issues of violence as well as lesbian concerns. You might ask about the broad goals of their program. What role do they think they or the lesbian community in general should play in stopping battering? Who do they think is responsible for battering? Where do they stand on involvement of the justice system in lesbian battering? If the agency doesn't have a clear stand that the person who batters is responsible for it, and if they aren't open to discussing the pros and cons involving police and courts, or if their attitudes toward battering are significantly different from yours, look for help elsewhere.

Confidentiality

Confidentiality is likely to be a special issue for you, and certainly you have a right to keep your situation private, though there may also be some reasons not to. But if it is your choice not to have anyone in the community know who is battering you, or even that it is happening, ask agency representatives about their record keeping and who has access to the files. Don't accept blanket reassurances, but ask to speak to the director or the person who understands how the system works in order to get detailed information. Where are the files kept? How detailed are they? Who has access to them? How will you gain access to them if you want to read them? If you plan to go to a group or counseling session, find out if there is a community center atmosphere in which many people may see you come and go. If so, you may encounter acquaintances who will ask innocent, but disturbing, questions. If you're not clever at deflecting questions like "What are you here for?" you might be better off seeking help somewhere else.

Counseling Services

Once you're satisfied that your confidentiality will be maintained or have decided it isn't an issue, then you need to find out which available service suits your needs. If there is no special program for women who have been battered, you might still get some help. You may want to join a general support or therapy group, in which you can discuss your relationship. Talk to the leader about what you want and find out whether she is empathic to your situation and whether her support will continue no matter what decisions you make. Ask her to think about whether the members of the group will be understanding, rather than impatient with you for not living up to their images of what a woman, a feminist or lesbian should be. You might ask her to explain your situation and needs to the group, or to give you time to do it yourself, postponing commitment until you know what their responses are.

If your need for privacy is great or you don't want to be associated with lesbian-serving agencies, you can make similar inquiries of shelter or safe home personnel, or crisis lines for battered women. Many of them will be able to offer supportive crisis counseling and information about housing, welfare, and the police, but you will have to ask them in each instance whether they have special reason to know that what they are saying applies to lesbians as well as heterosexuals. In some instances, they may not have the information but will be willing to find out for you. If so, let them do it. It will take some pressure off you, as well as giving them an opportunity to inform themselves, which will benefit the next lesbian who calls.

Finding Support

It may be that the best decision for you is to be completely open about the battering. To say out loud what is happening can be a strong message to yourself that you are not the one to blame and that you are not ashamed. It can also be a message to the lesbian community that yes, this really is happening right in our back yard, and we need to start taking care of it. Of course, you won't want to take the risk of speaking out unless you have an idea you will get at least some support. You will need most of your energy to deal with your fear, your anger and your sorrow. There may not be much strength left to fight a difficult political battle within your own community (though for some people that can enhance courage rather than diminish it). Try speaking to one friend or community activist at a time and see what kind of response you get. If it's negative, don't give up, but feel out the next person carefully, until you've found a couple of people who will stand by you.

If you decide there is no support for you in the community or you are so much in the closet that you dare not even ask for it, you may be better off to find an individual counselor who is familiar with battering and knowledgable about lesbian issues or at least willing to learn. No matter what your lifestyle or what decision you make, the support of caring, understanding people is essential to get through your ordeal with the least amount of emotional scarring.

Chapter 24

EMOTIONAL ABUSE

If you've been physically assaulted by an intimate partner, you're almost certain to have been subjected to emotional abuse as well. Perhaps the worst of it has been the continual or chronic terror of being beaten or killed. Maybe it's been the more subtle erosion of your self-esteem and capacity to act independently, or the shame and humiliation you endure on a daily basis. Perhaps, like nearly all women who are subjected to both, you experience emotional abuse as even harder to take than the physical abuse.

It might be that you've rarely or never been physically assaulted, but threats have kept you in fear and caused you gradually to lose your sense of identity, as you've given in to the ideas and demands of your partner. If the abuser has neither hit nor threatened you, but has used more subtle methods to manipulate, control and debilitate you, you might feel more submissive, confused and given to self-blame than many women who've been severely beaten. A woman who has a black eye or broken bone knows something has been done to her, but emotional abuse is sometimes so complex and bewildering it is difficult to name. If it can't be identified clearly, the person it's directed toward may believe she's imagining it.

Much of *Getting Free* implicitly provides ways to defend against or recover from emotional abuse. A continuum of emotional abuse is described in the introductory chapter, "Who The Book Is For." But you won't find an analysis, a refined definition or a special section on the subject. When *Getting Free* was written I was still struggling, as were many of the women subjected to emotional abuse, to identify it in specific terms. We were searching for ways to delineate it from the ordinary irritability and occasional name-calling that most couples engage in from time to time. In fact, much of that behavior is abusive, but it may not be permanently damaging until it reaches the level of a campaign to reduce the partner's sense of self-worth and to maintain control. Because the abusive person may establish control over the other, it is most damaging when it is a pattern of behavior on the part of just one partner, though it may also be harmful when it's mutual psychological combat.

UNDERSTANDING THE CHART OF COERCION

Because it's so hard for many of us to get a clear view of emotional abuse, in this chapter I'm going to use a framework that creates some distance from it. In her book, *Rape In Marriage*, Diana Russell reprinted a Chart of Coercion from an Amnesty International publication, *Report on Torture*, depicting the brainwashing of prisoners of war; she suggested that it also describes the "torture of wives." Most people who brainwash their intimate partners use methods similar to those of prison guards, who recognize that physical control is never easily accomplished without the cooperation of the prisoner. The most effective way to gain that cooperation is through subversive manipulation of the mind and feelings of the victim, who then becomes a psychological, as well as a physical, prisoner. These methods form the core of emotional abuse. In the following discussion of brainwashing and the exercise to help you identify it, I have modified the language of the Chart of Coercion categories for readability, but maintained their essential meaning.

Biderman's Chart of Coercion

General Method	Effects and Purposes
Isolation	Deprives victim of all social support [for the] ability to resist.
	Develops an intense concern with self.
	Makes victim dependent upon interogator.
Monopolization of Perception	Fixes attention upon immediate predicament; fosters introspection.
	Eliminates stimuli competing with those controlled by captor.
	Frustrates all actions not consistent with compliance.
Induced Debility and Exhaustion	Weakens mental and physical ability to resist.
Threats	Cultivates anxiety and despair.
Occasional Indulgences	Provides positive motivation for compliance.
Demonstrating "Omnipotence"	Suggests futility of resistance.
Degradation	Makes cost of resistance appear more damaging to self esteem than capitulation.
	Reduces prisoner to "animal level" concerns.
Enforcing Trivial Demands	Develops habit of compliance.

Isolation

Isolation is the most effective way to set the stage for brainwashing, since once the victim is away from emotional supports and reality checks, the rest of the process is relatively easy. A prisoner may be placed alone in a cell, to increase dependency on the guards and a subsequent willingness to obey. Religious fanatics sometimes surround a potential recruit and repetitively hammer into his or her consciousness a rigid ideology, while the victim is cut off from previous relationships and competing ideas. Women who are battered are often kept from contact with almost everyone except the person who batters, so that the self-interested, demeaning or threatening messages can saturate her senses.

A man who batters often carries on a process of gradually weaning a wife or girlfriend away from everyone else she is close to through a combination of demands, threats and manipulation. He may complain about her maintaining a friendship with a former boyfriend, then make critical remarks about her divorced women friends being a bad influence, and later insist that she not talk on the telephone when he is home. He may insult her friends, acquaintances and relatives, so that they voluntarily stay away or the woman feels too embarrassed to invite them into her home. He may stay at the woman's side, except when he is at work, and if he does decide to leave her alone he either telephones periodically to be sure she is at home or convinces her that he has spies who watch her and report to him. Sometimes he does have spies. The woman may unwittingly collude in his campaign to isolate her, because she is either too depressed to want to be with other people or too ashamed to let others see her if she is bruised. The violent partner may also threaten that if she talks to anyone he will beat, or even kill her.

Lesbians may abuse their partners in similar ways. There are often additional excuses for abuse. For instance, a lesbian who is afraid to claim her identity may demand that her "out-of-the-closet" lover drop her lesbian friends and, in effect, join her in the closet. The abused partner may be coerced into hiding many of her true ideas and feelings because they seem threatening to the abusive woman's job or relationships.

The abused woman, whether lesbian or heterosexual, may be allowed to see people, especially if the abuser wants her to work, but the isolation may still occur on a more subtle, emotional level. For instance, she is not allowed to speak of what is done to her behind the closed doors, and she may be terrified of the abuser's violence if she inadvertantly lets someone know what she is subjected to. To be on the safe side, she becomes unnaturally silent or superficial. She may also be convinced that if her friends or colleagues knew about the violence they would believe it was her own fault. Under those circumstances she is emotionally and socially isolated from everyone, because she hides her feelings, her thoughts and the pattern of her life from them and they don't really know her.

Humiliation Or Degradation

Once the woman stops interacting openly with other people, the abuser's influence becomes paramount. She is bombarded with misinformation and distorted values, and there is no one to reinforce her own ideas of the truth. This process of isolation and the self-doubt it creates are effective in gaining power over another person. But there is more. The abuser may criticize the woman for minor flaws, sometimes in public, or remind her of humiliating experiences. He may continually tell her she is bad, stupid and crazy, as well as a slut, cunt or worse. He may also subject her to sexual innuendos about her behavior with other men, flaunt his relationships with other women, insult her or simply ignore her.

Lesbians may, in addition to those abuses, call their partners names that demean their sexual orientation and the very relationship that in happier moments is treasured. The abused lesbian is called a goddamned dyke or "femme" or "butch." Or she's accused of really loving men.

Some abusers find extreme and bizarre ways to degrade a partner, such as raping her in front of the children or forcing her to eat from a pet dish. The sense of extreme humiliation makes the woman feel she deserves to be treated as less than human and may also cause her to think no one but the abusive partner would ever want anything to do with her. When the abuser occasionally treats her well, she is so hungry for any crumb of care that she accepts it gratefully. Eventually, the awareness of her dependence and her gratitude for the smallest attention contribute even more to the woman's sense of degradation, and she abuses herself with litanies of self-blame.

Trivial Demands And Focus On The Whims Of The Abuser

The abusers insist on compliance with trivial demands, related to all facets of life: food, clothing, money, household arrangements, children and conversation. They monitor their partner's appearance, criticize her values, her language and her childcare practices. They insist on precise mealtimes with prescribed menus, which may change and be contradictory from day to day or moment to moment.

The abused woman may at first think that her partner is unreasonable, and argue back. Later, either because she wants to live in peace or because she is afraid, she tries to comply. After all, what difference does it make if the dinner has to be served at precisely five after six, or if she is forced to wear yellow even though it looks ghastly on her? In the long run maybe it's good for the children to always have their toys put away when their father is home. A woman with an abusive male partner tries to read his mind, anticipate his wishes and deflect his wrath. Soon it becomes apparent that there is no end to his demands, and her time and energy are focused on him and his imminent rage over anything she does that may turn out to be "wrong." Everything becomes important in terms of how it will affect him, and her desires, feelings, and ideas become insignificant. Eventually she doesn't even know what she wants, feels and thinks. He monopolizes all of her perceptions with his trivial demands, so that she loses her perspective on the enormity of her total situation.

An abusive lesbian might insist she knows what is "correct"

about the lesbian lifestyle, as if there is only one. She will criticize her partner's clothes as being too "femme," too "butch" or too "dykey" and her sexual practices as being "sick" or too much like heterosexuals'. A woman who is just coming out as a lesbian may be particularly vulnerable to these verbal assaults. Her focus changes from her own preferences in style and habits to what she projects will keep her partner from being displeased with her.

Demonstration Of Power And Threats

The abusers persuade the woman that they are the ones who know the correct way that everything should be done. When their behavior results in disastrous consequences, as it often does, the partner is blamed. Abusers may even claim to have supernatural powers. Usually they claim to be superior intellectually and to know the ways of the world. Because the abused woman has been brought so low herself, she may come to believe this. As early as the initial honeymoon period she may have developed the idea that her partner is brilliant, worldly, accomplished and knowledgable, and he or she will have done everything possible to encourage it. Abusers may also have moments, especially after a beating, when they "confess" that they think they're inadequate or worthless; the contrast of these moments of vulnerablity with their usual pose of being all-powerful endears them to the woman and gives her hope for some open communication. Their supposed superiority and her inferiority reinforce their power over her, and inhibit her ability to create change.

Threats are an almost natural concomitant to all of these processes. The person who batters threatens to leave the partner, threatens to harm her children or other family members, tells her "I'll fix you so no one will ever want you," and threatens to kill. Since some of these actions are carried out, the woman can never be sure when the abuser will follow through on the others. She is coerced into obedience to unreasonable demands and increases her attention on the abuser and away from herself. Her focus is on what she can do to preserve her short-term safety, and it distracts her from considerations of how to work toward a plan for real security in the long range.

The person who is not physically abusive may first force the woman into actions that embarrass or humiliate her, then threaten to tell her family or friends about it. A lesbian may threaten her closeted partner with making their relationship known to her boss or family. An abusive man may tell his partner that he will take her children away, destroy objects of sentimental value or harass and humiliate her in the presence of her work colleagues or boss, or use other methods to cause her to lose her job. He often controls all the money even if she earns it, and may periodically take her car keys or checkbook away if she doesn't obey him. If she doesn't give in to his demands, he may begin to put into practice one of these threats. Emotionally abusive people are sometimes remarkably imaginative. They can be just as frightening to their partners as are physically violent partners.

Helplessness And Exhaustion

The chronic physical injury from beatings creates an on-going state of exhaustion. The woman who is subjected to these techniques of brainwashing becomes worn out by her tension, fear and her continual rushing about in the effort to arrange her partner's world effectively enough to avoid abuse. She must also strain to keep her fear, sorrow and rage from showing, since any display of emotion is likely to be ridiculed or punished. Physical weakness, self-doubt and self-loathing, reinforced by her partner's insistence that she is stupid, crazy and does not know how to do anything, finally convince the emotionally abused woman that she is incapable of taking care of herself or of making a move to sever her relationship.

Occasional Indulgences

If there is a moment in which the woman sees hope of escaping or becomes desperate enough to take any risk to get away, the abuser often senses it and comes through with some form of indulgence, whether a new car, a night out or a seemingly loving, affectionate offering of time together. Hope that the abuser will change replaces the woman's fear or despair, and she decides to continue working on the relationship.

Some of the brainwashing techniques in each of the categories mentioned above are extreme, but not uncommon. Some abusers use them in a disciplined and regular manner, some sporadically. But even mild and occasional use of the techniques is often effective in gaining power. When they are combined with physical abuse they are reliable methods of keeping a woman in a relationship and guaranteeing obedience. These methods are not the only means of emotional abuse. There are no doubt countless ways a person can manipulate the emotions of an intimate partner in negative ways, but I will mention only two more.

Emotional Distance

Psychological unavailability or emotional distance is known to have an extremely devastating effect on children, but little is known of its impact on adults. It is such a common complaint of women about their male partners that it has been a standing cartoon subject for many years. The man sitting behind the newspaper at the breakfast table while his wife sets fire to it to get his attention is just one of the many variations on the theme. A woman often thinks there is something wrong with her for wanting the man she's involved with to be present. She wants him to talk, to listen, to express feelings, to understand the nuances of her conversation. If he is focused on the paper or the television or only pretending to listen, then the woman begins to feel like a non-person. If she doesn't have other people in her life to let her know she is heard and understood and cared about in a way that reflects who she really is, she may eventually begin to doubt her judgment and her worth.

"Crazy-Making"

Another method of emotional abuse is "crazy-making." It is difficult to describe because it has many manifestations. In the movie *Gaslight* the husband regularly turns down the gas lights and when his wife complains about it, he says she's imagining that they've changed. In its extreme form, such a man may remove his wife's possessions from their usual place, and when she says they are missing, complain of her inability to keep track of things. Then he replaces them and accuses her of imagining they were missing. That's expert "crazy-making."

Many people who abuse their partners deny and minimize their faults, and often tell lies about such trivial matters that the woman wonders if she is mistaken about what she thinks is true. "Who would lie about something so unimportant? I must have misunderstood." When she has "misunderstood" numerous times, and that notion is reinforced by her partner — "I never said that. You must be imagining things" — she begins to doubt her judgment. Small contradictions — "I never eat well-done steak"/"I always want my steak rare" — can have a similar effect.

Because there are no socially prescribed roles for lesbians, an abusive woman may use her partner's ambivalence or confusion about who does what tasks to confuse her with continually shifting ideas or demands about what, if any, roles they each should play. Being dependent or doing domestic tasks, for instance, may be rewarded on Friday and demeaned on Saturday. A transfer of guilt from the abuser to the victim sometimes causes the victim to feel crazy. "You brought it on yourself. You love to be beaten," the abusive man says, and eventually the woman asks herself, "Could I love it, subconsciously? Is it my fault?" Abusers may often be troubled by fears, anger and depression, and may try to get rid of those feelings by blustering, threatening and dominating a woman or an entire household. Then they feel some release, and the others feel frightened, angry or depressed. They may then be criticized for those feelings while the abuser brags that he or she doesn't let feelings get out of control that way. When the others wonder what's wrong with themselves, they're beginning to get a little "crazy."

Some abusive people are adept at picking out a trait that a woman is most pleased about and using it against her. This can happen two ways. Treasuring her independence of spirit or her analytic ability, for instance, can be made to seem like a flaw. Independence becomes rejection or selfishness, and analytic ability is called "logic-chopping," "coldness" or "showing off." When the woman begins to believe that her virtues are her flaws, her ability to make other judgments becomes impaired as well. Another tactic is to convince the abused partner that she really isn't humorous or smart or artistically talented. A lesbian who is pleased by her growing comfort with her lesbian identity may be told by her abusive partner that she has no right to call herself a lesbian unless she comes out to her boss, her grandmother and her neighbors. When an abused woman begins to doubt that she has that one special trait she has always felt secure about, the rest of her self-concept is quickly called into question.

PROBLEMS OF IDENTIFYING ABUSE

Why have workers in the battered women's movement emphasized physical rather than emotional abuse? Perhaps because we recognize that everyone emotionally abuses to some extent, and if we are all guilty then we don't want to blame anyone else, for fear we will in turn be held responsible. Or we thought emotional abuse wasn't "so bad," because after all it was so common. We didn't realize "how bad" it can be. A lie? An unreasonable demand? A name called? An occasional manipulation? Not really listening? Oh, come on! Everybody does those things. That's no big deal. There's some truth to that, except when one person is using it as a way of controlling another, or frightening her or destroying her self-concept; except when it's a pattern that characterizes the relationship and gives one person almost all the power; except when one person becomes so uncertain of herself she can't trust her judgment and thinks she doesn't have the right to make judgments.

We also didn't know how to name emotional abuse. It's not clear-cut like a black eye. It is often subtle and it's also confusing if the one who's abused is also emotionally abusive. "It isn't fair to call that abusive, because I do that too." It should be remembered that even if both partners do it, it is still abuse. Sometimes it's hard to tell whether a person is being abused by a partner or abuses herself. What about a woman who is neurotic, who has a very low self-concept, who continually defers to her partner, who hands over her power to others? Isn't it possible the emotional abuse isn't really being done to her at all and that she's imagining it? Sure, it's possible, but probably it's being at least reinforced by the partner.

IDENTIFYING EMOTIONAL ABUSE AND USING *GETTING FREE* TO DIMINISH IT

If you wonder about whether you're being emotionally abused fill out the following checklist to determine if that's what's happening to you. If you're being subjected to brainwashing, "crazy-making" or psychological neglect, start diminishing its impact by doing the indicated exercises in *Getting Free*.

Activity 38   *Emotional Abuse Checklist*

Are You Isolated?

A.

	often	sometimes	never
1. Does your partner ridicule or insult people you like?	___	___	___
2. Is your partner jealous of your friends, family and even pets?	___	___	___
3. Does your partner intercept your mail or telephone calls?	___	___	___
4. Does your partner become angry or upset, dampening your enthusiasm, just before, or during a social event you've looked forward to?	___	___	___

B.

	often	sometimes	never
1. Do you discourage people from telephoning you at home because your partner resents sharing your time?	___	___	___
2. Do you have fewer contacts and activities with friends and family than before you began the relationship?	___	___	___
3. Do you feel uneasy about being with your partner and your friends at the same time?	___	___	___
4. Do you feel nervous or frightened of what your partner will say or do if you are even a few minutes late from work, shopping, or visiting others?	___	___	___

If you have many affirmative answers to the questions above, you're in danger of becoming so isolated from the support and perspective of other people that you eventually won't be able to evaluate what's being done to you, or to recognize a dangerous situation or person. If you had many "Yes" answers to "B," it might be that you've adapted so well to the isolation your partner has imposed that you've started isolating yourself. You can begin to break the pattern by reading Chapter 12, "An End To Isolation" and Chapter 13, "Reaching Out."

Is Your Attention Monopolized By The Abusive Person?

often sometimes never

1. *Do you feel your clothing, opinions and decisions must have your partner's approval?*

2. *Do you feel overpowered by your partner's presence whether or not he or she is with you?*

3. *Do you speak carefully, or avoid speaking, so you won't risk upsetting your partner?*

4. *Do you time your activities to avoid their being noticed by your partner?*

5. *Do you often feel you're "walking on egg shells"?*

If you checked many answers in this group, you're focusing so much of your attention on your partner's opinions and reactions that you'll soon lose sight of your own rights and feelings and desires. This monopolization of your attention by your partner, in combination with isolation from other people, may lead you in the direction of excessive dependency on your partner. If you had several "always" or "sometimes" responses, read Chapter 4 and do Activities 5 and 6 so that you can begin to focus on what you need and want for yourself.

Does Your Partner Claim To Be All-Powerful?

often sometimes never

1. *Does your partner claim to be exceptionally bright or knowledgable, or to have extraordinary powers?*

2. *Does your partner claim to be more aware of the ways of the world than you are?*

3. *Does your partner claim to have friends and contacts who will report your activities when you are away from home?*

4. *Does your partner claim to know the "right" way to do things, and that you don't know what's "right"?*

If you checked two or more of the items above, you may eventually be persuaded by your partner that he or she is omnipotent or at least greatly superior to you, and that you aren't competent to make your own decisions. Read Chapter 10, "You Can Be Your Own Counselor" and do Activities 14 through 17 to gain a more positive perspective on what you do that's "right" or smart or competent or loving.

Does Your Partner Enforce Trivial Demands?

often sometimes never

1. *Does your partner insist that activities take place in precise ways or at precisely designated times?*   ___ ___ ___

2. *Does your partner interrupt your work or other things that are important to you, to get her or his needs met?*   ___ ___ ___

3. *Does your partner demand that you wear only approved clothing, jewelry, etc?*   ___ ___ ___

4. *Does your partner insist you perform menial services, or inspect your work and make hyper-critical comments?*   ___ ___ ___

5. *Does your partner demand detailed reports of hourly activities?*   ___ ___ ___

If your partner enforces trivial demands, you may feel either like a servant or an incompetent child. You'll focus on the narrow mechanical tasks expected of you, and give up making your own judgments about their value. To counter those demands, do the activities in "A Courageous Act A Day" and consider taking an assertion training course. (This category is not meant to imply that people who emotionally abuse don't also make outrageous demands. They often start with minor issues, which build up to greater ones, or the abuser may start with something so unacceptable that when he or she moves to something less dramatic, it may seem, by comparison, more manageable. These demands may involve "loans" of money, never repaid, or use of a car that's mistreated or not returned in time for you to keep an important engagement, or a host of other items.)

Are You Exhausted, Debilitated Or Dependent?

often sometimes never

1. Do you feel inadequate doing tasks you used to do easily and well? ___ ___ ___

2. Do you suffer from minor or major illnesses? ___ ___ ___

3. Do you have feelings of dread? ___ ___ ___

4. Do you feel you couldn't manage your life without your partner? ___ ___ ___

Checks after these questions indicate that the trivial demands of your partner are wearing you down. You may feel debilitated or dependent for reasons that aren't clear. Ask youself how you feel when you're not with your partner. If that hasn't happened in a long time, try to get away even for a few days to see how you feel when the pressure is off. You might have a great deal more energy. If these feelings persist for a long time see a counselor. Meanwhile do Activities 15, 16 and 19A and B.

Do You Feel Humiliated or Degraded?

often sometimes never

1. Does your partner force you to do things that are against your religious or moral values? ___ ___ ___

2. Does your partner ridicule the traits you admire or value most in yourself? ___ ___ ___

3. Does your partner tell you no one else would want you? ___ ___ ___

4. Has your partner talked you into doing something, and then made you feel guilty or ashamed about it? ___ ___ ___

5. Does your partner keep you up late, asking about real or imagined sexual or romantic incidents? ___ ___ ___

6. Does your partner force you to apologize for things you didn't do? ___ ___ ___

7. Does your partner insist you ask permission to spend money for household or personal items, whether the money is a community fund or your own income? ___ ___ ___

8. Does your partner call you names with sexual connotations such as "slut" or "whore"? ___ ___ ___

9. Does your partner flaunt relationships or flirt with others while in your presence? ___ ___ ___

The above questions ask about activities and demands that cause you to feel humiliated and degraded. It seems as if such experiences would motivate a person to end a relationship, but often that's not so. People who have experienced such things often stay involved because they're ashamed to face anyone else, and they hope that they can "fix" the relationship, which will make the humiliation seem to have been for a good cause. A course in assertiveness may help you say no to some of your partner's degrading demands. But if your partner is violent, make a plan for your safety before you try something new. Chapters 12, "An End To Isolation" and 13, "Reaching Out" will help you find ways to meet people and make friends who will encourage you to feel good about yourself.

Does Your Partner Threaten You?

	often	sometimes	never
1. Does your partner threaten to make public the things you've done or that you've told in private moments?	___	___	___
2. Does your partner threaten to leave you or divorce you, whenever you have arguments?	___	___	___
3. Does your partner tell you that suicide or mental illness will result if you leave or withdraw your love or affection?	___	___	___
4. Does your alcoholic partner hint at the probability of drinking again, unless you do what is required and be certain not to upset him or her?	___	___	___
5. Does your partner threaten to "punish you or teach you a lesson" if you "misbehave"?	___	___	___
6. Does your partner threaten to take your car keys, money or checkbook, if you don't comply with demands?	___	___	___
7. Does your partner use bodily or facial expressions or noises to show extreme anger and loss of control, in order to frighten you?	___	___	___
8. Has being hit or beaten in the past made you fear it happening again, if you don't comply?	___	___	___
9. Does your partner keep guns, knives or other weapons close at hand?	___	___	___

Whether you're threatened with the loss of your partner, the responsibility of your partner's mental illness or suicide, or injury to yourself, the use of power makes it certain you can't have a relationship of mutual respect and love. If you checked questions 5 through 8, you may be in serious danger. One way to diminish those threats is to ignore them, but you do that at risk of being seriously injured. This may be the point at which you'll consider leaving your partner. If you want help in making that decision, read Section 1, *Making The Decision To Leave Or Stay*, and do the activities.

Does Your Partner Occasionally Indulge Your Wishes?

	often	sometimes	never
1. *Just as you are thinking of separating, or when you've been abused, or for no reason at all, does your partner pamper you with gifts?*	___	___	___
2. *Does your partner suddenly do something you have been requesting for a long time?*	___	___	___
3. *Does your partner become unexpectedly understanding about something that would ordinarily cause him or her to exhibit anger?*	___	___	___
4. *Does your partner impress you with exceptional sensitivity to your feelings and desires?*	___	___	___
5. *After your partner has "put you down" are you then indulged with affection or special care?*	___	___	___

This category Occasional Indulgences is the one that "hooks you." These things may not happen very often, but there's always the hope that they are expressions of the real character of your partner, and that they'll surface on a regular basis. Do Activities 23 through 25 to get a perspective on how the positive things your partner has done compare with the abuse. Be sure to include all the most humiliating, demeaning and other emotional abuses in the "Most Dangerous" list. They are dangerous to your mental health.

Does Your Partner Do Things That Make You Feel Crazy?

A.   *often sometimes never*

1. Does your partner suggest you're "stupid" or "crazy"
   if you disagree with him or her?   ____ ____ ____

2. Does your partner apologize and say the abuse is a
   sign of deep love and fear of losing your love?   ____ ____ ____

3. Does your partner insist that the two of you are in a
   battle against a world full of enemies?   ____ ____ ____

4. After abusing you, does your partner express so much
   sorrow, guilt or self-hate, that you become the one
   who comforts your partner?   ____ ____ ____

5. Has your partner burdened you with shameful,
   embarrassing or criminal secrets, that only you know
   about?   ____ ____ ____

6. Does your partner lie about insignificant things?   ____ ____ ____

7. Does your partner make contradictory demands?   ____ ____ ____

8. Does your partner contradict the positive things others
   say about you?   ____ ____ ____

9. Does your partner say negative things about a trait
   you like about yourself, such as "wishy-washy,"
   "intellectual," "stuffy," etc?   ____ ____ ____

10. Does your partner do unrequested favors, then get
    angry or hurt when you don't do something in
    return?   ____ ____ ____

B.

often sometimes never

1. Do you distrust your feelings about yourself, your partner or others? ___ ___ ___

2. Do you feel ashamed of past deeds that once made you proud? ___ ___ ___

3. Are you afraid no one would like you if they knew the "the real you"? ___ ___ ___

4. Do you believe you're the only one who can save your partner from ruin, depression, alcoholism, insanity or suicide? — and yet, that you're the dependent one? ___ ___ ___

5. Does it just "happen" that when you are preparing for an upcoming test, job interview, evaluation, or an important event, you're distracted and worried by a crisis in your partner's life or work that seems more important? ___ ___ ___

6. Does your partner cause you to question your long-time friendships? ___ ___ ___

7. Are you confused about what is love and what is hate? Or right and wrong? ___ ___ ___

8. Does your partner bombard you with words, sometimes of many syllables, until you think he or she must know what they're talking about, and you give in to their position? ___ ___ ___

Most of these questions indicate that the abuser is doing something to make the partner weak, but checks after "A" questions indicate your partner is engaging in "crazy-making" or "gaslighting" behavior, and after "B" show to what extent you're beginning to take responsibility for it. The latter is especially likely if you're kept away from other people and if the "crazy-maker" demonstrates other kinds of power. Becoming involved with other people will help to validate your sanity. Read Chapters 12, "An End To Isolation" and 13, "Reaching Out."

Is Your Partner Emotionally Distant Or Neglectful?

Does your partner: often sometimes never

1. Ignore you or grunt absentmindedly when you begin
   a conversation?   ____   ____   ____

2. Groan, complain or ridicule you, when you cry,
   worry, or ask for emotional support?   ____   ____   ____

3. Refuse to confide in you, when he or she is worried,
   hurt or scared?   ____   ____   ____

4. Ignore your wish for sex, or refuse to do what excites
   or satisfies you?   ____   ____   ____

5. Make light of your triumphs, discourage your plans,
   disparage your success?   ____   ____   ____

6. Refuse to share her or his plans, or hopes for success? ____   ____   ____

7. Ignore your need for assistance when you're sick, tired
   or over-scheduled?   ____   ____   ____

Have you:

1. Given up asking your partner for companionship?   ____   ____   ____

2. Stopped asking for empathy or emotional support?   ____   ____   ____

3. Given up asking, when you're sick, tired or need your
   partner's help?   ____   ____   ____

4. Stopped asking your partner about his or her plans,
   worries, or triumphs?   ____   ____   ____

5. Developed a habit of avoiding sex, whenever possible,
   but enduring it as a tolerable routine, when it's
   unavoidable?   ____   ____   ____

If many of these situations are prevalent in your relationship, your partner is psychologically unavailable to you, and neglecting you, which is a form of abuse. If most of your checks were in part "B," you may have been minimizing the neglect, since you've learned that it's all you can expect of your partner. You may not be able to get what you want from your partner, but you can diminish the pain of neglect by spending time with friends who pay attention to you and finding work that gives you satisfactions. Read Chapters 11, 12, 13 and 17.

MAKING CHANGES

After you've finished Activity 38, if you're still not sure whether you or your partner is the abusive person, reverse the questions that begin "Does your partner..." and do the exercise again, to check out what you are doing. If both of you are emotionally abusive, and if you're not being battered, you may benefit from the help of a counselor or another person who has some objectivity. The third person can help you monitor your abuse of each other, and provide a relatively safe atmosphere in which you can each admit your vulnerability and ask for consideration.

You may have begun to emotionally abuse your partner in moments of helpless fury, to retaliate against physical or sexual abuse, and it may momentarily have given you a sense of power. But the ability to lower someone else's self-esteem is not real power. It doesn't enable you to live the kind of life you want. In addition, it may cause you to feel guilty or even to believe you deserve your partner's retaliation. The theme of *Getting Free* is that you can make changes in yourself, and this is another example. Decide whether you want to be abusive and whether you want to be free of another's abuse. Then act to make the changes you want.

If you don't have a pattern of abusing your partner, but your partner emotionally abuses you, a counselor might still be useful, if only to back up your position that your partner is abusive and can change. The comments after the checklist urge you to begin expanding your social contacts, and now is a good time to begin. If your partner resists your move to seek professional help or to be active and socialize with other people, that's further evidence that he or she has an investment in keeping you the way you are.

Maybe friends tell you you're brainwashed, but you claim, for instance, that your partner doesn't prevent you from seeing other people, that you stay home because you like to be alone or because it's your choice to stay with your partner. If friends persist in their opinions, you may want to insist they mind their own business, or you might want to allow for the possibility that if you are brainwashed you don't know it. You could decide to prove to yourself and to them that you're making your own choices. If you want to take a risk and are willing to act with an open mind you can decide to go out on your own to see friends or enroll in a class. If you're not being brainwashed, your partner will probably be glad you're doing something for yourself and will encourage you. If he or she puts obstacles in your way, complains a lot or "explains" all the reasons you don't need to be out on your own, it should be clear that you're not free to develop yourself without being made to pay a price.

The worst part of emotional abuse is that the person victimized by it eventually takes on the role of her abuser and begins to demean, degrade and humiliate herself. That is why it works so well, when it does. Brainwashing causes many women to be so debilitated, so dependent and so overwhelmed by dread that they look as if they could never become autonomous, active, optimistic people. Yet they do it. They are able to break away from abusive partners and to recover their self-esteem and autonomy.

Since you've read this far, you've probably named the problem and know what changes you want to make. You may feel overwhelmed by the tasks ahead of you, but you've already taken several important steps. Even if you can't affect your partner as much as you'd like, you can begin to react differently and to view yourself in a new light. You can take satisfaction in whatever work you do at home or on a paid job. You can begin to do pleasurable things and to allow yourself to consciously enjoy them. Your particular, individual inner resources have been untapped for a time, but you're using them now and the more you use them the more they will expand. You're on your way to a new way of life in which you'll struggle, learn to appreciate yourself, and interact with others who appreciate you. You'll find rewards in being with people and being alone, and you'll use new skills to meet conflict and criticism assertively and peaceably. That is the miracle of the human spirit.

RESOURCES

Chapter 1   Social and Political Aspects of Abuse

Davidson, Terry. *Conjugal Crime*. New York: Hawthorn Books, 1978.
An overview of the problem of battering, the book includes the author's
own story of life with her abusive father, a minister. It provides advice
to battered women who decide to stay with their partners and those
who leave, and how to deal with children, friends and family,
counselors and clergy. The directory of shelters is no longer accurate.

Dobash, R. Emerson and Russell Dobash. *Violence Against Wives: A Case
Against Patriarchy*. New York: The Free Press, 1979.
The authors' approach is intellectual, political and personal. They view
battering in the context of history and widespread acceptance of men's
dominance of women. They studied the police system and
interviewed victims of violence; there are numerous quotations from
battered wives describing their specific reactions to their situations.
Although the victims are all Scottish women, their stories are just like
those of American women.

Fleming, Jennifer Baker. *Stopping Wife Abuse*. New York: Anchor
Books/Doubleday, 1979.
About fifty pages are directed to the battered woman herself, and the
rest of the book is designed for professionals and others who want to
help battered women. Includes chapters on counseling, children,
legislation, research, shelters and a long chapter on the legal system.

Martin, Del. *Battered Wives*. San Francisco: Volcano Press, 1981.
An update of the first book about battering. It's a comprehensive
overview and includes reports of research, but is very readable. A
good book for victims, professionals and the general public.
The full address of the publisher, Volcano Press, is: 330 Ellis Street, #518
Dept. B, San Francisco, California, 94102.

Tavris, Carol and Carole Offir. *The Longest War: Sex Differences in
Perspective*. New York: Harcourt Brace Jovanich, Inc., 1977.

This is a highly readable presentation of various perspectives on sex differences, inequities and roles.

Chapter 2   Marriage and the Family

Bird, Caroline. *The Two Paycheck Marriage: How Women at Work Are Changing Life in America*. New York: Pocket Books, 1979.

Levitan, Sar A. and Richard S. Belous. *What's Happening to the American Family*. Baltimore: The Johns Hopkins University Press, 1981.

Mitchell, Joyce Slayton. *Be a Mother and More: Career and Life Planning for Young Women*. New York: Bantam Books, 1980.
Mitchell helps teen-aged and other young women understand that the question of whether to be a mother or work for pay is not the appropriate one for most of them. The real question is how to plan life so that young women can integrate all of their roles in the most satisfying way. The book includes stories of single and married mothers, full-time mothers and those who also work outside the home.

Chapter 3   Is It Ever Right to Break Up the Family?

Butler Sandra. *Conspiracy of Silence: The Trauma of Incest*. New York: Bantam Books, 1978.
A discussion of incestuous assaults by adult males against female children including first person accounts of the actions told by the children, their mothers and the men. The author treats the subject within the context of sex roles.

Finkelhor, David. *Sexually Victimized Children*. New York: The Free Press, 1979.
A readable academic study, including a description of various theories about incest.

Giovannoni, Jeanne M. and Rosina M. Becerra. *Defining Child Abuse*. New York: The Free Press, 1979.
Discusses the difficulties of defining child abuse, and the changes in that definition historically and within various cultural groups. Comparisons are made between the definitions of various professional workers and non-professionals.

Sanford, Linda T. *Silent Children: A Parent's Guide in the Prevention of Child Abuse*. New York: Anchor Press Doubleday, 1980.

Wheat, Patte with Leonard L. Lieber. *Hope for the Children: A Personal History of Parents Anonymous*. Minneapolis: Winston Press, 1979.
Stories of formerly abusive parents are woven through this history of Parents Anonymous, a self-help organization for parents who abuse or neglect their children.

Chapter 4   What Do You Owe Yourself?

Baer, Jean. *How To Be an Assertive (Not Aggressive) Woman in Life, in Love, and on the Job*. Signet, 1976.

Butler, Pamela E. *Self-Assertion For Women: A Guide to Becoming Androgynous*. New York: Harper and Row, 1976.

Fleming, Jennifer Baker and Carolyn Kott Washburne. *For Better, For Worse: A Feminist Handbook on Marriage and Other Options*. New York: Charles Scribner's Sons, 1977.
"Options" is the important word here. Reading about various ways women have exercised their rights in and out of marriage may help you realize that you have rights. It's unlikely your current mate will recognize them, but you can find other people who will, once you see what they are.

Friedan, Betty. *The Feminine Mystique*. New York: Dell, 1963.
Although some of the information is now dated, this first popular book on the contemporary women's movement is still pertinent to women's lives.

French, Marilyn. *The Women's Room*. New York: Summit Books, 1977.
A novel that catalogues women's lives as it tells of the tedium, risks, tragedies, laughs and triumphs of a woman both as a suburban housewife before the women's movement took hold, and as a divorcee and "older woman" student.

Morgan, Robin. *Sisterhood is Powerful. An Anthology of Writings from the Women's Liberation Movement*. New York: Random House, 1970.

Chapter 5   "But I Still Love Him"

Branden, Nathaniel. *The Psychology of Romantic Love*. New York: Bantam Books, 1980.

Goldstine, Daniel, Katherine Larner, Shirley Zuckerman and Hilary Goldstine. *The Dance-Away Lover: And Other Roles We Play in Love, Sex, and Marriage*. New York: Ballantine Books, 1977.

Peck, M. Scott, M.D., *The Road Less Traveled: A New Psychology of Love, Traditional Values and Spiritual Growth*. New York: Simon and Schuster, 1978.

Peele, Stanton with Archie Brodsky. *Love and Addiction*. New York: New American Library, 1976.

Chapter 6   Making the Decision

Goodman, Ellen. *Turning Points*. New York: Fawcett, 1980.
These are stories of people — mostly women — who have made significant changes in their lives and relationships. Some have come about with slow careful planning, others have been sudden and sometimes forced.

McNulty, Faith. *The Burning Bed*. New York: Bantam Books, 1981.
This is the true story of a battered wife who burned her ex-husband while he slept. Gripping as a novel, it may help you realize the danger of the last resort, when a victim is pushed beyond endurance.

Miller, Gordon Porter. *Life Choices: How to Make Decisions Take Control of Your Life and Get the Future You Want*. New York: Bantam Books, 1981.

Viscott, David, M.D. *Risking*. New York: Pocket Books, 1977.
After discussing risktaking in general and such issues as control and esteem, Viscott turns to particular kinds of risks: autonomy, change, love. He includes useful "Do's and Don'ts of Risking."

Willison, Marilyn Murray. *Diary of a Divorced Mother*. New York: Bantam Books, 1981.

Chapter 7   Getting Help from Doctors, Police and Prosecutors

Ehrenreich, Barbara and Deidre English. *For Her Own Good: 150 Years of the Experts' Advice to Women*. New York: Anchor Press/Doubleday, 1978.

Fleming, Jennifer Baker. *Stopping Wife Abuse*. New York: Anchor Books/Doubleday, 1979.

Chapter 8   Making Legal Decisions

Antoniak, Helen M.S.W., Nancy Lynch Scott and Nancy Worcester. *Alone: Emotional, Legal and Financial Help for the Widowed Or Divorced Woman*. Millbrae, California: Les Femmes, 1979.

The address of Les Femmes is 231 Adrian Rd., Millbrae, Ca. 94030.

DeCrow, Karen. *Sexist Justice: How Legal Sexism Affects You*. New York: Vintage books, 1975.

Gillers, Stephen. *The Rights of Lawyers and Clients: An American Civil Liberties Union Handbook*. New York: Discus Books/Avon, 1979.

Ross, Susan C. *The Rights of Women: An American Civil Liberties Union Handbook*. New York: Discus Books/Avon, 1973.

Women In Transition, Inc. *Women In Transition: A Feminist Handbook on Separation and Divorce*. New York: Charles Scribner's Sons, 1975.

Woolley, Persia. *The Custody Handbook*. New York, Summit Books, 1979.

Chapter 9   Getting Help from a Counselor

Halas, Celia, Ph.D. and Roberta Matteson, Ph.D. *I've Done So Well – Why Do I Feel So Bad?* New York: Macmillan, 1978.

Miller, Jean Baker, M.D. *Toward a New Psychology of Women*. Boston: Beacon Press, 1976.

Robson, Elizabeth and Gwenyth Edwards. *Getting Help: A Woman's Guide To Therapy*. New York: E. P. Dutton, 1980.

Smith, Dorothy and Sara J. David, eds. *Women Look at Psychiatry*. Vancouver, Canada: Press Gang Publishers, 1975.
The full address for Press Gang Publishers is 821 E. Hastings St., Vancouver, B.C. Canada.

Chapter 10   You Can Be Your Own Counselor

Briggs, Dorothy Corkille. *Celebrate Yourself*. New York: Doubleday, 1977.

Burns, M.D. *Feeling Good: The New Mood Therapy*. New York: New American Library, 1980.

Davis, Martha, Ph.D., Elizabeth Robbins Eshelman and Matthew McKay Ph.D. *The Relaxation & Stress Reduction Workbook*. Richmond, California: New Harbinger Publications, 1980.

Gaylin, Willard, M.D., *Feelings*. New York: Ballantine Books, 1979.

Gendlin, Eugene T. Ph.D., *Focusing*. New York: Bantam Books, 1981.

Greenburg, Dan with Marcia Jacobs. *How To Make Yourself Miserable*. New York: Random House, 1966.
To appreciate this book you have to be able to laugh at yourself a little, even in the midst of tragedy. Underneath the humor are some sound and serious messages.

Jongeward, Dorothy and Dru Scott, *Women As Winners: Transactional Analysis for Personal Growth*. Reading, Massachusetts: Addison-Wesley, 1977.

Lewinsohn, Peter M., et al. *Control Your Depression*. Englewood Cliffs, New Jersey: Prentice-Hall, 1978.

Rubin, Theodore Isaac, M.D. *The Angry Book*. New York: Macmillan, 1969.

Sharon B. Berlin, *Behavioral Methods in Social Work*. Steven Paul Schinke, ed. (New York: Aldine Publishing Co., 1981) pp 135-136, "Women and Self-Criticism."

Chapter 12   An End to Isolation

Coleman, Emily and Betty Edwards. *Brief Encounters: How to Make the Most of Relationships that May Not Last Forever*. Garden City, New York: Anchor Press/Doubleday, 1980.
Don't let the unusual ideas put you off. There are some good ones to try, so just keep reading.

Gambrill, E.D. and C.A. Richey. *It's Up To You: Developing Assertive Social Skills*. New York: Harper and Row, forthcoming.

Powell, Barbara. *Overcoming Shyness: Practical Scripts For Overcoming Shyness*. New York. McGraw-Hill, 1979.

Chapter 13   Reaching Out

McGinnis, Alan Loy. *The Friendship Factor: How to Get Closer to the People You Care For*. Minneapolis: Augsburg, 1979.
This book is about increasing and maintaining intimacy among friends, lovers and family. The author, a minister, has sensible things to say about expressing need, being loyal and resolving problems.

Fast, Barbara. *Getting Close*. New York: Berkeley, 1979.

Leefeldt, Christine and Ernest Callenbach. *The Art of Friendship*. New York: Berkeley, 1981.

Chapter 14   The First Week

Colgrove, Melba, Ph.D., Harold H. Bloomfield, M.D. and Peter McWilliams. *How to Survive the Loss of a Love*. New York, Bantam Books, 1981.

Newman, Mildred and Bernard Berkowitz with Jean Owen. *How To Be Your Own Best Friend*. New York: Random House, 1971.

Pogrebin, Letty Cottin. *Growing Up Free: Raising Your Child in the 80s*. New York: Bantam Books, 1981.

Yglesias, Helen. *Starting Early, Anew, Over and Late*. New York: Rawson, Wade, 1978.
These are stories of the author's various "starts," of three young people's early successes, and of sixteen others who started something new or again in mid- or late life. Some of them are public personalities, others are not. Their "starts" are in vocations and relationships and styles of life.

Chapter 15   Protecting Yourself and The Children

Phillips, Debora with Robert Judd. *How To Fall Out of Love*. New York: Fawcett, 1978.

About And For Children:

Briggs, Dorothy Corkille, *Your Child's Self-Esteem*. New York: Dolphin/ Doubleday, 1975.

Gardner, Richard A., M.D., *The Boys and Girls Book About Divorce*. New York: Bantam Books, 1980.

Pogrebin, Letty Cottin. *Growing Up Free: Raising Your Child In the 80s*. New York: Bantam Books, 1981.

Rofes, Eric, ed., *The Kids Book of Divorce, By For And About Kids*. Lexington, Mass Lewis, 1981.
Written by children in a private school as part of their class work. For children 11 to 14.

Turow, Rita. *Daddy Doesn't Live Here Anymore: A Guide for Divorced Parents*. New York: Anchor Press/Doubleday, 1978.

Chapter 16   The Practical Questions of Welfare and Housing

Milwaukee County Welfare Rights Organization. *Welfare Mothers Speak Out*. New York: W. W. Norton, 1972.

Sheehan, Susan. *A Welfare Mother*. New York: New American Library, 1976.

Chapter 17   The Economics of Single Life

Chesler, Phyllis and Emily Jane Goodman. *Women, Money & Power*. New York: Bantam Books, 1977.

Porter, Sylvia. *Sylvia Porter's New Money Book For the 80s*. New York: Avon, 1980.
This is the big-selling money book, and Porter is a respected economist. She also makes numerous sexist assumptions, which may reinforce your ideas that when it comes to money, you don't have quite the same rights, interests or abilities as does the man in your life. If you decide to read it, be very, very careful to read between the lines.

Scheele, Adele, Ph.D. *Skills For Success: A Guide to the Top for Men and Women*. New York: Ballantine Books, 1979.

Van Caspel, Venito. *Money Dynamics for the 80s*. Reston, Virginia: Reston Publishers, 1980.

Chapter 18   Sexuality

Barbach, Lonnie Garfield. *For Yourself: The Fulfillment of Female Sexuality*. New York: Anchor Press/Doubleday, 1975.

Boston Women's Health Book Collective. *Our Bodies, Ourselves: A Book By And For Women*. New York: Simon and Schuster, 1973.

Baetz, Ruth. *Lesbian Crossroads: Personal Stories of Lesbian Struggles & Triumphs*. New York: William Morrow, 1980.

Brown, Gabrielle, Ph.D., *The New Celibacy: How To Take A Vacation From Sex — And Enjoy it!* New York: Ballantine Books, 1980.

Hite, Shere. *The Hite Report*. New York: Dell, 1977.
Hite's scientific method has been widely criticized. The quotations from many many women who talked about their sexuality are helpful to any woman who feels herself alone with her sexual idiosyncracies.

Martin, Del and Phyllis Lyon. *Lesbian/Woman*. Glide, 1972.

Tavris, Carol and Susan Sadd. *The Redbook Report on Female Sexuality*. New York: Dell, 1977.
Because this survey of 100,000 married women discovered surprisingly good news about women's sexual satisfaction, you might find yourself becoming depressed or self-critical because you missed out on it. Another way to look at it is that if you want to look for it, there are apparently men out there who can be good sexual partners.

Vida, Ginny. *Our Right to Love: A Lesbian Resource Book*. New York: Prentice Hall, 1978.

Chapter 19   The New Romance

Adams, Jane. *Sex and The Single Parent*. New York: Coward, McCann and Geoghegan, 1978.
Describes how parents handle their sex lives in relations to their children.

Gould, Roger L., M.D., *Transformations: Growth and Change in Adult Life*. New York: Simon and Schuster, 1978.

Halpern, Howard Ph.D., *Cutting Loose: An Adult Guide to Coming to Terms with Your Parents*. New York: Bantam Books, 1981.
Understanding your relationship with your parents and the roles you each play will help you avoid destructive repetitive patterns.

Krantzler, Mel. *Learning To Love Again*. New York: Bantam Books, 1979.

Sunila, Joyce. *The New Lovers: Younger Men/Older Women*. New York: Fawcett, 1980.

Vizinczey, Stephen. *In Praise Of Older Women: The Amorous Recollections of Andras Vajda*. New York: Ballantine Books, 1965.
If you're an "older woman," it isn't necessarily all over for you. There are some men out there who positively value older women as sexual partners. This novel talks about one of them.

Chapter 20   The Long Haul

Edwards, Marie and Eleanor Hoover. *The Challenge Of Being Single*. New York: New American Library, 1975.

McConnel, Adeline and Beverly Anderson. *Single After 50: How To Have The Time Of Your Life.* New York: McGraw-Hill, 1980.

Peterson, Nancy L. *Our Lives For Ourselves: Women Who Have Never Married.* New York: C.P. Putnam's, 1981.

Westoff, Leslie Aldridge. *Breaking Out Of The Middle-Age Trap.* New York: New American Library, 1980.

Chapter 22   Teen Abuse

Adams, Caren and Jennifer Fay and Jan Loreen-Martin. *No Is Not Enough: Helping Teen-agers Avoid Sexual Assault.* San Luis Obispo, CA: Impact Publishers (P.O. Box 1094, San Luis Obispo, CA 93406), 1984.

Bateman, Py. *Acquaintance Rape Awareness and Prevention for Teenagers.* Seattle: Alternatives to Fear (1605-17th Avenue, Seattle, WA 98122), 1982.

Bateman, Py and Gayle Stringer. *Where Do I Start? A Parent's Guide for Talking to Teens About Acquaintance Rape.* Dubuque, IA: Kendall/Hall Publishing Company, 1984.

Fay, Jennifer J. and Billie Jo Flerchinger. *Top Secret: Sexual Assault Information for Teenagers Only.* Renton, WA: King County Rape Relief (305 So. 43rd, Renton, WA 98055), 1982.

Gordon, Sol. *The Teenage Survival Book.* New York: Book Times (130-5th Ave., New York, NY 10011), 1981.

Lindsay, Jeanne Warren. *Teenage Marriage.* Buena Park, CA: Morning Glory Press (6595 San Haroldo Way, Buena Park, CA 90620), 1984.

NiCarthy, Ginny. "Addictive Love and Abuse: A Course for Teenage Women." *The Second Mile: Contemporary Approaches in Counseling Young Women.* Seattle: New Directions for Young Women (312 S. Washington, Seattle, WA 98104), 1983.

NiCarthy, Ginny. *Assertion Skills for Young Women.* Seattle: New Directions for Young Women (312 S. Washington, Seattle, WA 98104), 1981.

Chapter 23   Lesbian Abuse

Lobel, Kerry. *Naming the Violence: Speaking Out About Lesbian Battering.*
Seattle: Seal Press, forthcoming 1986.

The Western Center on Domestic Violence (WCDV) has prepared
two important resource packets: one on battering in lesbian
relationships, and another on issues of homophobia and heterosexism.
Both packets are available from the Center. Write to WCDV, 870 Market
Street, Suite 1058, San Francisco, CA 94102.

Articles on lesbian abuse periodically appear in *Off Our Backs* (1841
Columbia Road NW, Room 212, Washington, D.C. 20009), *Gay
Community News* (167 Tremont Street, Boston, MA 02111), and *Plexus*
(545 Athol Avenue, Oakland, CA 94606), among other publications.

Other Resources

Violence Against Women:

Most of these books are serious studies, intended more for academic
people than for the general public, but if you're not in crisis and you
want to know what the sociologists and other thinkers are finding out
about this problem, thumb through these books to see if they will
answer your needs.

Chesler, Phyllis. *Mothers On Trial: The Battle for Children and Custody.* New
York: McGraw-Hill, 1986.
This book can be extremely discouraging if you're thinking about
leaving and afraid of losing child custody. It can also be read as a
guide to how you can guard against your partner's efforts to take
custody away from you. You may want to take the section on men
who batter to your lawyer so she or he will understand the
seriousness of your situation.

Fortune, Marie. *Sexual Violence: The Unmentionable Sin: An Ethical and
Pastoral Perspective.* New York: Pilgrim Press, 1983.

Pagelow, Mildred Daley. *Family Violence.* New York: Praeger, 1984.
This is the best current overview of the research, covering date
battering, child abuse, elder abuse and exploring the current
knowledge about the question of whether abuse is learned in families.

Russell, Diana E. H. *Rape in Marriage.* New York: Macmillan Pub. Co.,
1982.

Schechter, Susan. *Women and Male Violence: The Visions and Struggles of the Battered Women's Movement.* Boston: South End Press, 1982.

Walker, Lenore. *The Battered Woman Syndrome.* New York: Springer Publishing Co., 1984.

Self-help Books:

Black, Claudia. *It Will Never Happen to Me: Children of Alcoholics.* Denver: MAC Publications (1850 High Street, Denver, CO 80218), 1981.

Black, Claudia. *Repeat After Me.* Denver: MAC Publications (1850 High Street, Denver, CO 80218), 1981.

Halpern, Howard. *How to Break Your Addiction to a Person.* New York: Bantam Books, 1982.

Schaef, Anne Wilson. *Co-dependence: Misunderstood—Mistreated.* Minneapolis: Winston Press, 1986.

Sonkin, Daniel Jay and Michael Durphy. *Learning to Live Without Violence: A Handbook for Men.* San Francisco: Volcano Press, 1982.

White, Evelyn C. *Chain Chain Change: For Black Women Dealing with Physical and Emotional Abuse.* Seattle: Seal Press, 1985.

Zambrano, Myrna M. *Mejor Sola Que Mal Acompañada: Para la Mujer Golpeada/For the Latina in an Abusive Relationship.* Seattle: Seal Press, 1985.

ABOUT THE AUTHOR

Ginny NiCarthy, MSW, was the founder and director of the Abused Women's Network in Seattle and a former director of Seattle Rape Relief. She has led groups for abused women since 1976, and for the past two years has co-led an abusive anger group for lesbians. She has taught junior and senior high school and has written a manual for youth workers, *Assertion Skills For Young Women*. She has conducted workshops on women's issues in the United States, Great Britain and Norway. She is co-author of *Talking It Out: A Guide to Groups for Abused Women* and is working on a book about women who have left abusive relationships. NiCarthy is currently a counselor with the Women's Counseling Group in Seattle.

Photo by Mary Rivard.

DATE DUE

4/16/05			
4/8/10			
GAYLORD			PRINTED IN U.S.A.

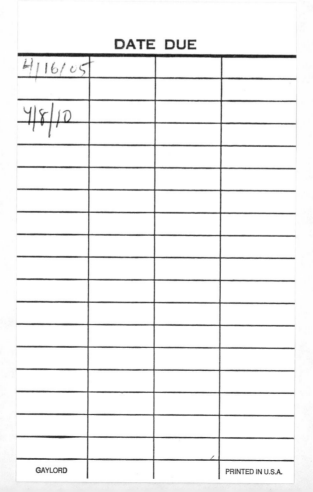